Русские в Китае
Заявки на службу в полиции Шанхая
1930-1942

Компиляция, аннотации
Кирилл В. Чащин

South Eastern Publishers
2017

Russians in China
Shanghai D-917 Police Applicants
1930-1942

Compiled, Edited and Annotated
by Kirill V. Chashchin

South Eastern Publishers
2017

South Eastern Publishers Inc.

228 Park Ave South,

New York, NY 10003-1502 USA

For more information e-mail info@sepublishers.com

or visit our website www.SEpublishers.com

Book design by B.B.Opastny

Printed in United States of America

First Edition: September 2017

ISBN 978-1-936531-16-5 (Paperback Edition)

ISBN 978-1-936531-17-2 (Ebook Edition)

Library of Congress Control Number: 2017952359

Table of Contents

Introduction

Here is our humble effort to create the small tribute to Russians who served in the Russian Regiment, Shanghai Volunteer Corps, during 1930s and 1940s.

It compromises the data gathered from the D.917 file of the Shanghai Municipal Police (full police biographies of applicants), their registration cards, and, where available, other documents from the Shanghai and Harbin Directories and SMP files.

Sources, methods and acknowledgments

We have started from the Shanghai Municipal Police file D/917, which is available at the National Archives and Records Administration (NARA), College Park, MD, USA, as a part of Record Group 263 "Records of the Central Intelligence Agency", Publication M1750.

The archive has documents with serial numbers from 251 to 392. Documents with earlier and later serial numbers did not survived.

We have applied artificial intelligence to the analysis of back sides of registration cards of Russians in Shangha in 1939-1946 (Microfilm Copy of Registration Cards of Russian Emigrants, 1940 - 1945, the part of the same NARA Publication M1750).

We then were able to recover the names of Shanghai Volunteer Corps Russian applicants whose applications were missing.

We also enriched the data with **External archival references to this person:** field which has references to those Shanghai registration cards, even though the original applications do not have them. They are referenced as per book "Russians in China. Genealogical Index 1926-1946" (ISBN 978-1936531158). All those documents are in possession of author.

You can ask for a copy of relevant documents by writing me at kir@rusgenproject.com.

We have kept the documents in their chronological order. Last names index in Russian language was created to facilitate the search for particular person. The index included, in addition to files' subjects, other persons mentionned in D/917 documents, especially "Known to" references. So you should not be surprised to find the female names in the index. Those usually relatives and landlords of applicants.

Explanations

We have routinely omitted the page numbers from the D.917, as well as the notes that *Applicant is registered with the Russian Emigrants' Committee*, or that *Applicant did not come to police notice*, or *There is nothing in the Municipal Police records detrimental to his character* or *While in Shanghai he did not come to the notice of the Municipal Police in connection with any activities of an undesirable nature*, which were the standard indications of no criminal records.

We allowed for the variety in English spellings of Russian names and places to remain, correcting only obvious typing mistakes. You never know in which spelling someone will search for his ancestor.

Most of the text of those files is in English language. We sometimes put the Russian language notes to records, but we hope they are short, help understand the document and are mostly self-explaining.

Statistics and facts

The youngest applicant was born in 1922 (around 18 years old), oldest was 56 years old. Average age was 25 years at the time of application.

Fourteen persons applied twice, probably after the unsuccessfull first attempt.

Largest part of applicants were born in Harbin, slighly less in Vladivostok, the remaining were spread evenly from Warsaw to Tokyo.

There are a number of Russians who applied to the Shanghai volunteer corps after serving in the troops of notorious warlord Chang Chung Chang (a.k.a. Zhang Zongchang, a.k.a. Chang Tsung-ch'ang). They represent an interesting gang and indexed separately at the end of the index.

Along those relatively straighforward applications there is a long file on certain Lev Nicolaevich Primortsev. We decided to leave it where it was filed chronologically.

All primary sources used are the public domain documents.

Abbreviations

SMC - Shangai Municipal Council

SMP - Shanghai Municipal Police

SVC - Shanghai Volunteer Corps.

SSD - Shanghai Special District Court

YMCA - Young Man Christian Association

H.B.M. - Her British Majesty

Recovered files #1-250 (1930-Dec 1938)

Full Name in Russian: Костин Федор Семенович
Report date: -
Report number: -
External archival references to this person: SH/61178
Notes: No date, no number.

Full Name in Russian: Семибратов Яков Семенович
Report date: -
Report number: -
External archival references to this person: SH/110309
Notes: No date, no number.

Full Name in Russian: Сергиевский Лев Николаевич
Report date: -
Report number: -
External archival references to this person: SH/110435
Notes: No date, no number.

Full Name in Russian: Чудинов Иван Сергеевич
Report date: -
Report number: -
External archival references to this person: SH/21634
Notes: No date, no number.

Full Name in Russian: Щирский-Чернский Иван Яковлевич
Report date:
Report number:
External archival references to this person: SH/110090
Notes: No date, no number.

Full Name in Russian: Юшков Афанасий Гаврилович
Report date: -
Report number: -
External archival references to this person: SH/140057
Notes: No date, no number.

Full Name in Russian: Рымович Владислав Владиславович
Report date: -
Report number: -
External archival references to this person: SH/101781
Notes: Запрос Л. Гроссе. Без даты и номера.

Full Name in Russian: Ступин Иннокентий Васильевич
Report date: *
Report number: 3
External archival references to this person: SH/120995
Notes: Опечатка - в индексе указан как Стутин.

Full Name in Russian: Тархов Василий Алексеевич
Report date: 1930
Report number: 5
External archival references to this person: SH/121366
Notes: Дата указана условно.

Full Name in Russian: Васильев Николай Николаевич
Report date: -
Report number: 7
External archival references to this person: SH/130774
Notes: No date.

Full Name in Russian: Иванченко Фромель Роберт Борис Георгиевич
Report date: -
Report number: 12
External archival references to this person: SH/50386
Notes: Без отчества в индексе.

Full Name in Russian: Трофимов Василий Зиновьевич
Report date: -
Report number: 16
External archival references to this person: SH/122190
Notes: No date.

Full Name in Russian: Воронцов Михаил Владимирович
Report date: *
Report number: 16
External archival references to this person: SH/131669

Notes: No date.

Full Name in Russian: Емельянов А. С.
Report date: 26.7.1941
Report number: 18
External archival references to this person: SH/140884
Notes: плохо читается. Опечатка в карточке. Должно быть 1931 г.

Full Name in Russian: Зарембо Петр Дмитриевич
Report date: -
Report number: 18
External archival references to this person: SH/140348
Notes: упомянут В. Гроссе. Дата определена по другой карточке с тем
же номером.

Full Name in Russian: Щекин Алексей Алексеевич
Report date: -
Report number: 19
External archival references to this person: SH/110011
Notes: No date.

Full Name in Russian: Щекин Андрей Алексеевич
Report date: *
Report number: 19
External archival references to this person: SH/110013
Notes: No date.

Full Name in Russian: Непомнящий Борис Павлович
Report date: *
Report number: 21
External archival references to this person: SH/81573
Notes: No date.

Full Name in Russian: Козловский Владимир Иванович
Report date: *
Report number: 25
External archival references to this person: SH/61563
Notes: No date.

Full Name in Russian: Федосеев Валентин Гаврилович
Report date: *
Report number: 27
External archival references to this person: SH/31403
Notes: No date.

Full Name in Russian: Шастин Николай Меркурьевич
Report date: *
Report number: 40
External archival references to this person: SH/110687
Notes: No date.

Full Name in Russian: Альткласс Борис
Report date: 27.10.1931
Report number: 62
External archival references to this person: SH/10424

Full Name in Russian: Нестеров Владимир
Report date: 23.1.1934
Report number: 74
External archival references to this person: SH/81721
Notes: Нет отчества. Карточка не его.

Full Name in Russian: Байгильдин Ибрагим Сафович
Report date: 24.1.1934
Report number: 76
External archival references to this person: SH/11476

Full Name in Russian: Батуев Игорь Леонидович
Report date: 20.2.1934
Report number: 77
External archival references to this person: SH/11455

Full Name in Russian: Нилус Александр Евгеньевич
Report date: 20.2.1934
Report number: 77
External archival references to this person: SH/81963

Full Name in Russian: Законов Петр Михайлович
Report date: 7.3.1934

Report number: 78
External archival references to this person: SH/140261

Full Name in Russian: Калитилин Алексей Николаевич
Report date: 26.3.1934
Report number: 79
External archival references to this person: SH/51052

Full Name in Russian: Волчков Георгий Васильевич
Report date: 12.4.1934
Report number: 81
External archival references to this person: SH/131416
Notes: В карточке опечатка - указан 1932 вместо 1934

Full Name in Russian: Диго Виктор Николаевич
Report date: 12.4.1934
Report number: 81
External archival references to this person: SH/30107
Notes: нет отдельной карточки.

Full Name in Russian: Адрианов Николай Владимирович
Report date:
Report number: 82
External archival references to this person: SH/10125
Notes: Без даты.

Full Name in Russian: Никитин Андрей Петрович
Report date: 3.5.1934
Report number:
External archival references to this person: SH/81874
Notes: Без номера.

Full Name in Russian: Захаров Владимир Исидорович
Report date: 15.5.1934
Report number: *
External archival references to this person: SH/140237
Notes: No date.

Full Name in Russian: Добровольский Александр Петрович
Report date: 15.5.1934

Report number: *
External archival references to this person: SH/30321
Notes: Без номера.

Full Name in Russian: Скобяев Павел Флегонтович
Report date: 15.5.1934
Report number: *
External archival references to this person: SH/111833
Notes: Без номера.

Full Name in Russian: Петер Владимир Анатольевич
Report date: 25.5.1934
Report number: 85
External archival references to this person: SH/91212

Full Name in Russian: Дюдин Борис Алексеевич
Report date: 2.6.1934
Report number: *
External archival references to this person: SH/30682
Notes: Без номера.

Full Name in Russian: Скаредов Олег Николаевич
Report date: 12.6.1934
Report number: *
External archival references to this person: SH/111787
Notes: Без номера.

Full Name in Russian: Рудин Сильвестр Николаевич
Report date: 22.6.1934
Report number: 88
External archival references to this person: SH/101635
Notes: Рудин-Донченко

Full Name in Russian: Попов Василий Евграфович
Report date: 2.7.1934
Report number: -
External archival references to this person: SH/100021
Notes: Без номера.

Full Name in Russian: Глебов Вадим Иванович
Report date: 12.9.1934
Report number: *
External archival references to this person: SH/40444
Notes: Без номера.

Full Name in Russian: Тархов Борис Николаевич
Report date: 2.11.1934
Report number: *
External archival references to this person: SH/121368
Notes: 2 раза

Full Name in Russian: Андогский Всеволод Александрович
Report date: 8.11.1934
Report number: *
External archival references to this person: SH/10510
Notes: Без номера.

Full Name in Russian: Чердынцев Дмитрий Владимирович
Report date: 8.11.1934
Report number: *
External archival references to this person: SH/21251

Full Name in Russian: Марков Георгий Алексеевич
Report date: 15.11.1934
Report number: 97
External archival references to this person: SH/70781

Full Name in Russian: Тарасов Сергей Александрович
Report date: 15.11.1934
Report number: 97
External archival references to this person: SH/121315

Full Name in Russian: Токмаков Владимир Вениаминович
Report date: 15.11.1934
Report number: 97
External archival references to this person: SH/121817

Full Name in Russian: Мелешко Александр Максимович
Report date: 19.11.1934

Report number: 98
External archival references to this person: SH/71101
Notes: 2 раза

Full Name in Russian: Дронников Сергей Николаевич
Report date: 19.11.1934
Report number: 98
External archival references to this person: SH/30591

Full Name in Russian: Салищев Петр Петрович
Report date: 19.11.1934
Report number: 98
External archival references to this person: SH/101903

Full Name in Russian: Редров Георгий Геннадьевич
Report date: 18.12.1930
Report number: 100
External archival references to this person: SH/100836
Notes: В карточке опечатка - указан 1930 вместо 1934

Full Name in Russian: Краковцев Владимир Михайлович
Report date: 6.3.1935
Report number: *
External archival references to this person: SH/61603

Full Name in Russian: Робустов Викентий Александрович
Report date: 18.3.1935
Report number: *
External archival references to this person: SH/101129

Full Name in Russian: Бородина Мария Николаевна
Report date: 4.6.1935
Report number: 107
External archival references to this person: SH/20652
Notes: упомянута

Full Name in Russian: Гинх Глеб Николаевич
Report date: 21.6.1935
Report number: 109
External archival references to this person: SH/41522

Full Name in Russian: Сычев-Данилевский Константин Павлович
Report date: 14.12.1935
Report number: 110
External archival references to this person: SH/111716

Full Name in Russian: Волошин Константин Васильевич
Report date: 14.12.1935
Report number: 110
External archival references to this person: SH/131546

Full Name in Russian: Дубович Эльмень Виктор Иоганович
Report date: 27.12.1935
Report number: *
External archival references to this person: SH/30480
Notes: Без номера.

Full Name in Russian: Лысик Александр Александрович
Report date: 4.2.1936
Report number: 113
External archival references to this person: SH/81193

Full Name in Russian: Мезенцев Николай Иванович
Report date: 13.5.1936
Report number: *
External archival references to this person: SH/71463
Notes: Без номера.

Full Name in Russian: Фуфелев Иннокентий Гаврилович
Report date: 29.5.1936
Report number: 118
External archival references to this person: SH/31433

Full Name in Russian: Мельников Игорь Иродионович
Report date: 29.5.1936
Report number: 118
External archival references to this person: SH/71171

Full Name in Russian: Вальтер Михаил Александрович
Report date: 3.6.1936
Report number: *

External archival references to this person: SH/131790
Notes: Без номера.

Full Name in Russian: Романов Леонид Тимофеевич
Report date: 10.6.1936
Report number: 20
External archival references to this person: SH/101272
Notes: В карточке опечатка. Должен быть номер 120.

Full Name in Russian: Шевелев Ростислав Борисович
Report date: 19.6.1936
Report number: 121
External archival references to this person: SH/110950

Full Name in Russian: Горлинский Александр Викторович
Report date: 21.6.1935
Report number: 122
External archival references to this person: SH/40989
Notes: В карточке опечатка. Должно быть 1936 г.

Full Name in Russian: Носков Борис Артемьевич
Report date: 21.6.1936
Report number: 122
External archival references to this person: SH/82032

Full Name in Russian: Примаков Петр Гаврилович
Report date: 21.6.1936
Report number: 122
External archival references to this person: SH/100390

Full Name in Russian: Турлук-Кортус Виктор Иванович
Report date: 25.6.1936
Report number: -
External archival references to this person: SH/122050
Notes: Без номера.

Full Name in Russian: Короткевич Лев Михайлович
Report date: 2.7.1936
Report number: 124
External archival references to this person: SH/61001

Full Name in Russian: Янчевский Дмитрий Владимирович
Report date: 25.7.1936
Report number: 126
External archival references to this person: SH/132075

Full Name in Russian: Эпов Владимир Алексеевич
Report date: 25.7.1936
Report number: 126
External archival references to this person: SH/140941

Full Name in Russian: Евстафиев Леонид Борисович
Report date: 27.7.1936
Report number: 127
External archival references to this person: SH/31107

Full Name in Russian: Приходько Виталий Степанович
Report date: 3.8.1936
Report number: 128
External archival references to this person: SH/100370

Full Name in Russian: Стогней Николай Константинович
Report date: 7.8.1936
Report number: 129
External archival references to this person: SH/120817

Full Name in Russian: Петренко Василий Георгиевич
Report date: 15.8.1936
Report number: 131
External archival references to this person: SH/91253
Notes: 2 раза

Full Name in Russian: Урович Константин Константинович
Report date: 23.9.1936
Report number: 133
External archival references to this person: SH/130474

Full Name in Russian: Григорьев Леонид Васильевич
Report date: 28.9.1936
Report number: 134
External archival references to this person: SH/41299

Full Name in Russian: Фокин Леонид Васильевич
Report date: 30.9.1936
Report number: 135
External archival references to this person: SH/31713
Notes: 2 раза

Full Name in Russian: Диканов Евгений Евгеньевич
Report date: 30.9.1937
Report number: 135
External archival references to this person: SH/30113
Notes: Опечатка в дате. Должно быть 30.9.1936

Full Name in Russian: Жаров Леонид Георгиевич
Report date: 3.10.1936
Report number: 136
External archival references to this person: SH/140559
Notes: 2 раза

Full Name in Russian: Голубков Г.
Report date: 16.10.1936
Report number: 137
External archival references to this person: SH/40688
Notes: Карточка без даты. Дата определена экстраполяцией. Лицо отсутствует в индексе.

Full Name in Russian: Гончаренко Иосиф Маркович
Report date: 16.10.1936
Report number: 137
External archival references to this person: SH/40796

Full Name in Russian: Стоцкий Владимир Владимирович
Report date: 16.10.1936
Report number: 137
External archival references to this person: SH/120883
Notes:

Full Name in Russian: Тевзадзе Гиго Парменович
Report date: 17.10.1936
Report number: 138
External archival references to this person: SH/121643

Notes: Вероятно ошибка в дате. Указано 21.12.1936, скорее всего
17.10.1936

Full Name in Russian: Миронов Георгий Михайлович
Report date: 17.10.1936
Report number: 138
External archival references to this person: SH/71810

Full Name in Russian: Писарев Борис Николаевич
Report date: 29.10.1936
Report number: 140
External archival references to this person: SH/91626
Notes: Год на карточке не указан. Дата определена экстраполяцией.

Full Name in Russian: Рухлядев Владимир Викторович
Report date: 29.10.1936
Report number: 140
External archival references to this person: SH/101483

Full Name in Russian: Петров Виктор Петрович
Report date: 6.11.1936
Report number: 141
External archival references to this person: SH/91301

Full Name in Russian: Круглик Игорь Иллиодорович
Report date: 8.12.
Report number: 143
External archival references to this person: SH/61918
Notes: В карточке год не указан.

Full Name in Russian: Лашкевич Георгий Алексеевич
Report date: 8.12.
Report number: 143
External archival references to this person: SH/70373
Notes: В карточке год не указан.

Full Name in Russian: Пономарев Владимир Иосифович
Report date: 8.12.1936
Report number: 144
External archival references to this person: SH/92166

Full Name in Russian: Шестаков Феодор Алексеевич
Report date: 8.12.1936
Report number: 143
External archival references to this person: SH/110889

Full Name in Russian: Третьяков Степан Алексеевич
Report date: 8.12.1936
Report number: 143
External archival references to this person: SH/122127

Full Name in Russian: Нежин Валентин Александрович
Report date: -
Report number: 145
External archival references to this person: SH/81660
Notes: В карточке без даты.

Full Name in Russian: Теславский Евгений Николаевич
Report date: 25.1.1937
Report number: 146
External archival references to this person: SH/121626

Full Name in Russian: Попов Владимир Иванович
Report date: 4.2.1937
Report number: 148
External archival references to this person: SH/100037

Full Name in Russian: Шевелев Олег Владимирович
Report date: 4.2.1937
Report number: 148
External archival references to this person: SH/110952

Full Name in Russian: Покачалов Анатолий Васильевич
Report date: 9.2.1937
Report number: 149
External archival references to this person: SH/91914

Full Name in Russian: Муханов Александр Вивианович
Report date: 16.3.1937
Report number: 150
External archival references to this person: SH/72023

Full Name in Russian: Тешин Николай Павлович
Report date: 16.3.1937
Report number: 150
External archival references to this person: SH/121622

Full Name in Russian: Ценин Константин Федорович
Report date: 16.3.1937
Report number: 150
External archival references to this person: SH/130135

Full Name in Russian: Скалин Николай Иванович
Report date: 22.3.1937
Report number: 151
External archival references to this person: SH/111775
Notes: Опечатка в индексе - Сколин

Full Name in Russian: Утюжников Михаил Ильич
Report date: 22.3.1937
Report number: 151
External archival references to this person: SH/130560

Full Name in Russian: Жаров Леонид Георгиевич
Report date: 27.3.1937
Report number: 153
External archival references to this person: SH/140559
Notes: 2 раза

Full Name in Russian: Алексеев Василий Васильевич
Report date: 17.4.1937
Report number: 156
External archival references to this person: SH/10360

Full Name in Russian: Фоминых Александр Григорьевич
Report date: 17.4.1937
Report number: 156
External archival references to this person: SH/31747

Full Name in Russian: Найденьшев Евгений Петрович
Report date: 17.4.1937
Report number: 156

External archival references to this person: SH/81402

Full Name in Russian: Носков Семен Васильевич
Report date: 17.4.1937
Report number: 156
External archival references to this person: SH/82044

Full Name in Russian: Тауц Борис Львович
Report date: 17.4.1937
Report number: 156
External archival references to this person: SH/121430

Full Name in Russian: Баронов Евгений Александрович
Report date: 15.5.1937
Report number: *
External archival references to this person: SH/11334
Notes: Без номера.

Full Name in Russian: Зоренко Харитон Кириллович
Report date: 15.5.1937
Report number: *
External archival references to this person: SH/140722
Notes: Без номера. 2 раза.

Full Name in Russian: Велюхов Илья Михайлович
Report date: 28.5.1937
Report number: 150
External archival references to this person: SH/131035
Notes: 2 раза. Вероятно опечатка в номере или дате.

Full Name in Russian: Егоров Милий Николаевич
Report date: 1.6.1937
Report number: 159
External archival references to this person: SH/30831

Full Name in Russian: Максимов Федорищев Виктор Петрович
Report date: 1.6.1937
Report number: 159
External archival references to this person: SH/71075

Full Name in Russian: Гелемиев Борис Тихонович
Report date: 3.6.1937
Report number: 159
External archival references to this person: SH/40141
Notes: Опечатка в индексе.

Full Name in Russian: Стрельчук Николай Михайлович
Report date: 18.6.1937
Report number: 160
External archival references to this person: SH/120923

Full Name in Russian: Грищев Михаил Степанович
Report date: 25.7.1937
Report number: 161
External archival references to this person: SH/41357
Notes: Вероятно ошибка в дате, должно быть 25.6.1937

Full Name in Russian: Меньков Владимир Михайлович
Report date: 2.7.1937
Report number: 162
External archival references to this person: SH/71314
Notes: 2 раза

Full Name in Russian: Попов Александр Евграфович
Report date: 2.7.1937
Report number: 162
External archival references to this person: SH/100019

Full Name in Russian: Усанков Л. А.
Report date: 19.7.1937
Report number: 163
External archival references to this person: SH/130489
Notes: Нет отдельной карточки.

Full Name in Russian: Мелешко Александр Максимович
Report date: 28.7.1937
Report number: 168
External archival references to this person: SH/71101
Notes: 2 раза

Full Name in Russian: Сосновский Валентин Михайлович
Report date: 28.7.1938
Report number: 168
External archival references to this person: SH/120391
Notes: Опечатка в дате. Должно быть 28.7.1937

Full Name in Russian: Сомнительнов Геннадий Иванович
Report date: 28.7.1937
Report number: 168
External archival references to this person: SH/120276

Full Name in Russian: Чернышев Алексей Петрович
Report date: 11.8.1937
Report number: 169
External archival references to this person: SH/21442

Full Name in Russian: Якунин Дмитрий Федорович
Report date: 29.8.1937
Report number: 170
External archival references to this person: SH/132049

Full Name in Russian: Аткачунас Константин Иосифович
Report date: 1.9.1937
Report number: 171
External archival references to this person: SH/10934
Notes: Transport Company, S.V.C.

Full Name in Russian: Скуев Викторин Валерьевич
Report date: 1.9.1937
Report number: 171
External archival references to this person: SH/111840

Full Name in Russian: Уженин Федор Сергеевич
Report date: 3.9.1937
Report number: 177
External archival references to this person: SH/130457

Full Name in Russian: Комарницкий Владимир Федорович
Report date: 4.9.1937
Report number: 172

External archival references to this person: SH/60511

Full Name in Russian: Богословский Николай Владимирович
Report date: 5.9.1937
Report number: 173
External archival references to this person: SH/20229

Full Name in Russian: Коротков Александр Степанович
Report date: 5.9.1937
Report number: 174
External archival references to this person: SH/61006

Full Name in Russian: Скарятин Георгий Александрович
Report date: 5.9.1937
Report number: 175
External archival references to this person: SH/111795

Full Name in Russian: Степанов Борис Иванович
Report date: 7.9.1937
Report number: 176
External archival references to this person: SH/120738

Full Name in Russian: Бельдин Виталий Лаврентьевич
Report date: 10.9.1937
Report number: 178
External archival references to this person: SH/12013

Full Name in Russian: Сычев Игорь Ефимович
Report date: 16.9.1937
Report number: 180
External archival references to this person: SH/111718

Full Name in Russian: Шмулевский Леонид Израелевич
Report date: 22.9.1937
Report number: 182
External archival references to this person: SH/111257

Full Name in Russian: Сосновский Леонид Михайлович
Report date: 20.10.1937
Report number: 183

External archival references to this person: SH/120389

Full Name in Russian: Тарасов Николай Николаевич
Report date: 28.10.1937
Report number: 184
External archival references to this person: SH/121317

Full Name in Russian: Махов Сергей Гурьевич
Report date: 4.11.1937
Report number: 185
External archival references to this person: SH/81264

Full Name in Russian: Ханжин Владимир Михайлович
Report date: 8.11.1937
Report number: 186
External archival references to this person: SH/41711

Full Name in Russian: Тельных Виктор Антонович
Report date: 8.11.1937
Report number: 186
External archival references to this person: SH/121525

Full Name in Russian: Меньков Владимир Михайлович
Report date: 15.11.1937
Report number: 187
External archival references to this person: SH/71314
Notes: 2 раза

Full Name in Russian: Новожилов Василий Сергеевич
Report date: 22.11.1937
Report number: 187
External archival references to this person: SH/82149

Full Name in Russian: Языков Иннокентий Афанасьевич
Report date: 22.11.1937
Report number: 187
External archival references to this person: SH/132198

Full Name in Russian: Марков Гавриил Иванович
Report date: 28.11.1937

Report number: 188
External archival references to this person: SH/70804

Full Name in Russian: Спирин Павел Григорьевич
Report date: 13.12.1937
Report number: 189
External archival references to this person: SH/120510

Full Name in Russian: Жемчужин Борис Владимирович
Report date: 15.12.1937
Report number: 184
External archival references to this person: SH/50714

Full Name in Russian: Ломаев Семен Алексеевич
Report date: 24.12.1937
Report number: 190
External archival references to this person: SH/80897

Full Name in Russian: Лукин Георгий Димитриевич
Report date: 4.1.1938
Report number: 193
External archival references to this person: SH/80921

Full Name in Russian: Андреев Алексей Иванович
Report date: 9.1.1938
Report number: 192
External archival references to this person: SH/10515
Notes: 2 раза

Full Name in Russian: Андреев Михаил Иванович
Report date: 9.1.1938
Report number: 192
External archival references to this person: SH/10529
Notes: 2 раза

Full Name in Russian: Андреев Валентин Иванович
Report date: 9.1.1938
Report number: 192
External archival references to this person: SH/10541

Full Name in Russian: Попов Александр Владимирович
Report date: 13.1.1938
Report number: 191
External archival references to this person: SH/100029

Full Name in Russian: Нарышкин Юрий Сергеевич
Report date: 13.1.1938
Report number: 193
External archival references to this person: SH/81442

Full Name in Russian: Веретенников Иннокентий Капикович
Report date: 28.1.1938
Report number: 194
External archival references to this person: SH/131077

Full Name in Russian: Бедрин Венедикт Васильевич
Report date: 5.3.1938
Report number: 199
External archival references to this person: SH/11539

Full Name in Russian: Жуков Виктор Григорьевич
Report date: 7.3.1938
Report number: 200
External archival references to this person: SH/50865

Full Name in Russian: Макаров Борис Николаевич
Report date: 7.3.1938
Report number: 200
External archival references to this person: SH/81325

Full Name in Russian: Шимохин Александр Петрович
Report date: 14.3.1938
Report number: 202
External archival references to this person: SH/111033

Full Name in Russian: Павлов Леонид Витальевич
Report date: 19.3.1938
Report number: 205
External archival references to this person: SH/90932

Full Name in Russian: Вольский Владимир Александрович
Report date: 21.3.1938
Report number: 207
External archival references to this person: SH/131569

Full Name in Russian: Велюхов Илья Михайлович
Report date: 30.3.1938
Report number: 208
External archival references to this person: SH/131035
Notes: 2 раза

Full Name in Russian: Алябьев Евгений Гаврилович
Report date: 6.4.1938
Report number: 210
External archival references to this person: SH/10400

Full Name in Russian: Денисов Георгий Иннокентьевич
Report date: 6.4.1938
Report number: 210
External archival references to this person: SH/22053

Full Name in Russian: Иванчин Иван Иванович
Report date: 6.4.1938
Report number: 210
External archival references to this person: SH/50393

Full Name in Russian: Лисуненко Георгий Петрович
Report date: 6.4.1938
Report number: 210
External archival references to this person: SH/80736

Full Name in Russian: Данилов П. Т.
Report date: 12.4.1938
Report number: 211
External archival references to this person: SH/21876
Notes: Нет отдельной карточки.

Full Name in Russian: Голос Виталий Е.
Report date: 12.4.1938
Report number: 211

External archival references to this person: SH/40067

Full Name in Russian: Пятаков Петр Михайлович
Report date: 12.4.1938
Report number: 211
External archival references to this person: SH/91518

Full Name in Russian: Колесников Георгий Николаевич
Report date: 19.4.1938
Report number: 212
External archival references to this person: SH/60373

Full Name in Russian: Петров Никита Никитич
Report date: 23.4.1938
Report number: 213
External archival references to this person: SH/91287

Full Name in Russian: Васильев Вадим Петрович
Report date: 2.5.1938
Report number: 214
External archival references to this person: SH/130786

Full Name in Russian: Поляков Николай Леонидович
Report date: 14.5.1936
Report number: 217
External archival references to this person: SH/92004
Notes: Опечатка в карточке. Должно быть 14.5.1938 г.

Full Name in Russian: Кирьяков Константин Сергеевич
Report date: 14.5.1938
Report number: 216
External archival references to this person: SH/51831

Full Name in Russian: Третьяков Николай Александрович
Report date: 14.5.1938
Report number: 216
External archival references to this person: SH/122129

Full Name in Russian: Габескирия Георгий Михайлович
Report date: 14.5.1938

Report number: 217
External archival references to this person: SH/31964

Full Name in Russian: Луполов Иосиф Иосифович
Report date: 14.5.1938
Report number: 217
External archival references to this person: SH/80932

Full Name in Russian: Циммерман Борис Давидович
Report date: 14.5.1938
Report number: 217
External archival references to this person: SH/140598

Full Name in Russian: Павлов Мартиан Петрович
Report date: 3.6.1938
Report number: 221
External archival references to this person: SH/90930

Full Name in Russian: Кардашьянц Степан Мамиконович
Report date: 5.7.1938
Report number: 224
External archival references to this person: SH/51328

Full Name in Russian: Толстогузов Виктор Степанович
Report date: 9.7.1938
Report number: 225
External archival references to this person: SH/121878

Full Name in Russian: Попов Константин Александрович
Report date: 3.8.1938
Report number: 227
External archival references to this person: SH/100054

Full Name in Russian: Андреев Алексей Иванович
Report date: 16.8.1939
Report number: 230
External archival references to this person: SH/10515
Notes: 2 раза. Опечатка в карточке. Должно быть 16.8.1938 г.

Full Name in Russian: Сердюк Анатолий Николаевич
Report date: 16.8.1938
Report number: 230
External archival references to this person: SH/110368

Full Name in Russian: Талавиков Георгий Константинович
Report date: 22.8.1938
Report number: 231
External archival references to this person: SH/121253
Notes: Таловиков?

Full Name in Russian: Шаврин Николай Всеволодович
Report date: 22.9.1938
Report number: 234
External archival references to this person: SH/110711

Full Name in Russian: Шестаков Михаил Иванович
Report date: 22.9.1938
Report number: 234
External archival references to this person: SH/110885

Full Name in Russian: Андреев Михаил Иванович
Report date: 13.10.1938
Report number: 236
External archival references to this person: SH/10529
Notes: 2 раза

Full Name in Russian: Попов Георгий Константинович
Report date: 14.10.1938
Report number: 237
External archival references to this person: SH/100056

Full Name in Russian: Амбарянц Петр Георгиевич
Report date: 20.10.1938
Report number: 239
External archival references to this person: SH/10460
Notes: 2 раза

Full Name in Russian: Новицкий Олег Вениаминович
Report date: 20.10.1938

Report number: 239
External archival references to this person: SH/82133

Full Name in Russian: Полетика Феодосий Сергеевич
Report date: 20.10.1938
Report number: 239
External archival references to this person: SH/91969

Full Name in Russian: Мельников Семен Иванович
Report date: 25.10.1938
Report number: 240
External archival references to this person: SH/71175

Full Name in Russian: Нежин Георгий Александрович
Report date: 25.10.1938
Report number: 240
External archival references to this person: SH/81662

Full Name in Russian: Безручко Павел Георгиевич
Report date: 15.11.1938
Report number: 241
External archival references to this person: SH/11970

Full Name in Russian: Кулинберг Виктор Сергеевич
Report date: 15.11.1938
Report number: 242
External archival references to this person: SH/60718

Full Name in Russian: Франк, де Виктор Николаевич
Report date: 25.11.38
Report number: 244
External archival references to this person: SH/31790

Full Name in Russian: Цируленко Анатолий Трофимович
Report date: 13.12.1938
Report number: 250
External archival references to this person: SH/130190

Full text files #251-392 (13 Dec 1938-26 Aug 1940)

Full Name in English:	Fedoroff Stepan Ivanovitch
Full Name in Russian:	Фёдоров Степан Иванович
Birth Year:	1920
Birth Place:	Vladivostok, Maritime Province
Report Title:	S.I. Fedoroff, applicant for enlistment in the Russian Regiment, S. V. C.
Report date:	13 December 1938
Report number:	251

Stepan Ivanovitch Fedoroff, was born on August 28, 1920 in Vladivostok, Maritime Province, His late father, a Chinese, was engaged in commercial business in that city. The applicant arrived in Shanghai together with his mother in 1926. From 1927 to 1929 he attended the Russian Commercial School. Upon the death of his mother in 1929 he was placed by the French Consular Authorities in the St. Francis Xavier's college in which he studied up to October, 1936.

Full Name in English:	Annaukhkoff (Hill) Alexey Prokopievitch
Full Name in Russian:	Аннаухов (Хилл) Алексей Прокопьевич
Birth Year:	1918
Birth Place:	Krasnoyarsk, Siberia
Private Address:	Route Bourgeat, 331
Report Title:	Alec Hill, applicant for enrolment in "B" Company, S. V. C.
Report date:	21/12/1938
Report number:	252

Alexey Prokopievitch Annaukhkoff (Hill), Russian, was born on March 29, 1918 at Krasnoyarsk, Siberia. His aunt, E. Boubnoff, was married to Mr. G. C. Hill, H.B.M. Consul-General in Vladivostok. In 1924, the applicant was unofficially adopted by Mr. and Mrs. Hill and has since been known under the name of Hill. He arrived in Harbin from Vladivostok in 1927 together with Mr. and Mrs. Hill and resided there until 1929 when he left Harbin for England, where until 1933 he attended the St. Georges Scholl on the Isle of Wight. He arrived in the Shanghai in 1933. In the beginning of 1935 he entered the Public and Thomas Hanbury School, graduating from same in 1937.

In June 1938 he obtained his present position with Alexander Clark Co., (Shanghai) Ltd.

Mr. G.C. Hill died in Shanghai in 1935 and at present the applicant is residing together with Mrs. Hill at 331 Route Bourgeat.

Full Name in English:	Nikolaeff Semen Nikolaevitch
Full Name in Russian:	Николаев Семен Николаевич
Birth Year:	1912
Birth Place:	Simbirsk Province, Russia
Report Title:	S.N. Nikolaeff, applicant for enlistment in the Russian Regiment, S.V.C.
Report date:	23 December 1938
Report number:	253

Semen Nikolaevitch Nikolaeff, Russian, was born on September 1, 1912 in Simbirsk Province, Russia. From 1918 to 1927 he resided together with his parents on the Saghalin Island. In 1927, he proceed to Harbin and until 1931 worked there as a bus conductor and subsequently as a bus driver. He arrived in Shanghai in June 1931 and soon afterwards obtained a position as a chauffeur with Mr. M. Artischeff, proprietor of a dairy farm in the French Concession. On March 14, 1932, he joined and the Russian Regiment, S.V.C. in which he served until October 31, 1937, when he resigned on his own accord. Upon leaving the Regiment, he worked casually as a driver and for the past six months was employed by the City Express Transportation Company, 613/55 Avenue Joffre.

Full Name in English:	Sahno Ivan Ivanovitch
Full Name in Russian:	Сахно Иван Иванович
Birth Year:	1913
Birth Place:	Harbin. Manchuria
Private Address:	Astor Rd, 24
Report Title:	I. I. Sahno, G.K. Baklanoff and V.V. Russian, applicants for enlistment in the Russian Regiment, S.V.C.
Report date:	9 January 1939
Report number:	254

Ivan Ivanovitch Sahno, Russian, was born on June 17, 1913 in Harbin. Manchuria. He first came to Shanghai in 1934 and according to his own statement, lived here for a period being unemployed and supported by his father. On February 2, 1935 he joined the Auxiliary Detachment of the French Police in which he served until 8-5-35 when he deserted in order to proceed to Harbin. He returned to Shanghai in April, 1938 and worked casually until September of the same year when he was engaged by Calatroni, Hsieh & Co., as a godown keeper. He left that employment on his own accord recently in order to join the Russian Regiment.

The applicant's mother and mother and brother left Harbin for the U.S.S.R. in 1936. His sister at present is residing in Harbin.

On his first arrival in Shanghai he registered with the Council of United Russian Organisations (SORO) but at present is registered with the Russian Emigrants' Committee, 118/1 Moulmein Road.

Full Name in English:	Baklanoff Georgy Makarovitch
Full Name in Russian:	Бакланов Георгий Макарович
Birth Year:	1902
Birth Place:	Barnaul, Siberia
Private Address:	Macgregor Rd, 91
Report Title:	I. I. Sahno, G.K. Baklanoff and V.V. Russian, applicants for enlistment in the Russian Regiment, S.V.C.
Report date:	9 January 1939
Report number:	254

External archival references to this person: SH/11147

Georgy Makarovitch Baklanoff, Russian, was born on May 15, 1902, in Barnaul, Siberia. He is reported to have escaped from the U.S.S.R. to Manchuria in 1931 and subsequently resided in Harbin. He arrived in Shanghai in the s.s. "Tsingtao Maru" on December 7, 1938. He is registered with the Russian Emigrants' Committee, 118/1 Moulmein Road on the strength of passport No. 10844 issued by the Harbin Police on 1-8-38.

Being a new arrival in Shanghai, the applicant is not known in the local Russian community.

Full Name in English:	Russian Vladislav Victorovitch
Full Name in Russian:	Русский Владислав Викторович
Birth Year:	1920
Birth Place:	Irkutsk, Siberia
Private Address:	Kungping Terrace, 48
Report Title:	I. I. Sahno, G.K. Baklanoff and V.V. Russian, applicants for enlistment in the Russian Regiment, S.V.C.
Report date:	9 January 1939
Report number:	254

Vladislav Victorovitch Russian, Russian, was born on January 6, 1920 at Irkutsk, Siberia. He is reported to have left Russia together with his parents in 1921 and subsequently resided in Harbin. From 1927 to 1930 he resided in Tientsin. He arrived in Shanghai from the latter city in 1930 and here for a period studied in the Russian Commercial School and later entered the St.. Jeanne d'Arc College, graduating from same in the beginning of 1936. In August of the same year he joined the Auxiliary Detachment of the French police in which he served until September 1937 when he left the service on account of poor health.

He is registered with the Russian Emigrants' Committee. 118/1 Moulmein Road, on the strength of passport No.21098, issued by the Police Bureau of the City Government of Shanghai on 17-5-37.

Full Name in English:	Kazantzeff Nikolai Lookianovitch
Full Name in Russian:	Казанцев Николай Лукьянович
Birth Year:	1911
Birth Place:	Harbin, Manchuria
Report Title:	N.L. Kazantzeff. N.N. Hoodikovsky and G.M. Sity, applicants for enlistment in the Russian Regiment, S.V.C.
Report date:	10 January 1939
Report number:	255
External archival references to this person:	SH/51665

Nikolai Lookianovitch Kazantzeff, Russian, was born on April 4, 1911 in Harbin, Manchuria. He arrived in Shanghai from Harbin in April 1934 and in July of the same year was engaged by the China General Omnibus Company as a ticket Inspector. Leaving this place of employment on his own accord in February 1937 he worked casually mostly as a salesman or a chauffeur. On November 1, 1938 he was fined <invisible>6.00 by the 1st Shanghai Special District Court for driving a Motor Truck without a permit. The applicant's sister, who is believed to be in Singapore at present, was married to K.I. Ivanoff, notorious swindler, who recently committed suicide in Bangkok.

Full Name in English:	Hoodikovsky Nikolai Nikolaevitch
Full Name in Russian:	Худиковский Николай Николаевич
Birth Place:	Chita, Siberia

Report Title:	N.L. Kazantzeff. N.N. Hoodikovsky and G.M. Sity, applicants for enlistment in the Russian Regiment, S.V.C.
Report date:	10 January 1939
Report number:	255

External archival references to this person: SH/50026

Nikolai Nikolaevitch Hoodikovsky, Russian, was born on August 28, <invisible> at Chita, Siberia. He is reported to have left Russia together with his parents in 1923 and subsequently resided in Harbin. The applicant arrived here on the 1-1-30 in the s.s. "Tsingtao Maru", together with his two sisters, travelling on visa No. 3049 issued on 17-12-38 by the Harbin Police. His father, a doctor by profession, is at present residing in Harbin.

Full Name in English:	Sity Georgy Michailovitch
Full Name in Russian:	Сытый Георгий Михайлович
Birth Year:	1920
Birth Place:	Imianpo Station, Chinese Eastern Railway
Report Title:	N.L. Kazantzeff. N.N. Hoodikovsky and G.M. Sity, applicants for enlistment in the Russian Regiment, S.V.C.
Report date:	10 January 1939
Report number:	255

External archival references to this person: SH/111714

Georgy Michailovitch Sity, Russian, was born on April 1, 1920 at Imianpo Station, Chinese Eastern Railway. He resided at that station until his departure to Shanghai and holds passport No. 99, issued on 24-5-38, by the Imianpo Police. He arrived in Shanghai on 30-12-38 in the s.s. "Dairen Maru" and stayed at 150. Route der Soeurs, Apt. 2, with his sister, Z.M. Sity, the wife of a certain Looneff, who is better known under his stage name, Karmelinsky, and who is reported to be in the U.S.S.R. at present.

Full Name in English:	Sogrin Nikolai Michailovitch
Full Name in Russian:	Согрин Николай Михайлович
Birth Year:	1907
Birth Place:	Perm Province, Russia
Report Title:	N.M. Sogrin, applicant for enrolment in the no.3 (Volunteer) Company, S.V.C.
Report date:	18 January 1939
Report number:	256

External archival references to this person: SH/141016, 141017

Nikolai Michailovitch Sogrin, Russian, was born on April 20, 1907 in Perm Province, Russia. He is reported to have left Russia, together with his two brothers in 1920 and subsequently resided in Harbin. Upon graduating from a local high school and the school of accountancy he was employed by Vorontzeff Bros. and Co. as a bookkeeper at their oil factory at Hailar Station, Chinese Eastern Railway, from April 1926 to October 1927, after which he worked as a lumber contractor of the Chinese Eastern Railway up to 1930. In the beginning of 1931, he proceeded to Tsingtao where he was employed as a manager and representative of Vorontzeff Bros. & Co. After liquidation of the branch office of the above company in that city, he proceeded to Shanghai arriving here in September 1933. Here he worked casually until March 1934 when he was engaged by the China General Omnibus Company as a ticket inspector. Leaving this position on his own accord in September 1937 he secured an employment with A.A. Reyer and was placed in charge of their chartered lighters company as a bookkeeper at their general office, 97 Yuen Hing Yuen Road.

The applicant is registered with the Russian Emigrants' committee, 118/1 Moulmein Road, and with the Police Bureau of the City Government of Shanghai (Reg. Cert. No. 13348 issued on 8-9-37).

Full Name in English:	Sorochinsky Sergey Arsentievitch
Full Name in Russian:	Сорочинский Сергей Арсентьевич
Birth Year:	1905
Birth Place:	Bouhedu Station, Chinese Eastern Railway
Private Address:	Chlisan Rd, 21, Room 4
Report Title:	S. Sorochinsky, D. Chelpanoff, A. Koolinberg, G. Arhangelsky, B. Mramornoff, N. Riaudin and V. Leviy, applicants for enlistment in the Russian Regiment, S.V.C.
Report date:	25 January 1939
Report number:	257

External archival references to this person: SH/120336

Sergey Arsentievitch Sorochinsky, Russian, was born on March 23, 1905, at Bouhedu Station, Chinese Eastern Railway. Upon graduating from a local primary school he worked as a chauffeur for various periods in Harbin, Hailar and other railway station on the Chinese Eastern Railway until May 1938 when he proceeded to Tientsin, where, according to his own statement, he worked in the same capacity until September of the same year when he left for Shanghai. Here on September 25, 1938 he joined the Auxiliary Detachment of the French Police, from which he resigned on his own accord on 28-12-38. Being a new arrival in Shanghai he is little known locally.

Full Name in English:	Chelpanoff Dionisy Yakovlevitch
Full Name in Russian:	Челпанов Дионисий Яковлевич
Birth Year:	1906
Birth Place:	Tomsk Province, Siberia
Private Address:	Wayside Rd, 96
Report Title:	S. Sorochinsky, D. Chelpanoff, A. Koolinberg, G. Arhangelsky, B. Mramornoff, N. Riaudin and V. Leviy, applicants for enlistment in the Russian Regiment, S.V.C.
Report date:	25 January 1939
Report number:	257

External archival references to this person: SH/21222

Dionisy Yakovlevitch Chelpanoff, Russian, was born on March 10, 1906 in Tomsk Province, Siberia. He is reported to have escaped from the U.S.S.R. to Manchuria in 1930 and subsequently worked in the Railway Police at Eshaho Station, Chinese Eastern Railway. In September 1938 he proceeded to Tientsin and there joined the Railway Guards and was stationed at a coal mine, situated between Tsinanfu and Tsingtao. In December 1938 he was arrested for insubordination and after being kept prisoner for 17 days at the so called "White House" in Tientsin, he was deported to Shanghai, arriving here on 8-1-39.

He holds passport No. 1928 issued on 27-9-38 by the Police Bureau of the Greater Tientsin.

Full Name in English:	Koolinberg Alexey Sergeyevitch
Full Name in Russian:	Кулинберг Алексей Сергеевич
Birth Year:	1919
Birth Place:	Petrograd, Russia
Private Address:	Macgregor Rd., 121
Report Title:	S. Sorochinsky, D. Chelpanoff, A. Koolinberg, G. Arhangelsky, B. Mramornoff, N. Riaudin and V. Leviy, applicants for enlistment in the Russian Regiment, S.V.C.
Report date:	25 January 1939
Report number:	257

External archival references to this person: SH/60718

Alexey Sergeyevitch Koolinberg, Russian, was born on May 15, 1919 at Petrograd, Russia, He is reported to have left Russia together with his parents in 1921 and subsequently resided in Harbin. In 1934 he left Harbin for Chefoo, where he entered the Yih Wen Commercial College. Upon graduating from same in 1937, he proceeded to Tsingtao, where for the following year he resided together with his mother and his step father, Mr. Goldobin, who until recently was the owner of a bakery in that city. He arrived in Shanghai from Tsingtao on 6-1-39, travelling on passport No. 18462 issued on 7-2-38 by Tsingtao Police. His brother, V. Koolinberg, is at present serving in the Russian Regiment, S.V.C.

Full Name in English:	Arhangelsky Georgy Victorovitch
Full Name in Russian:	Архангельский Георгий Викторович
Birth Year:	1920
Birth Place:	Harbin, Manchuria
Private Address:	Rue Bourgeat, 611/13
Report Title:	S. Sorochinsky, D. Chelpanoff, A. Koolinberg, G. Arhangelsky, B. Mramornoff, N. Riaudin and V. Leviy, applicants for enlistment in the Russian Regiment, S.V.C.
Report date:	25 January 1939
Report number:	257

External archival references to this person: SH/10744

Georgy Victorovitch Arhangelsky, Russian, was born on May 16, 1920 in Harbin, Manchuria. Upon graduating from a local high school in 1938 he proceeded to Shanghai, arriving here on 1-1-39. His brother is at present employed as a radio operator with Moller & Company.

Full Name in English:	Mramornoff Boris Alexeyevitch
Full Name in Russian:	Мраморнов Борис Алексеевич
Birth Year:	1911
Birth Place:	Amur Region, Siberia
Private Address:	Great Western Rd, 61
Report Title:	S. Sorochinsky, D. Chelpanoff, A. Koolinberg, G. Arhangelsky, B. Mramornoff, N. Riaudin and V. Leviy, applicants for enlistment in the Russian Regiment, S.V.C.
Report date:	25 January 1939
Report number:	257

External archival references to this person: SH/80067

Boris Alexeyevitch Mramornoff, Russian, was born on September 6, 1911 in Amur Region, Siberia. He is reported Harbin. In 1927 he joined the Russian Detachment of Marshal Chang Chung Chang's Army in which he served until 1929 when the Detachment was disbanded. He then returned to Harbin. He first arrived in Shanghai in the end of 1930 and in February 1931 joined the Russian Regiment, S.V.C, in which he served until August 1932, when he resigned on his own accord. During the same month he proceeded to Mukden and joined there the Railway Guards, in which capacity he worked until June 1935, when he returned to Shanghai. In July of the same year he joined the Auxiliary Detachment of the French Police in which he served until his dismissal on 11-1-39 for assaulting a Chinese.

Full Name in English:	Riaudin Nikolai Alexeyevitch
Full Name in Russian:	Ряудин Николай Алексеевич
Birth Year:	1917
Birth Place:	Tomsk, Siberia
Private Address:	Av. Du Roi Albert, 373
Report Title:	S. Sorochinsky, D. Chelpanoff, A. Koolinberg, G. Arhangelsky, B. Mramornoff, N. Riaudin and V. Leviy, applicants for enlistment in the Russian Regiment, S.V.C.
Report date:	25 January 1939
Report number:	257
External archival references to this person:	SH/101002

Nikolai Alexeyevitch Riaudin, Russian, was born on April 24, 1917 in Tomsk, Siberia. He is reported to have left Russia together with his parents in 1922 and subsequently resided in Harbin until September 1931, when he left for Shanghai. Here he entered the Russian Commercial School in which he studied up to 1933. In February 1933 he obtained an employment with Foch Pharmacy, 901 Avenue Joffre, as an apprentice. He worked there until July 1935, after which he left for Harbin. Returning to Shanghai in the end of 1935 he joined the Russian Regiment, S.V.C. on 16-12-35, on 16-1-38 he resigned on his own accord and on 30-1-38 joined the Auxiliary Detachment of the French Police, in which he served until 1-1-39 when he resigned on his own accord.

Full Name in English:	Leviy Vassily Dimitrievitch
Full Name in Russian:	Левый Василий Дмитриевич
Birth Year:	1911
Birth Place:	Pogranichnaya Station, Chinese Eastern Railway

Private Address:	Route Paul Henry, 94 Appt. 5.
Report Title:	S. Sorochinsky, D. Chelpanoff, A. Koolinberg, G. Arhangelsky, B. Mramornoff, N. Riaudin and V. Leviy, applicants for enlistment in the Russian Regiment, S.V.C.
Report date:	25 January 1939
Report number:	257

External archival references to this person: SH/80531

Vassily Dimitrievitch Leviy, Russian, was born on March 22, 1911 at Pogranichnaya Station, Chinese Eastern Railway. He first arrived in Shanghai in April 1931 and November of the same year returned to Harbin. Until 1934, he attended the 1st Harbin School of Dentistry. In the beginning of 1935 he proceeded to Tientsin, where, according to his own statement, he worked as a dentist until 1937 after which he returned to Harbin. He arrived in Shanghai from Harbin in August 1938 and in September of the same year joined the Auxiliary Detachment of the French Police, in which he served until December 1938, when he was dismissed for overstaying his leave. He holds passport No. 21136 issued on 21-12-37 by the Harbin Police.

Full Name in English:	Sitzinsky Franz Nikolaevitch
Full Name in Russian:	Сицинский Франц Николаевич
Birth Year:	1920
Birth Place:	Kamchatka Region, Siberia
Private Address:	Route De Rahn, 30-32
Report Title:	F.N. Sitzinsky, E.V. Gvozdoff and O.I. Trostiansky, applicants for enlistment in the Russian, S.V.C.
Report date:	27 January 1939
Report number:	258

External archival references to this person: SH/111750

Franz Nikolaevitch Sitzinsky, Russian was born on December 14, 1920 in Kamchatka Region, Siberia. He is reported to have escaped from the U.S.S.R. to Manchuria together with his parents in 1930 and subsequently resided in Harbin until 1932 when he proceed to Shanghai. Here he entered the Ecole Remi, in which he studied up to 1935. In the end of the same year he was engaged as a messenger by W. Futterer, 1201-1203 Bubbling Well Rd. He worked with this firm, first as a messenger and later as a shop assistant, until 21.1.39 when he resigned on his own accord.

Full Name in English:	Gvozdoff Boris Vladimirovitch
Full Name in Russian:	Гвоздев Борис Владимирович

Birth Year:	1920
Birth Place:	Nikolsk-Ussuryish, Maritime Province, Siberia.
Private Address:	101 Av bu Roi Albert, Apt 3
Report Title:	F.N. Sitzinsky, E.V. Gvozdoff and O.I. Trostiansky, applicants for enlistment in the Russian, S.V.C.
Report date:	27 January 1939
Report number:	258

External archival references to this person: SH/41615

Boris Vladimirovitch Gvozdoff, Russian, was born on May 24, 1920 at Nikolsk-Ussuryish, Maritime Province, Siberia. He is reported to have left Russia together with his parents in 1922 and for the following five years resided in Tientsin after which he left for Harbin.

On November 11, 1938 he arrived in Shanghai and on November 25, of the same year joined the Auxiliary Detachment of the French Police, in which he served until 18.1.39 when he resigned on his own accord.

Full Name in English:	Trostiansky Oleg Ivanovitch
Full Name in Russian:	Тростянский Олег Иванович
Birth Year:	1921
Birth Place:	Echo Station, Chinese Eastern Railway
Private Address:	Rue Bourgeat, 368 Apt 8
Report Title:	F.N. Sitzinsky, E.V. Gvozdoff and O.I. Trostiansky, applicants for enlistment in the Russian, S.V.C.
Report date:	27 January 1939
Report number:	258

External archival references to this person: SH/130037

Oleg Ivanovitch Trostiansky, Russian, was born on March 25, 1921 at Echo Station, Chinese Eastern Railway. He arrived in Shanghai from Harbin on 12.1.39, travelling on passport No. 3186 issued on 30.8.38 by the Harbin Police.

Being a new arrival in Shanghai he is not known locally.

Full Name in English:	Voropay Vassily Vassilievitch
Full Name in Russian:	Воропай Василий Васильевич
Birth Year:	1911
Birth Place:	Petrograd, Russia

Report Title:	V.V. Voropay, applicant for enrolment in the Transport Company, S.V.C.
Report date:	27 January 1939
Report number:	259

External archival references to this person: SH/131681

Vassily Vassilievitch Voropay, Russian, was born on October 16, 1911 at Petrograd, Russia, He is reported to have arrived in Shanghai from Vladivostok together with his parents in 1922.

In 1924 he entered the St. Francis Xavier's College in which he studied up to 1930. Upon leaving the college he worked casually until October 1934 when he was engaged by the China General Omnibus Company as a ticket inspector.

He worked in this capacity until 9-1-39 when he was dismissed for coming late for duty.

When interviewed, the applicant expressed his desire to withdraw his application for enrolment in the Transport Company, S.V.C., stating that he hoped to obtained a position on board of one of the vessels of Jardine, Matheson & Co., Ltd., in near future and consequently would be unable to attend the regular drills, parades etc.

Full Name in English:	Ambariantz Peter Georgievitch
Full Name in Russian:	Амбарянц Петр Георгиевич
Birth Year:	1920
Birth Place:	Chanchun, Manchuria
Private Address:	Chapoo Rd, 408
Report Title:	P.G. Ambariantz and V.F. Zabal, applicants for enlistment in the Russian Regiment, S.V.C
Report date:	February 9, 1939
Report number:	260

External archival references to this person: SH/10460

Peter Georgievitch Ambariantz, Russian of Armenian origin, was born on July 2, 1920 at Chanchun, Manchuria. He arrived in Shanghai in the beginning of 1932 and soon afterwards entered the St. Francis Xavier's College, which he attended up to 1934. From 1934 to 1937 he studied at the Anglo-French College, Range Road. Upon leaving the latter College he worked for a short period in the Willie's Theatre, 408 Chapoo Road, the manager of which, Mr. Gotlieb is his step-father.

On June 25, 1938, the applicant was charged with Larceny at the 1st S.S.D. Court and was sentenced to 4 months imprisonment. However, upon his appeal to the High Court, the fact that he did not play an active part in the crime and that it was his first offence was taken in to consideration, and he was given the same sentence suspended for two years.

Applicant's brother, S.G. Ambariantz, is at present serving in the Russian Regiment, S.V.C.

Full Name in English:	Zabal Vladimir Fedorovitch
Full Name in Russian:	Забаль Владимир Федорович
Birth Year:	1913
Birth Place:	Verhneudinsk, Siberia
Private Address:	Ward Rd, 24
Report Title:	P.G. Ambariantz and V.F. Zabal, applicants for enlistment in the Russian Regiment, S.V.C
Report date:	February 9, 1939
Report number:	260

Vladimir Fedorovitch Zabal, Russian, was born on December 19, 1913 at Verhneudinsk, Siberia. He is reported to have arrived in Harbin in 1919 and to have resided in that city until his departure to Shanghal. He arrived here on 29-1-39, travelling on passport No.20877 issued on 8-12-38 by the Harbin Police.

His brother N.F. Zabal is at present serving in the Russian Regiment, S.V.C.

Full Name in English:	Onischuck Victor Kuzmitch
Full Name in Russian:	Онищук Виктор Кузьмич
Birth Year:	1919
Birth Place:	Harbin, Manchuria
Report Title:	V.K. Onischuck, applicant for enrolment in the Signals Company, S.V.C.
Report date:	February 13, 1939
Report number:	261
External archival references to this person: SH/90208	

Victor Kuzmitch Onischuck, Russian, was born on May 5, 1919 in Harbin, Manchuria. He resided in Haroin until 1925, when he together with his mother and his step father, Mr. Tyvoniuk, a musician by profession, proceeded to Hankow. He arrived in Shanghai from the latter city in 1927. Here he entered the Public and Thomas Hanbury School for Boys graduating from same in 1936. From February 1937 to July 1937, he attended the Shanghai Business College, after which he obtained an employment with the American-Asiatic under-Writers an office clerk. He left that concern in December 1938 and in January 1939, secured his present position as a clerk with the American Express Company.

Full Name in English:	Belkin Georgy Andreyevitch
Full Name in Russian:	Белкин Георгий Андреевич
Birth Year:	1898
Birth Place:	Transbaikal Province, Siberia
Private Address:	Av Joffre, 1002/2
Report Title:	G.A. Belkin, applicant for enrolment in the Transport Company, S.V.C.
Report date:	February 15, 1939
Report number:	262
External archival references to this person:	SH/11644

Georgy Andreyevitch Belkin, Russian, was born on April 27, 1898 in Transbaikal Province, Siberia. He is reported to have left Russia in 1920 and subsequently resided in Hailar, Manchuria, until the outbreak of the Sino-Russian hostilities in 1929, after which he proceeded to Mukden. According to his own statement, while in Hailer he operated a photo-studio and later worked in the same capacity in Mukden. He arrived in Shanghai from Mukden in April 1931 and soon afterwards opened a photo-studio at 728 Avenue Joffre, which was later removed, first to 1205 Bubbling well Road in 1934 and then (in 1935) to 999 Avenue Joffre. At present he is a staff photographer of the newspaper "Evening Echo" and works independently as a photographer at his home, 1002/2 Avenue Joffre.

Full Name in English:	Zalevsky Maximilian Nikolai Victor
Full Name in Russian:	Залевский Максимилиан Николай Виктор
Birth Year:	1918
Birth Place:	Vladivostok, Siberia
Report Title:	M.N.V. Zalevsky, applicant for enrolment in the Transport Company, S.V.C
Report date:	February 15, 1939.
Report number:	263

Maximilian Nikolai Victor Zalevsky was born on December 12, 1918 at Vladivostok, Siberia. He is reported to have left Vladivostok for Manchuria together with his parents in 1922 and to have subsequently resided in Harbin until 1923 when he proceeded to Shanghai. Here in 1924 he entered the Shanghai American School in which he studied up to 1933. Later he attended the Gonzaga, graduating from same in 1937. In August 1937 he obtained employment with the "Shanghai Evening Post and Mercury" and worked in that concern until September 1938. In October of the same year he secured his present position as a manager of the Shipping Department of the Shotter, Madar and Co., 225-6 Saesoon House.

The applicant claims to be a pole by birth, however, he is registered with the Police Bureau of the City Government of Shanghai as a Russian Emigrant.(Reg. Cert. No. 22092 issued on 2-6-37).

Applicant's father, who until recently lived separately from his family, came to the notice of the Municipal Police in November 1931, when a complaint was made at the Wayside Police Station by one Ling Ching Keoung, Zaleveky's former partner in the Wine Factory on East Seward Road, accusing Zalevsky of having misappropriated the sum of 9,000.00 dollars. However, as the case was of a purely civil nature, no police action was taken in connection with the matter.

Full Name in English:	Borodin Victor Sergeyevitch
Full Name in Russian:	Бородин Виктор Сергеевич
Birth Year:	1916
Birth Place:	Vladivostok, Maritime province, Siberia
Report Title:	V.S. Borodin, applicant for enrolment in the Transport Company S.V.C.
Report date:	February 23, 1939
Report number:	264
External archival references to this person: SH/20654	

Victor Sergeyevitch Borodin, Russian, was born on March 23, 1916 at Vladivostok, Maritime province, Siberia. He arrived in Shanghai from Vladivostok in 1923. In 1924 he entered the St. Francis Xavier's College, graduating from same in December 1934. During 1936 he attended the radio operator's school of the Russian Mercantile Marine Association, 12 Rue du Consulat. In January 1936 he secured a position as a radio operator with Moller & co., in which capacity he was employed until January 1939. At present he is employed in the same capacity at Moller's Wireless station in Shanghai, 14 Edinburgh Road.

Full Name in English:	Piterskih Nikolai Kalinovitch
Full Name in Russian:	Питерских Николай Калинович (Калинникович)
Birth Year:	1916
Birth Place:	Harbin, Manchuria
Report Title:	N.K. Piterskih, applicant for enrolment in No. 3(Volunteer) Company-Russian, S.V.C.
Report date:	February 28, 1939
Report number:	265
External archival references to this person: SH/91669	

Nikolai Kalinovitch Piterskih, Russian, was born on December 3, 1916 at Harbin, Manchuria. He arrived in Shanghai from Harbin towards the end of 1935 and worked here casually until January 1937 when he was engaged by Bill's Motors, Fed. Inc. U.S.A. as an assistant mechanic. He was dismissed from this concern in December of the same year for disobedience of orders. In January 1938 he secured his present position as a mechanic with Jenny's Motors, 177 Rue Amiral Courbet.

Full Name in English:	Pepeliaeff Kirill Yakovlevitch
Full Name in Russian:	Пепеляев Кирилл Яковлевич
Birth Year:	1898
Birth Place:	Barnaul, Siberia
Private Address:	Av Du Roi Albert, 588
Known to:	Mr.A. Goroshrevich, 568 Av. Du Roi Albert.
Report Title:	K.Y. Pepeliaeff, N.F. Vajenin, A.F. Lange, N.P. Melnikoff and A. Vergassoff, applicant for enlistment in the Russian Regiment, S.V.C.
Report date:	March 3, 1939
Report number:	266
External archival references to this person:	SH/91035

Kirill Yakovlevitch Pepeliaeff, Russian, was born on July 15, 1898 at Barnaul, Siberia. He is reported to have left Russia at Barnaul, Siberia. He is reported to have left Russia in 1921 and subsequently resided in Harbin until 1931 and subsequently resided in Harbin until 1931 when he proceeded to Shanghai. Here on 15-3-32 he joined the Russian Regiment, S.V.C., in which he served until 1-1-34 when he resigned on his own accord. In March 1933 he was engaged by the China General Omnibus Company as a driver. In August 1834 he left that place of employment and proceeded to Harbin. He returned to Shanghai on January 23, 1939.

Full Name in English:	Vajenin Nikolai Fedorovitch
Full Name in Russian:	Важенин Николай Федорович
Birth Year:	1920
Birth Place:	Kulja, Sinkiang Province, China
Private Address:	Rue Paul Henry, 61
Known to:	Mr. C.V. Radetsky-Mirowliten, 635 Rue Ratard, House 5
Report Title:	K.Y. Pepeliaeff, N.F. Vajenin, A.F. Lange, N.P. Melnikoff and A. Vergassoff, applicant for enlistment in the Russian Regiment, S.V.C.
Report date:	March 3, 1939

Report number: 266
External archival references to this person: SH/130623

Nikolai Fedorovitch Vajenin, Russian, was born on May 1, 1920 at Kulja, Sinkiang Province, China. From 1922 to 1925 he resided in Tientsin after which he proceeded to Shanghai. Here in 1929 he entered that time he has been unemployed.

Full Name in English:	Lange Alexander Feodorovitch
Full Name in Russian:	Ланге Александр Федорович
Birth Year:	1912
Birth Place:	Omsk, Siberia
Private Address:	Av Du Roi Albert, 242/1
Known to:	E.A. Yaroov, 888 Wei-Hai-Wei Rd
Report Title:	K.Y. Pepeliaeff, N.F. Vajenin, A.F. Lange, N.P. Melnikoff and A. Vergassoff, applicant for enlistment in the Russian Regiment, S.V.C.
Report date:	March 3, 1939
Report number:	266

External archival references to this person: SH/70228

Alexander Feodorovitch Lange, Russian, was born on June 4, 1912 at Omsk, Siberia. He is reported to have left Russia together with his parents in 1918 and to have subsequently resided in Harbin until 1922 when he proceeded to Shanghai. On July 28, 1931 he joined the Russian Regiment, S.V.C., in which he served until 31-1-32 when he resigned on his own accord. From April 1932 to October 1934 he was employed as an assistant welder with Shanghai Arcwelding Company, 9-A Yang Terrace, Weihaiwei Road. From December 1934 to November 1936 he worked as an assistant foreman on the Kiaochow-Tainan Railway, Taingtao. Returning to Shanghai in December 1936, he was re-engaged by the former Company, which at that time was known as Arcwelding and Diecasting Works Ltd., 781 Wuting Road. In January 1939 he left this employment owing to the closure of the company.

Full Name in English:	Melnikoff Nikolai Petrovitch
Full Name in Russian:	Мельников Николай Петрович
Birth Year:	1918
Birth Place:	Toronto, Italy
Private Address:	Rue Ratard, 741/22
Known to:	Mr. N.V. Nikolsky, 741/22 Rue Rathard.
Report Title:	K.Y. Pepeliaeff, N.F. Vajenin, A.F. Lange, N.P. Melnikoff and A. Vergassoff, applicant for enlistment in the Russian Regiment, S.V.C.

Report date: March 3, 1939
Report number: 266
External archival references to this person: SH/71167

Nikolai Petrovitch Melnikoff, Russian, was born on December 16, 1918 at Toronto, Italy. According to his own statement, his parents arrived in Harbin from Italy in 1920 and have since been reading in that city. The applicant graduated from a local high school in 1936 and consequently worked as a baker in various bakeries and confectionaries in that city. He arrived in Shanghai on February 14, 1939. Being a new arrival here, he is not known locally.

Full Name in English:	Vergassoff Amroola
Full Name in Russian:	Вергасов Амрула
Birth Year:	1919
Birth Place:	Verhneoudinsk, Siberia
Private Address:	Joffre Terrace, 47
Known to:	Mr.A. Yamalitdindff, 682/18 Rue Borgeat.
Report Title:	K.Y. Pepeliaeff, N.F. Vajenin, A.F. Lange, N.P. Melnikoff and A. Vergassoff, applicant for enlistment in the Russian Regiment, S.V.C.
Report date:	March 3, 1939
Report number:	266

External archival references to this person: SH/131083

Amroola Vergassoff, Russian of Tartar Origin, Was born on January 21, 1919 at Verhneoudinsk, Siberia. He is reported to have lost his parents in 1920 and to have since been taken care of by certain Mr. and Mrs. YAUSHEFF, Russians of Tartar origin. According to his own statement, he resided in Tientsin from 1920 to 1929, after which he proceeded to Tsingtao together with Mr. and Mrs. YAUSHEFF, who are still residing in the latter city. He arrived in Shanghai on February 14, 1839.

Full Name in English:	Hrapoff Evgeny Alexandrovitch
Full Name in Russian:	Храпов Евгений Александрович
Birth Year:	1913
Birth Place:	Irkutsk, Siberia
Report Title:	E.A. Hrapoff, application for enrolment in the Transport Company, S.V.C
Report date:	March 6, 1939
Report number:	267

External archival references to this person: SH/42115

Evgeny Alexandrovitch Hrapoff, Russian, was born on October 11, 1913 at Irkutsk, Siberia. He is reported to have arrived in Shanghai from Vladivostok in 1923. From 1924 to 1928 he attended the Commercial Scholl of the Russian Orthodox Confraternity, after which he studied in the English Universal Service School (Now defunct) for one year. For the following three years he worked in various garages, first as an apprentice and later as a mechanic.

In December 1932 he was engaged by the China General Omnibus Company Ltd. as a mechanic and at present is employed by the same company in their theirs vulcanizing department.

Full Name in English:	Cherniavsky Alexander Nikolaevitch
Full Name in Russian:	Чернявский Александр Николаевич
Birth Year:	1910
Birth Place:	Kuban Province, Russia
Private Address:	Yu Yuen Road, 1315
Report Title:	A.N. Cherniavsky, application of enrolment in the Transport Company S.V.C.
Report date:	March 7, 1939
Report number:	268
External archival references to this person:	SH/21414

Alexander Nikolaevitch Cherniavsky, Russian, was born on September 6, 1910 in Kuban Province, Russia. He is reported to have left Russia in 1918 and to have subsequently resided in Harbin until 1927, after which he came to Shanghai. From 1927 to 1932 he failed permanent employment but worked in casual jobs:- one time as an interior decorator, later as a reporter of the Russian daily newspaper "Slovo" and he is also reported to have served in the Russian Detachment of the S.V.C. from 10-5-30 to 10-6-30.

He left Shanghai for Canton in 1932 and after a short stay there, during which, according to his own statement, he was employed by the Shameen Police, returned to Shanghai. Upon his return here he was engaged by the S.S. Shoe Store, 199 Nanking Road as a shop assistant. Later he worked in the same capacity with the Shanghai Shoe Manufacturing Company, 21 Boone Road. From 1935 up to the present moment he has been unemployment and at present resides together with his mother, proprietrix of a boarding house, at 1315 Yu Yuen Road

On March 6, 1931, the applicant was fined $30.00 by 1ˢᵗ. S.S.D. Court on a charge of Amount with Intent to Cause Bodily Harm. (B.W. F.I.R.185/31)

Full Name in English:	Mishin Igor Alexeyevitch
Full Name in Russian:	Мишин Игорь Алексеевич
Birth Year:	1911
Birth Place:	Moscow, Russia
Report Title:	I.A. Mishin, application for enrolment in No. 3 (Vol) Company, S.V.C
Report date:	March 10, 1939
Report number:	269

Igor Alexeyevitch Mishin, Russian, was born on Febryuary19, 1911 at Moscow, Russia. He is reported to have left Russia in 1922 together with his parents and to have subsequently resided in Harbin until 1933, after which became to Shanghai. After a short stay in this city he proceeded to Kulin and resided there until 1934, when he returned to Shanghai. In the beginning of 1935 he left Shanghai for Hankow.

On August 28, 1938 he and four other Russians were arrested by the Chinese Authorities in Hankow. They were kept prisoners for six days after which they were released and advised to leave Hankow within 14 days. The applicant left Hankow on 17-9-38 and travelled to Shanghai via Hong Kong, arriving here on 5-10-38.

On February 11, 1939 he secured his present employment, as a supervisor with Fagan & Co., 281 Kiangse Road.

The application is registered with the Russian Emigrants' Committee, 118/1 Moulmein Road, on the strength of passport No.827 issued on 12-9-38 by the Hankow Police.

Full Name in English:	Igoshin Alexander Vladimirovitch
Full Name in Russian:	Игошин Александр Владимирович
Birth Year:	1921
Birth Place:	Harbin, Manchuria
Private Address:	Av. Joffre, 918, House 5, Room 8,
Report Title:	A.V. Igoshin, I.A. Mescheriakoff and G.A. Markevitch, applicants for enlistment in the Russian Regiment, S.V.C.
Report date:	March 8, 1939
Report number:	270
External archival references to this person:	SH/50138

Alexander Vladimirovitch Igoshin, Russian, was born on October 19, 1921 in Harbin, Manchuria. He arrived in Shanghai in December 1932 and soon afterwards entered the Commercial Scholl of the Russian Orthodox Confraternity in which he studied until 1937. On December 8, 1937 he joined the Auxiliary Detachment of the French Police in which he served until 15-6-38, when he resigned on his own accord. Since then he has been unemployed.

Full Name in English:	Mescheriakoff Igor Alexandrovitch
Full Name in Russian:	Мещеряков Игорь Александрович
Birth Year:	1921
Birth Place:	Harbin, Manchuria
Private Address:	Weihaiwei Road, 651, Apt. B.02
Report Title:	A.V. Igoshin, I.A. Mescheriakoff and G.A. Markevitch, applicants for enlistment in the Russian Regiment, S.V.C.
Report date:	March 8, 1939
Report number:	270

External archival references to this person: SH/71414

Igor Alexandrovitch Mescheriakoff, Russian, was born on January 4, 1921 in Harbin, Manchuria. He arrived in Shanghai from Harbin on February 25, 1939 and resided together with Dr. G.M. Krivoroochko, at 651, Weihaiwei Road, Apt. B.02.

Full Name in English:	Markevitch Georgy Alexandrovitch
Full Name in Russian:	Маркевич Георгий Александрович
Birth Year:	1921
Birth Place:	Nikolaevsk-on-Amur, Siberia
Private Address:	Rue Lafayette, 1232
Report Title:	A.V. Igoshin, I.A. Mescheriakoff and G.A. Markevitch, applicants for enlistment in the Russian Regiment, S.V.C.
Report date:	March 8, 1939
Report number:	270

External archival references to this person: SH/70765

Georgy Alexandrovitch Markevitch, Russian, was born on June 14, 1921 in Nikolaevsk-on-Amur, Siberia. He is reported to have escaped from the U.S.S.R. to Manchuria, together with his mother in 1929 and to have subsequently resided in Harbin. He arrived in Shanghai in 1932 and during the same year entered the Ecole Remi in which he studied up to 1938.

Full Name in English:	Serejnikoff Georgy Nikolaevitch
Full Name in Russian:	Сережников Георгий Николаевич
Birth Year:	1917
Birth Place:	Astrakan, Russia

Report Title:	G. Serejnikoff, applicant for enrolment in the Signals Company, S.V.C.
Report date:	March 20, 1939
Report number:	271

External archival references to this person: SH/110458

Georgy Nikolaevitch Serejnikoff, Russian, was born on November 26, 1917 at Astrakan, Russia. He arrived in Shanghai from Vladivostok in 1922 together with his parents. In 1929 he entered the First Russian School (now A.S. Poushkin Memorial School), graduating from same in 1937. During the same year he entered the Aurora University, in which he studied up to December 1938. In January 1939 he was engaged by the Shanghai Power Company as an apprentics in their chemical department.

Full Name in English:	Tihonoff Victor Alexandrovitch
Full Name in Russian:	Тихонов Виктор Александрович
Birth Year:	1920
Birth Place:	Handaohedze station, Chinese Eastern Railway
Private Address:	Rue Rathard, 547/2
Known to:	Mr N.D. Lichenfzoff 547/2 Rue Ratard
Report Title:	V.A. Tihonoff, Y.A. Beliakoff and B.A. Korosteloff, applicants for enlistment in the Russian Regiment, S.V.C.
Report date:	March 22, 1939
Report number:	272

External archival references to this person: SH/121682

Victor Alexandrovitch Tihonoff, Russian, was born on May 28, 1920 at Handaohedze station, Chinese Eastern Railway. He arrived in Shanghai from Harbin on March 11, 1939 and is not known locally.

Full Name in English:	Beliakoff Yury Alexandrovitch
Full Name in Russian:	Беляков Юрий Александрович
Birth Year:	1920
Birth Place:	Harbin, Manchuria
Private Address:	Route Vallon, 188/10
Known to:	Mr. N.Y. Fomin, 95 Route Mayen
Report Title:	V.A. Tihonoff, Y.A. Beliakoff and B.A. Korosteloff, applicants for enlistment in the Russian Regiment, S.V.C.
Report date:	March 22, 1939

Report number: 272
External archival references to this person: SH/11600

Yury Alexandrovitch Beliakoff, Russian, was born on October 26, 1920 in Harbin, Manchuria. He arrived in Shanghai in My 1936 and during the same month entered the First Russian School (now A.S. Poushkin Memorial School). Having graduated from same in 1937, he has since been studying in the Centre Technique Superieue, 200 Route Remi.

Full Name in English:	Korosteloff Boris Alexeyevitch
Full Name in Russian:	Коростелев Борис Алексеевич
Birth Year:	1920
Birth Place:	Harbin, Manchuria
Private Address:	Rue Lafayette, 1273
Known to:	Mr. V.i. Shaiditsky 79/2 Route Tenant De La Tour
Report Title:	V.A. Tihonoff, Y.A. Beliakoff and B.A. Korosteloff, applicants for enlistment in the Russian Regiment, S.V.C.
Report date:	March 22, 1939
Report number:	272

External archival references to this person: SH/60974

Boris Alexeyevitch Korosteloff, Russian, was born on December 10, 1920 in Harbin, Manchuria. He arrived in Shanghai in 1928 and in 1931 and in 1931 entered the commercial School of the Russian Orthodox Confranternity, in which he studied up to 1933. Upon leaving the school he was unemployed.

Full Name in English:	Kravchenko Rostislav Harlampievitch
Full Name in Russian:	Кравченко Ростислав Харлампиевич
Birth Year:	1919
Birth Place:	Nikolsk-Ussuriisk, Russia
Report Title:	R.H. Kravchenko, applicant for enrolment in the signal company S.V.C
Report date:	March 25, 1939
Report number:	273

External archival references to this person: SH/61715

Rostislav Harlampievitch Kravchenko, Russian, was born on January 28, 1919 in Nikolsk-Ussuriisk, Russia. He is reported to have arrived in Shanghai from Vladivostok in 1922 together with his parents. In 1931 he entered the Commercial School of the Russian Orthodox Confraternity and graduated from same in 1936. On February 1, 1939 he secured his present position in the cable slicing department of the Shanghai Telephone Company.

Full Name in English:	Petroff G.V.
Full Name in Russian:	Петров Георгий Васильевич
Report Title:	G.V. Petroff, applicant for enrolment in No.3 (Volunteer).
Report date:	March 29, 1939
Report number:	274
External archival references to this person:	SH/91285

With reference to the attached application of Mr. G.V. Petroff for enrolment in NO.3 (Volunteer) Company, S.V.C., I beg to report that the applicant has been a member of the said company since January 1932 and at present only applies to be transferred to the Class "A" Reservists.

The applicant has, for the past seven years, been employed with the China General Omnibus Company Ltd. as a ticket inspector.

Full Name in English:	Rozenberg Alexander Alfredovitch
Full Name in Russian:	Розенберг Александр Альфредович
Birth Year:	1910
Birth Place:	Harbin, Manchuria
Report Title:	A.A. Rozenberg, applicant for enlistment in No, 3 (volunteer) Company, S.V.C.
Report date:	29 March 1939
Report number:	275
External archival references to this person:	SH/101363

Alexander Alfredovitch Rozenberg, Russian, was born on November 2, 1910 in Harbin, Manchuria. Upon graduating from a local high school in 1930 he entered the 2nd Harbin School of Dentistry, graduating from same in 1933. He arrived in Shanghai in the beginning of 1934 and in September of the same year was engaged by Z.A. Gorovitz, Dental Surgeon, 97 Route Vallon, as an assistant dentist. In August 1938 he left that place of employment on his own accord and proceeded to Harbin. He returned to Shanghai in December of the same year and on 19-12-38 secured his present positions as a dentist with M. Klatchko, Dental Surgeon, 26 The Bund.

Full Name in English:	Looshnikoff Andrey Ivanovitch
Full Name in Russian:	Лушников Андрей Иванович

Birth Year:	1918
Birth Place:	Viatka Province, Russia
Private Address:	Rue Bourgeat, 344 room 7
Known to:	Mr. M. Merzliakoff 344 Rue Bourgeat. Room 7
Report Title:	A.I. Looshnikoff and A.B. Beloff, applicants for enlistment in the Russian Regiment, S.V.C.
Report date:	April 4, 1939
Report number:	276

External archival references to this person: SH/81020

Andrey Ivanovitch Looshnikoff, Russian, was born on August 28, 1918 in Viatka Province, Russia. He is reported to have left Russia in 1922 together with his parents and to have subsequently resided in Harbin Railway Police. He arrived in Shanghai on March 21, 1939 and is not known locally.

Full Name in English:	Beloff Antoly Emelianovitch
Full Name in Russian:	Белов Анатолий Емельянович
Birth Year:	1918
Birth Place:	Harbin, Manchuria
Private Address:	Hardoon Road, 314/3
Known to:	F.sgt. I.T. Aksenoff, Central Police station
Report Title:	A.I. Looshnikoff and A.B. Beloff, applicants for enlistment in the Russian Regiment, S.V.C.
Report date:	April 4, 1939
Report number:	276

External archival references to this person: SH/12020

Antoly Emelianovitch Beloff, Russian, was born on August 10, 1918 in Harbin, Manchuria. After graduating from a local middle school he, for the past two year, served in the Harbin Railway Police. He arrived in Shanghai on March 14, 1939 and resided at 314/3 Hardoon Road, together with his brother-in-law, I.T. Aksenoff, Sergeant of the Shanghai Municipal Police.

Full Name in English:	Beltatko Alexander Antonovitch
Full Name in Russian:	Белятко Александр Антонович
Birth Year:	1910
Birth Place:	Harbin, Manchuria
Report Title:	A.A. Beltatko, applicant for enrolment in the American Machine Gun Co., S.V.C.
Report date:	May 2, 1939
Report number:	278

SMP D.917 file

External archival references to this person: SH/11621

Alexander Antonovitch Beltatko, Russian, was born on April 10, 1910 in Harbin, Manchuria. After graduating from a local high school in 1927 he entered the Harbin Polytechnic Institute and graduated from same in July 1932. He arrived in Shanghai from Harbin in November 1935. From June 1936 to February 1937 he was employed as a draughtsman with the Auto Palace Co., Ltd. Since February 1937 he has been employed in the same capacity with the China Car & Foundry Co., Ltd., 21 Yuen-Ming-Yuen Road.

Full Name in English:	Elensky Evgeny Spiridonovitch
Full Name in Russian:	Еленский Евгений Спиридонович
Birth Year:	1909
Birth Place:	Viasemekaya Station, Ussoury Railway, Maritime Province, Russia
Report Title:	E. Elensky, applicant for enrolment in the American Machine Gun Co., S.V.C.
Report date:	May 2, 1939
Report number:	278

External archival references to this person: SH/30903

Evgeny Spiridonovitch Elensky, Russian, was born on September 21, 1909 at Viasemekaya Station, Ussoury Railway, Maritime Province, Russia. According to his own statement, he resided together with his parents in various places of the Chinese Eastern Railway zone from 1910 and in 1932 graduated from the Harbin Polytechnic Institute.

He arrived in Shanghai from Harbin in September 1933 and from March 1934 has been employed with Anderson, Meyer & Co., 21 Yuen-Ming-Yuen Road (Structural Department).

Full Name in English:	Volkoff Vladimir Ivanovitch
Full Name in Russian:	Волков Владимир Иванович
Birth Year:	1921
Birth Place:	Shanghai, China
Private Address:	Wei Hai Wei RD, 888
Known to:	Mr. S.S. Grigorieff
Report Title:	V.I. Volkoff and S.I. Danko, applicants for enlistment in the Russian Regiment, S.V.C.
Report date:	April 15 1939
Report number:	277

Vladimir Ivanovitch Volkoff, Russian, was born on July 21, 1921 in Shanghai, China. From 1923 to 1935 he resided for various periods in Bangkok, Tsingtao, Dairon and Mukden, together with the last four years he resided in Tientsin. He arrived in Shanghai from Tientsin on April 2,1939.

Full Name in English:	Danko Sergey llyitch
Full Name in Russian:	Данько Сергей Ильич
Birth Year:	1919
Birth Place:	Vladivostok, Maritime Province, Russia
Private Address:	Route Vallon, 242
Known to:	Mr. A.D. Lang 28 Route Dollfus
Report Title:	V.I. Volkoff and S.I. Danko, applicants for enlistment in the Russian Regiment, S.V.C.
Report date:	April 15 1939
Report number:	277

Sergey llyitch Danko, Russian, was born on November 15, 1919 at Vladivostok, Maritime Province, Russia. He is reported to have escaped from Vladivostok together with his parents in 1931 and to have subsequently resided in Harbin. He arrived in Shanghai on March 6, 1939 and resided at 242, route Vallon, together with his uncle, T.Y. Danko.

Full Name in English:	Elovitsky Tadeosh Genrichovitch
Full Name in Russian:	Еловитский Тадеуш Генрихович
Birth Year:	1903
Birth Place:	Vladivostok, Maritime Province, Russia
Private Address:	Av Joffre, 925
Known to:	Mr. A.A. Lordkipanidze, 1224 Av. Joffre
Report Title:	T. Elovitsky, G. Yumehanoff and V.Yumshanoff, applicants for enlistment in the Russian Regiment, S.V.C.
Report date:	May 1, 1936
Report number:	279

Tadeosh Genrichovitch Elovitsky, Russian, was born on March 27, 1903 in Vladivostok, Maritime Province, Russia. He is reported to have left Russia in 1921 and to have subsequently resided in Harbin. He arrived in Shanghai from Harbin in July

1929 and on August 1, 1929 joined the Russian Regiment, S.V.C. He served in the Regiment until September 1, 1934, when he resigned on his own accord during the same month he joined the Auxiliary Detachment of the French Police in which he served until 16-8-35 when he was dismissed for borrowing money from a money lender. He worked casually until May 1937 when he proceeded to Hankow, where he resided until April 11, 1939, after which he returned to Shanghai.

Full Name in English:	Yumshanoff Georgy Ivanovitch
Full Name in Russian:	Юмшанов Георгий Иванович
Birth Year:	1916
Birth Place:	Bukhedu, Chinese Eastern Railway
Known to:	Mr. M.L. Roubin, 524 Kiaochow Rd.
Report Title:	T. Elovitsky, G. Yumehanoff and V.Yumshanoff, applicants for enlistment in the Russian Regiment, S.V.C.
Report date:	May 1, 1936
Report number:	279
External archival references to this person:	SH/130449

Georgy Ivanovitch Yumshanoff, Russian, was born on November 28, 1916 at station Bukhedu, Chinese Eastern Railway. According to his own statement, he attended a Russian School in Harbin from 1928 to1933 after which he resided at station Bukhedu together with his parents for a period. Some time towards the end of 1934 he proceeded to Mukden where he was employed with Liddell Bros. & Co., Ltd. Until August, 1937. He is reported to have arrived in Shanghai from Dairen in February, 1938. Since his arrival until January 1939 he was employed as a mechanic with the Far Eastern Salvage Association, 2 French Bund.

Full Name in English:	Yumshanoff Vladimir Ivanovitch
Full Name in Russian:	Юмшанов Владимир Иванович
Birth Year:	1919
Birth Place:	Bukhedu, Chinese Eastern Railway
Private Address:	Kiaochow Rd, 524
Known to:	Mr. M.L. Roubin, 524 Kiaochow Rd.
Report Title:	T. Elovitsky, G. Yumehanoff and V.Yumshanoff, applicants for enlistment in the Russian Regiment, S.V.C.
Report date:	May 1, 1936
Report number:	279

Vladimir Ivanovitch Yumshanoff, Russian, was born on July 15, 1919 at station Bukhedu, Chinese Eastern Railway. He is reported to have graduated from the First Russian Middle School at Harbin in 1936, after which he was employed with Liddell Bros. & Co., Ltd. at Mukden from September 1936 to May 1937, and with the Laoning Press in the same city from December1937 to March 1938. He arrived in Shanghai from Deiren in April 1938 and until January 1939 was employed with the Far Eastern Salvage Association, 2 French Bund.

Full Name in English:	Charushnikoff Michail Alexandrovitch
Full Name in Russian:	Чарушников Михаил Александрович
Birth Year:	1912
Birth Place:	Vladivostok, Maritime Province, Russia
Report Title:	M.A. Charushnikoff, applicants for enrolment in the Transport Company, S.V.C.
Report date:	May 15, 1936
Report number:	280

External archival references to this person: SH/21184

Michail Alexandrovitch Charushnikoff, Russian, was born on November 21, 1912 at Vladivostok, Maritime Province, Russia. He is reported to have escaped from the U.S.S.R. together with his parents in 1926 and to have subsequently resided in Changchun, Manchuria. He arrived in Shanghai in the beginning of 1930 and soon afterwards obtained a position as an assistant mechanic with Bills Motors (Fed. Inc. U.S.A.). He left that place of employment of 1936 he proceeded to Amoy, where he resided together with his uncle-in-law, Mr. Ivanoff of the Chinese Maritime Customs. He returned to Shanghai in December 1936 and since February 1937 has been working as a mechanic in the Service Station of Mark L. Moody, 408 Rue Bourget.

Full Name in English:	Granovsky Pavel Innokiaentievitch
Full Name in Russian:	Грановский Павел Иннокентьевич
Birth Year:	1909
Birth Place:	Harbin, Manchuria
Report Title:	P.I. Granovsky, applicant for enlistment in the transport Company, S.V.C.
Report date:	May, 15 1939
Report number:	280

External archival references to this person: SH/41217

Pavel Innokiaentievitch Granovsky, Russian, was born in June 29, 1909 in Harbin, Manchuria. He first arrived in Shanghai in September 1928 and during the same month entered the Public School for Boys. During 1929 he attended the Shanghai American School and in the summer of 1930 left Shanghai for Teingtao, where he obtained a position as an assistant mechanic with Frazer Motors. In the end of the same year he was transferred to the Tientsin branch of the same company. He returned to Shanghai in the beginning of 1931 and soon afterwards obtained a position as an assistant mechanic with the China Motors, 702 bubbling Well Road. In the end of 1933 he left that place of employment on his own accord and on May 1, 1934 secured a similar position with the Export Motor Service, 604 Rue Ratard. This firm went into liquidation in February 1938 and since that date the applicant has been employed with the service station of Mark L. Moody, 408 Rue Bourgeat.

Full Name in English:	Koodriavtzeff Anatoly Nikitich
Full Name in Russian:	Кудрявцев Анатолий Никитич
Birth Year:	1921
Birth Place:	Harbin, Manchuria
Private Address:	Tongshan Rd, 694 /31
Known to:	Mr. N. V. Cattell 878 Bubbling Well Rd
Report Title:	A.N. Koodriavtzeff, applicant for enlistment in the Russian Regiment, S. V. C.
Report date:	May 20, 1939
Report number:	281
External archival references to this person:	SH/62170

Anatoly Nikitich Koodriavtzeff, Russian, was born on December 23, 1921, in Harbin, Manchuria. According to his own statement he graduated from a local middle school in 1937. He arrived in Shanghai from Harbin on May 5, 1939. Being a new arrival in Shanghai he is not known locally.

Full Name in English:	Lange Fedor Feodorovitch
Full Name in Russian:	Ланге Федор Федорович
Birth Year:	1907
Birth Place:	Omsk, Siberia
Private Address:	Av. Du Roi Albert, 242/1
Known to:	Mr. K.I. Kulchitsky, 42 Route De Grouchy
Report Title:	F.F. Lange, applicant for enlistment in the Russian Regiment, S.V.C.
Report date:	May 20, 1939
Report number:	282
External archival references to this person:	SH/70223, в карточке под фамилией Ланг.

Fedor Feodorovitch Lange, Russian, was born on May 11, 1907, in Omsk, Siberia. He is reported to have left Russia in 1920 and to have subsequently resided in Harbin until 1922, after which he processed to Shanghai. He served in the Russian Regiment, S. V. C. for the following periods:- 1-6-28 to 1-11-28 and from 1-10-30 to 6-3-32, leaving the regiment on his own accord on both occasions. Between July 7, 1932 and May 10, 1933 he worked as a foreman at the French Tramway Company's depot. Leaving that on his own accord, he worked casually until June 1935 when he was engaged as a foreman welder by the Shanghai Dockyard Ltd. On November 5, 1937 his services were dispensed with owing to a reduction in staff. From July 15, 1938 to April 12, 1939 he served as anti-piracy guard with the China Navigation Steamship Company.

On September 28, 1933 he was sentenced by the 1st Shanghai Special District Court to 12 days' imprisonment on a charge of Negligent Driving and Breach of Traffic Regulation No.34.

Full Name in English:	Semenin Nikolai Michailovitch
Full Name in Russian:	Семенин Николай Михайлович
Birth Year:	1920
Birth Place:	Harbin, Manchuria
Private Address:	Rue Ratard, 699
Known to:	Mr. M.G. Yakovkin, 118/1 Mulmein Rd.
Report Title:	N.M. Semenin applicant for enlistment in the Russian Regiment, S.V.C
Report date:	May 20, 1939
Report number:	283

Nikolai Michailovitch Semenin, Russian, was born on December 6, 1920, in Harbin, Manchuria. He arrived in Shanghai from Harbin in 1923 together with his adopted mother, Mrs. Zahir. From 1928 to 1932 he attended the Public School for Boys and during 1933 and 1934 the Commercial School of the Russian Orthodox Confraternity.

Full Name in English:	Popoff Alexander Ivanovitch
Full Name in Russian:	Попов Александр Иванович
Birth Year:	1921
Birth Place:	Vladivostok, Maritime Province, Russia
Report Title:	A.I. Popoff, application enrolment in No.3 (Vol) Company, "C" Bn., S.V.C.
Report date:	May 19, 1939
Report number:	284

Note: listed as Nikolay Ivanovich in SH/100045

Alexander Ivanovitch Popoff, Russian, was born on March 22, 1921, at Vladivostok, Maritime Province, Russia. He is reported to have left Russia in 1922 together with his mother and to have subsequently resided in Harbin until 1924, after which he proceeded to Shanghai. In 1930 he entered the St. Joan of Arc's College and graduated from same early in 1936. In January 1938 he entered the St. Francis Xavier's College and is due to graduate from same in the end of the present year. From April 1933 to October of the same year and from November 1936 to October 1937 he resided in Europe together with the mother.

In 1926 the applicant's mother married one Mr. K.T. Williams of the Chinese Maritime Customs, but divorced him during 1928.

Full Name in English:	Belovchikoff Pavel Vaseilievitch
Full Name in Russian:	Беловчиков Павел Васильевич
Birth Year:	1921
Birth Place:	Harbin, Manchuria
Report Title:	P.V. Belovchikoef, applicant for enrolment in No.3 (Vol.) Company, "C" battalion, S.V.C.
Report date:	May 31, 1939
Report number:	285

Pavel Vaseilievitch Helovchikoff, Russian, was born on July 12, 1921 in Harbin, Manchuria. He arrived in Shanghai from Harbin in 1927 together with his parents and resided here until 1936 after which he proceeded to Tientsin together with his father. He returned to Shanghai in May 1938 and in September of the same year was engaged as a bar boy by the BOE-BA-BO Cabaret, 1337 Yu Yuen Road. He left that place of employment in January, 1939 and from last worked as a delivery boy with the Alliance Bakery, 58-60 Route Pere Robert. He discontinued his work on or about 25th of this month.

Reference obtained from Mr. A. Irshenko, proprietor of the Alliance Bakery and Mr. V. Ivanchenko, proprietor of the Bee-Ba-Bo cabaret, are not in the applicant's favour. They describe him as an irresponsible youth of lazy habits, lacking education and discipline.

His father, who it is believed in Tientsin at present, forms the subject of criminal record, No.F1209, the particulare of which are as follows:

2nd S.S.D. Trespassing Acquitted 24.4.29 Court.

1st S.S.D. False Pretences Not guilty. 25.10.32 Court. (Verdict brought in as the complaint refused to attend court)

2nd S.S.D. Court receiving morphine injection. 1 year & 6 month imprisonment. 5.3.36.

3rd Branch Kiangsu High Court. Appeal Not guilty. 10.4.36

The applicant's mother who, it is reported, divorced her husband about 8 years ago, is at present married to or cohabiting with Private Kemper of the 4th Regiment, U.S.M.C.

Full Name in English:	Frank Samuel Fillipovitch
Full Name in Russian:	Франк Самуэль (Семен) Филипович
Birth Year:	1920
Birth Place:	Shanghai
Report Title:	S. Frank, applicant for enrolment in the Jewish Company, S.V.C
Report date:	May 30, 1939
Report number:	286

External archival references to this person: SH/31797

Samuel Fillipovitch Frank, Russian Jew, Was born on February 8, 1920 in Shanghai. In 1929 he entered the Public & Thomas Hanbury School in which he studied up to 1936. In September of the same year he entered the Chemical Department of Henry Lester Institute for Technical Education. He discontinued his studies upon the outbreak of Sino-Japanese hostilities in August 1937.

From January 1939 he has been employed with the China Manufactures Representatives, 259 Kiangse Road. His father is a co-proprietor of that concern.

Full Name in English:	Drosdoff Alexander Petrovitch
Full Name in Russian:	Дроздов Александр Петрович
Birth Year:	1917
Birth Place:	Harbin, Manchuria
Report Title:	A. Drosdoff, applicant for enrolment in the American Troop Company, S.V.C
Report date:	May 30, 1939
Report number:	286

External archival references to this person: SH/30616

Alexander Petrovitch Drosdoff, Russian, was born on December 24, 1917 at Harbin, Manchuria. He arrived in Shanghai in 1924 together with his sister Miss M.P. Drosdoff. In 1930 he entered the Public and Thomas Hanbury School, graduating from same in 1935. In June 1936 he was engaged by I. Shickman, Fur & skin Dealer, and proceeded to training and later to Tientsin, where he worked in the head office of the above concern. He left that place of employment on his own accord in June 1938 and returned to Shanghai. In November of the same year he secured his present employment as a chief clerk with the Globe Wireless, Ltd., 51 Canton Road.

The applicant has four sisters, two of whom are reported to be in Hongkong at present and the other two reside in Shanghai.

Since 1930 the applicant is reported to have resided together with Mr. A.M. Deca, Portuguese, who, it is believed, intends to adopt the applicant in the near future.

He is not registered with the Russian Emigrants Committee or with any other Russian Public association and is not in presentation of any document of identity.

Full Name in English:	Uvadieff Naphtaly Aronovitch
Full Name in Russian:	Увадьев Нафталий Аронович
Birth Year:	1920
Birth Place:	Tashkent, Russian Turkestan
Report Title:	N. Uvadieff, applicant for enrolment in the Jewish Company, S.V.C
Report date:	May 30, 1939
Report number:	286
External archival references to this person:	SH/130573

Naphtaly Aronovitch Uvadieff, Russian Jew, was born on August 17, 1920 at Tashkent, Russian Turkestan. He resided together with his parents in Tashkent, Manchouli Station and Urga for various periods where, according to his own statement, his father was engaged in commercial activities. He arrived in Shanghai from Urga in 1927 together with his parents. During the same year he entered the Public and Thomas Hanbury School, graduating from same in December 1938. At present he is employed as an overseer with the Shanghai Cotton Waste and Linter Company, 128

Until 1929 the applicant and his family were Soviet Citizens after which they renounced their allegiance to the Soviet Government and at present are registered with the Russian Emigrants Committee, 118/1 Moulmein Road, as Russian emigrants.

Full Name in English:	Sidamonidze Constantin Urievitch
Full Name in Russian:	Сидамонидзе Константин Юрьевич
Birth Year:	1921
Birth Place:	Maritime Province, Russia
Report Title:	C.U. Sidamonidze applicant for enrolment in the signals company, S.V.C.
Report date:	May 30 1939

Report number: 287
External archival references to this person: SH/111529

Constantin Urievitch Sidamonidze, Russian of Georgian origin, was born on February 22, 1921, in Maritime Province, Russia. He is reported to have left Russia together with his mother and brother during the same year and to have subsequently resided in Harbin until 1929, after which he proceeded to Shanghai. In 1930 he entered the Commercial School of the Russian Orthodox Confraternity, graduating from same in July 1938. In November of the same year he secured his present position as a cable splicer with the Shanghai Telephone Company.

Full Name in English:	Fester Anatoly Edwardovitch
Full Name in Russian:	Фестер Анатолий Эдуардович
Birth Year:	1920
Birth Place:	Spassk, Maritime Province, Russia
Report Title:	A.E. Fester and A.P. Shavikin, applicants for enlistment in the Russian Regiment, S.V.C.
Report date:	May 27, 1939
Report number:	288
External archival references to this person:	SH/31538

Anatoly Edwardovitch Fester, Russian, was born on December 29, 1920, at Spassk, Maritime Province, Russia. He is reported to have escaped from the U.S.S.R. together with his parents in 1928 and to have subsequently resided in Pogranichnaya Station, Chinese Eastern Railway. He arrived in Shanghai in 1930 and in the beginning of 1931 entered the Ecole Remi. Upon leaving the school in 1936 he assisted his father who at that time was the owner of Fester Sausage Factory, 760 Route vallon. This factory closed down in June 1937 owing to business depression and since then up to May 1938 the applicant was employed with Lang & Semin Sausage Factory, 28 Route Dolfus. He left that place of employment on his own accords and from July 1938 to January 1939 worked with Saratov Sausage Factory, 126-128 Route Dufour.

Full Name in English:	Shavikin Alexander Pavlovitch
Full Name in Russian:	Шавикин Александр Павлович
Birth Year:	1921
Birth Place:	Tientsin
Report Title:	A.E. Fester and A.P. Shavikin, applicants for enlistment in the Russian Regiment, S.V.C.
Report date:	May 27, 1939
Report number:	288
External archival references to this person:	SH/110719

Alexander Pavlovitch Shavikin, Russian, was born on February 12, 1921 at Tientsin. He first arrived in Shanghai together with his parents during the same year and resided in this city until 1924 after which the family proceeded to manila, P.I. Returning to Shanghai in 1927 he attended the Ecole Remi from 1930 to 1935.

In March 1937, he and another Russian named O. Zaharoff stowed themselves away in the R.M.S. "Ranpura" bound for Hongkong. Upon arrival in that port they were discovered and detained by the Hongkong police until June 1937, when they were deported to Shanghai arriving here on 7/6/37 in the B.E. "Prosper". The applicant forms the subject of the criminal record No.F.1006, the particulars of which are as follows:-

2nd. S.S.D. Court.Larceny.   Acquitted 20-1-36.

1st. S.S.D. Court.   Looting.   3 months imprisonment suspended for 2 years. 23-3-38.

2nd. S.S.D. Court.   Assault.   3 months imprisonment or fine as $2.00 per day fine paid and released on 28-3-39.

It is understood that this applicant has already resigned from the Russian Regiment, S.V.C.

Full Name in English:	Kadoshnikoff Boris Dimitrievich
Full Name in Russian:	Кадушников Борис Дмитриевич
Birth Year:	1921
Birth Place:	Chita, Pransbaikal Province, Siberia
Report Title:	B.D. Kadoshnikoff, applicant for enrolment in the 3rd (Volunteer) Company, "Russian Regiment, S.V.C.
Report date:	06-01-1939
Report number:	289
External archival references to this person:	SH/50992

Boris Dimitrievich Kadoshnikoff, Russian, born on July 14, 1921 at Chita, Pransbaikal Province, Siberia. From his early childhood he is reported to have resided together with his parents first at Manchouli Station, Chinese Eastern Railway (1921 – 1927) and later at Mukden (1927-1930). In September, 1930 the family arrived in Shanghai from Mukden. The applicant attended the St. Francis Xavier's College from 1936 to January, 1939, after which he entered the Public & Thos. Hanbury School for Boys in which he is still studying.

He resides at Passage 66, House 48 Route Lorton together with his parents. His father, Mr. D.G. Kadoshnikoff, a journalist by occupation, has for the past several years been on the staff oh local Russian news paper "Slovo", 238 Avenue du Roi Albert.

The applicant is registered with the Russian Emigrants' Committee, Moulmein Road. In the Committee's register his date of birth was given on one occasion as 6-8-1922 and on another – as 6-8-1921.

Full Name in English:	Jookoff Mihail Vassilievich
Full Name in Russian:	Жуков Михаил Васильевич
Birth Year:	1922
Birth Place:	Shanghai
Private Address:	Tunsin Road, 221
Report Title:	M.V. Jookoff, applicant for enlistment in No.3 (Vol.) Company, "C" Bn., S.V.C.
Report date:	June 1, 1939
Report number:	290

External archival references to this person: SH/50842

Mihail Vassilievich Jookoff, Russian, born on September 4, 1922 at Shanghai. For the past several years he has been attending the Public & Thos. Hanbury School for Boys from which he is due to graduate in 1939.

His father, a Cossack of the Kuban clan by origin, is reported to have arrived in Shanghai from Persia via Mesopotamia and India in February, 1922 and has since been residing in this city. From 1924 to 1932 he was employed as manager of Stey's Dairy Farm, 92 Edinburgh road, and from 1-11-32 has been operating a dairy farm at 221 Tunsin Road on behalf of the Shanghai Milk Supply Company, Ltd.

The family resides at 221 Tunsin Road. They are registered with the Russian Emigrants' Committee, Moulmein Road. Recently they applied for a visa to enter Australia.

SMP 19 Aug 1941-N 900/20

Date: 27/June/1946

Subject: Soviet- Russian Residents of Wayside proposed Establishment of Club.

According to local Soviet press reports, Soviet- Russian residents of Wayside district propose to open in the near future their own small club. For this purpose an initiative group handed by V.V. JOUKOFF, V. HUDIK and B. MOCHALOFF, having permission from chairman of the Council of the Soviet Citizens' Society, rented the ground floor of premises No. 165 Chaoufoong Road comprised of several rooms. Repair work is in progress in the premises in question.

The aims of the new club include the organization of a reading room, library, chess circle. Lectures, conferences, parties, dancing and other forms of entertainment and recreation can be held in the club.

In its work the initiative group is said to have full assistance of the newly formed Society of Soviet Residence. Registration of prospective members is being carried daily from 7 p.m. to 9p.m. at the above address and when a sufficient number of members have been registered elections of the club's committee will be held.

Full Name in English:	Koshmann Julian Lucianovich
Full Name in Russian:	Кошман Юлиан Люцианович
Birth Year:	1921
Birth Place:	Shanghai
Private Address:	Av. Joffre, 905
Report Title:	J.L. Koshmann, applicant for enlistment in No.3 (Vol) Company, "C" Bn, S.V.C.
Report date:	8 June 1939
Report number:	291
External archival references to this person:	SH/61090

Julian Lucianovich Koshmann, Russian, born on July 4, 1921 at Shanghai. He is the son of the late Mr. L.P. Koshmann, an employee of a local Chinese steamship company who is reported to have perished in a shipwreck off Ningpo in 1932.

The applicant has been attending the Public & Thos. Hanbury School since 1933 and to graduate in 1939. He resides at 905 Avenue Joffre together with his mother, Mrs. A.I. Koshmann, who has been residing in Shanghai since 1923 and until the outbreak of the present Sino-Japanese hostilities conducted a boarding house at house 15, Lane 150 Kungping Road.

It is possible that the applicant in his eagerness to join the S.V.C. has overstated his age.

Full Name in English:	Trifonoff Leonid Grigorievich
Full Name in Russian:	Трифонов Леонид Григорьевич
Birth Year:	1921
Birth Place:	Chalantun, Manchuria
Private Address:	Bubbling Well Rd., 1525, 1ST Floor,
Known to:	Mr. A.J. Headincton, 220 Szechuen rd.
Report Title:	L.G. Trifonoff, applicant for enlistment in the Russian Detachment, S.V.C
Report date:	9/6/1939

Report number: 292
External archival references to this person: SH/122166

Leonid Grigorievich Trifonoff, Russian, born on April 22, 1921 at Chalantun, Manchuria, is reported to be the son of a retired employee of the Chinese Eastern Railway. He claims to have graduated from a middle school at Harbin in 1937. On 9-1-39 he arrived in Shanghai from Harbin aboard the s.s "Tsingtao Maru" and until recently resided at 1525 Bubbling Well Road together with his elder brother, Mr. E.G. Trifonoff, who has been employed with the Revenue Department, S.M.C., since May, 1938 as a superviser.

Full Name in English: Miller Isaac Solomonovich
Full Name in Russian: Миллер Исаак Соломонович
Birth Year: 1921
Birth Place: Harbin
Private Address: Weihaiwei Road, 5 Yang Terrace
Report Title: I.S. Miller, applicant for enlistment in the signals Company, S.V.C
Report date: June 13, 1939
Report number: 293
External archival references to this person: SH/71705

Isaac Solomonovich Miller, Russian of Jewish origin, born on December 13,1921 at Harbin. He is reported to have arrived in Shanghai from Harbin in 1929 together with his parents. Here he attended the Shanghai Jewish School until 1936, after which he studied in the Lester School of Technical Education for about six months (in 1937) and in the Public & Thos. Hanbury School from January to May, 1938. In May, 1938 he was engaged by the Shanghai Telephone Company as an apprentice and is still working in this capacity.

He resides at 5 yang Terrace, Weihaiwei Road, together with his parents, Mr. & Mrs S.B.F. Miller and his four brothers. The father and two elder sons are connected with Miller's Transport co., 106 Peking Road. Two brothers of the applicant, A.S. Miller and D.S. Miller, are reportd to be employed with the China General Omnibus Co., as mechanics and are members of the Transport Company, S.V.C.

Full Name in English: Volkoff Mihail Yakovlevich
Full Name in Russian: Волков Михаил Яковлевич
Birth Year: 1907
Birth Place: Shuanchenpo Station, Chinese Eastern Railway
Private Address: Route Lorton, 66/48

Report Title:	M.Ya. Volkoff, applicant for enlistment in No. 3 (Vol) Company, "C" Battalion, S.V.C.
Report date:	June 19, 1939
Report number:	294

External archival references to this person: SH/131466

Mihail Yakovlevich Volkoff, Russian, born on May 21,1907 at Shuanchenpo Station, Chinese Eastern Railway. According to his own statement, he attended a primary school until 1921, after which he studied in a technical school attached to the Central workshops of the Chinese Eastern Railway, Harbin. In 1923 he proceeded to the U.S.S.R. where he joined the army. In 1924 he fled back to Manchuria. For the following 14 years he resided in various places of the Chinese Eastern Railway Zone being engaged mainly in hunting and collecting material for various zoological museums etc. and now describes himself as a taxidermist.

He arrived in Shanghai from Harbin in June,1938 and has since been residing in this city, assisting in business his brother, V.Ya Volkoff, who is the proprietor of Arana Co., 90 Rue Tenant de la Tour, (X-ray & Electromedical Appar. Manufactures).

He is registered with the Russian Emigrants' Committee, Moulmein Road, on the strength of certificate of Residence No.4695 issued on 12-4-38 at Harbin. At present he resides at 66/48 Route Lorton.

Full Name in English:	Medi Nikolai Petrovich
Full Name in Russian:	Меди Николай Петрович
Birth Year:	1901
Birth Place:	Plotzk, Russia
Private Address:	Rue Tenant de la Tour, 411/19
Report Title:	N.P. Medi, applicant for enlistment in No.3 (Vol.) Company, "C" battalion, S.V.C.
Report date:	19/6/1939
Report number:	295

Nikolai Petrovich Medi, Russian, born on February 28, 1901 at Plotzk, Russia (at present belongs to Poland). Son of an officer of the Russian army he is reported to have graduated from the Habarovsk Military cadet school in 1918 and to have subsequently served in the ranks of the white army during the civil war in Siberia in 1918 – 1920. In 1921 he arrived in Harbin where he continued his education at the Harbin Law Faculty graduating in 1926. For the following 9 years he resided in Harbin, during which period he was employed for various periods by different firms and also served in the Railway Police for several months. He arrived in Shanghai from Harbin in December, 1935. Here he worked as a journalist in the Russian newspaper "New Trail" for about ten months (in 1936) and in the "Novosti Dnia" (in 1937), after which he left for Tientsin where from May to November, 1937 he was employed with the General Export Company. Returning to Shanghai in November, 1937 he worked as a private teacher for a short period, then as a translator in the newspaper "Slovo" for four months and from September, 1938 has been working as a journalist in the "Novosti Dnia".

In 1930 while in Harbin he became a naturalized Chinese citizen. However, he is registered with the Russian Emigrants Committee, Moulmein Road, and with the French Police as a Russian emigrant on account of the fact that he has no Chinese passport. He states that recently he applied to the Chungking Government for a Chinese passport.

He resides at 411/19 Rue Tenant de la Tour together with his wife, Mrs. N.N. Medi nee Lachinoff.

Full Name in English:	Boorkoff Sergey Alexandrovitch
Full Name in Russian:	Бурков Сергей Александрович
Birth Year:	1920
Birth Place:	Amur Region, Maritime Province
Private Address:	Route Vallon, 185
Known to:	Mr. I.S. Zaverniaeyf, 1242 Rue Lafayette tel 70901
Report Title:	S.A. Boorkoff, applicant for enlistment in the Russian Regiment, S.V.C
Report date:	July 11, 1939
Report number:	296
External archival references to this person: SH/21007	

Sergey Alexandrovitch Boorkoff, Russian was born on October 2, 1920 in Amur Region, Maritime Province, Russia. He is reported to have left Russia together with his parents in 1921 and to have subsequently resided in Harbin. He arrived in Shanghai from Harbin on May 16, 1939 and resided together with his parents at 185 Route Vallon. He has five sisters. The elder one is married to Abidor, Filipino, leader of the orchestra in the Del Monte Cabaret. The second one is married to Nalda, Filipino, a musician in the same orchestra, and the third one is employed as a bar attendant in Jose Cafe, Avenue du Roi Albert.

Full Name in English:	Koobley Ivan Nikitich
Full Name in Russian:	Коблей Иван Никитич
Birth Year:	1920

Birth Place:	Pogranichnaya Station, Chinese Eastern Railway.
Private Address:	Rue Lafayette, 1296
Known to:	Mr. K.A. Stekloff, 749 Bubble Well Rd, Room 203
Report Title:	I.N. Koobley, A.N, Rudniansky, L.C. Muller and N.K. Kartasheff, applicants for enlistment in the Russian Regiment, S.V.C
Report date:	July 11, 1939.
Report number:	297

External archival references to this person: SH/60688 фамилия Кублей

Ivan Nikitich Koobley, Russian, was born on November 20, 1920 at Pogranichnaya Station, Chinese Eastern Railway. He arrived in Shanghai from Harbin in 1930 and from 1931 to 1934 attended the Commercial School of the Russian Orthodox Confraternity. In 1936, he secured a position as an office assistant in the tea department of White & Co., Ltd., 81, Jinkee Road. In 1938 the company suspended dealing in tea and this department was taken over by one S.N. Sobelnikoff who established his business at 319, Route Cardinal Mercier. The applicant continued his work in the same capacity in the new enterprise until May 1939 when he resigned owing to ill health.

Applicant's brother, G.N. Koobley, has the following criminal record in Shanghai:

Drunk & Disorderly	1ˢᵗ.S.S.D.Court.	Fined $3.00 or 3 days detention. 3.2.38.
Larceny	1ˢᵗ.S.S.D. Court.	4 months imprisonment. 25.6.38.

Full Name in English:	Rudniansky Alexander Mihailovich
Full Name in Russian:	Руднянский Александр Михайлович
Birth Year:	1913
Birth Place:	Harbin, Manchuria
Private Address:	Route Vallon, 178
Known to:	Mr. Y. Novikoff,178 Route Vallon
Report Title:	I.N. Koobley, A.N, Rudniansky, L.C. Muller and N.K. Kartasheff, applicants for enlistment in the Russian Regiment, S.V.C
Report date:	July 11, 1939.
Report number:	297

External archival references to this person: SH/101643

Alexander Mihailovich Rudniansky, Russian, was born on September 15, 1913, in Harbin, Manchuria. He first arrived in Shanghai in the end of 1932 and after a short stay in this city proceeded to Mukden where he was engaged as a railway guard on Mukden Shanhaikan Railway. In April 1938 he left that place of employment and went to Tientsin. In December of the same year he secured a position as a guard at one of the coal mines situated off the Tsingtao-Tsinanfu Railway. According to his own statement, he left that position on his own accord in June 1939 and returned to Tientsin. On 25.6.39. he arrived in Shanghai.

His brother, M. Rudniansky, is a Lance Corporal in the Russian Regiment, S.V.C.

Full Name in English:	Muller Leo Makarovich
Full Name in Russian:	Мюллер Лео Макарович
Birth Year:	1918
Birth Place:	Vladivostok, Maritime Province, Russia
Private Address:	Rue Montauban, 29/503
Known to:	Mrs S.G. Topshoi, 207 Route Remi,
Report Title:	I.N. Koobley, A.N, Rudniansky, L.C. Muller and N.K. Kartasheff, applicants for enlistment in the Russian Regiment, S.V.C
Report date:	July 11, 1939.
Report number:	297

External archival references to this person: SH/80116 на карточке Лев Оскарович

Leo Makarovich Muller, Russian of German origin, was born on September 2, 1918 at Vladivostok, Maritime Province, Russia. He is reported to have left Russia together with his mother in 1922 and to have subsequently resided in Harbin, Manchuria.

He arrived in Shanghai in April 1936 and soon afterwards obtained a position as a radio-mechanic with Williams Radio Engineering Company, 681 B'Well Road. He left that concern just before the outbreak of the Sino-Japanese hostilities. During the first months of the conflict he worked casually as a chauffeur for various foreign and Japanese concerns in the Northern area. In the beginning of 1938 he established his own business, the "Shanghai Auto-driving School", 18 Linda Terrace, Avenue Joffre.

However, owing to the business depression he closed his enterprise in January 1939. Since then he has been unemployed.

Full Name in English:	Kartasheff Nikita Kuzmich
Full Name in Russian:	Карташев Никита Кузьмич
Birth Year:	1898
Birth Place:	Perm Province, Russia
Private Address:	Fearon Rd., 59

Known to:	Mr. P. Vdovkin,587 Av. Foch
Report Title:	I.N. Koobley, A.N. Rudniansky, L.C. Muller and N.K. Kartasheff, applicants for enlistment in the Russian Regiment, S.V.C
Report date:	July 11, 1939.
Report number:	297

External archival references to this person: SH/51464

Nikita Kuzmich Kartasheff, Russian, was born on March 30, 1898 in Perm Province, Russia. He arrived in Shanghai from Vladivostok in 1923. Here, he worked casually until 1926 when he was engaged as a chauffeur by the late Dr. Bari. In 1928 his services were dispensed with. From October 1, 1928 to August 20, 1931 he worked in the same capacity with the Asiatic Petroleum Co., (North Chine) Ltd.

Leaving that company on his own accord, he later worked as a chauffeur with the following concerns:-

Far Eastern Import and Export Company, 33 Route Vallon, from November 1933 to February 1934. The Taylor Garage Ltd., from June 1934 to September 1935. The Texas Co. (China) Ltd., from July 1936 to June 1939.

Full Name in English:	Dolgoff Ivan Nikitich
Full Name in Russian:	Долгов Иван Никитич
Birth Year:	1909
Birth Place:	Orloff Province, Russia
Report Title:	I. Dolgoff, applicant for enrolment in the Light Automatic (A.D.) Company, S.V.C
Report date:	July 20, 1939
Report number:	298

External archival references to this person: SH/30362

Ivan Nikitich Dolgoff, Russian, was born on November 14, 1909 in Orloff Province, Russia. He is reported to have left Russia in 1920 and to have subsequently resided first in Manchouli and from 1923 in Harbin. In September 1931 he arrived in Shanghai from Harbin. In April 1932 he secured a position as a draughtsman with the Cathay Ceramics Co., (Inc. U.S.A.), 24 and Bund. He left that place of employment of his own accord in November 1937 and from December of the same year was employed as a shipping clerk with the Yee Tsoong Tobacco Co., 175 Soochow Road.

Full Name in English:	Mihailoff-Mitchell Arcady Alexeyevitch
Full Name in Russian:	Михайлов Митчелл Аркадий Алексеевич
Birth Year:	1910

Birth Place:	Habarovsk, Siberia
Report Title:	A. Mihailoff-Mitchell, applicant for enrolment in the Light Automatic (A.D.) Company, S.V.C
Report date:	July 20 1939
Report number:	298
External archival references to this person:	SH/71537

Arcady Alexeyevitch Mihailoff-Mitchell, Russian, was born on December 14, 1910 at Habarovsk, Siberia. In 1923 he arrived in Shanghai from Vladivostok. In September of the same year he entered the Thomas Hanbury School for Boys and graduated from same in December 1926. Then he worked casually until September 1930 when he obtained a position as a supervisor with the China Printing & Finishing Company Ltd. at one of their mills in Pootung. In February 1931 he left that company of his own accord and in April of the same year secured a position as a meter inspector with the French Tramway & Electric Company.

In September 1935 his services were dispensed with owing to a reduction in staff. From September 1937 to September 1938 he was employed in the Transportation Department of the Scharpf, Guenter & Co., 666 Szechuen Road. In October, 1938 he secured his present position as Assistant Publicity Manager with the Bann's Studio, 104 Bubbling well Road.

Full Name in English:	Chirkovich Viacheslav Petrovitch
Full Name in Russian:	Чиркович Вячеслав Петрович
Birth Year:	1920
Birth Place:	Grodekovo Station, Ussuri Region, Siberia
Private Address:	Route Bourgeat, 690
Report Title:	V.P. Chirkovich, applicant for enrolment in No.3 (Volunteer) Company, "C" Battalion, S.V.C.
Report date:	July 26, 1939
Report number:	299

Viacheslav Petrovitch Chirkovich, Russian, was born on December 17, 1920 at Grodekovo Station, Ussuri Region, Siberia. He arrived in Shanghai from Vladivostok together with his parents in 1922 and in 1923 proceeded to Harbin. He returned to Shanghai in January 1935 and in February of the same year entered the Commercial School of the Russian Orthodox Confraternity, graduating from same in June 1939. On June 26, 1939 he was engaged as a motorcycle driver in the Delivery Department of Bakerite Company (Fed. Inc. U.S.A.), 1432 Sinza Road, and at present resides together with his mother at 690 Route Bourgeat.

Full Name in English:	Pavloff Vassily Iosifovitch
Full Name in Russian:	Павлов Василий Иосифович
Birth Year:	1917
Birth Place:	Transbaikal Province, Russia
Private Address:	Route Remi, 141/9
Known to:	Mr. T.F. Romanoff 141/9 Route Remi
Report Title:	V.I. Pavloff and U.A. Beleliubsky, applicants for enlistment in the Russian Regiment, S.V.C
Report date:	July 29, 1939
Report number:	300
External archival references to this person:	SH/90903

Vassily Iosifovitch Pavloff, Russian, was born on March 20, 1917 in Transbaikal Province, Russia. He is reported to have left Russia together with his parents in 1919 and to have subsequently resided in Harbin, Manchuria. In August 1934 he arrived in Shanghai from Harbin and in October of the same year joined the Russian Regiment, S.V.C. In April 1939 he left the Regiment of his own accord and in May of the same year joined the Auxiliary Detachment, French Police. On June 26, 1939 he resigned from the Detachment on the excuse that he wanted to proceed to Harbin.

Full Name in English:	Beleliubsky Uriy Alexandrovitch
Full Name in Russian:	Белелюбский Юрий Александрович
Birth Year:	1910
Birth Place:	Riazan Province, Russia
Private Address:	Kungping Rd, 15
Known to:	Mr. N. Jarikoff, 144 Route Des Soeurs
Report Title:	V.I. Pavloff and U.A. Beleliubsky, applicants for enlistment in the Russian Regiment, S.V.C
Report date:	July 29, 1939
Report number:	300

Uriy Alexandrovitch Beleliubsky, Russian, was born on April 11, 1910 in Riazan Province, Russia. According to his own statement, he left Russia together with the parents in 1920 and subsequently resided in Harbin, Manchuria. In July 1932 he arrived in Shanghai from Harbin and in August of the same year joined the Russian Regiment, S.V.C.

On October 31, 1937 he left the Regiment of his own accord. Soon afterwards he obtained a position as a chauffeur with Marden & Co. and later worked in the same capacity with the British Transportation Company, 299 Kiukiang Road.

On May 19, 1939 he was charged with Fighting at the Shanghai First Special District Court and sentenced to a $7.00 fine or seven Days' imprisonment. He served the sentence and was released on May 26, 1939.

Full Name in English:	Oksakovsky Anatoly Leontievitch
Full Name in Russian:	Оксаковский Анатолий Леонтьевич
Birth Year:	1908
Birth Place:	Chernigoff Province, Russia
Report Title:	A.L. Oksakovsky, application for enrolment in No.3 (Vol) Company, S.V.C
Report date:	July, 31, 1939
Report number:	301
External archival references to this person:	SH/90128

Anatoly Leontievitch Oksakovsky, Russian, was born on July 30, 1908 in Chernigoff Province, Russia, He is reported to have left Russia together with his parents in 1917 and to have subsequently resided in Harbin, Manchuria. In October 1936 he arrived in Shanghai from Harbin. In January 1937 he and another Russian, M. Ilvis, established their own business under the style Universal Advertising Company, 309 Route Cardinal Mercier. In June of the same year he suspended conducting the business owing to the lack of funds and proceeded to Tientsin. In June 1938 he returned to Shanghai and on August 9, 1938 was engaged as a draughtsman by Noller & Company, 12 The Bund.

Full Name in English:	Choodovsky Dimitry Nikolaevitch
Full Name in Russian:	Чудовский Дмитрий Николаевич
Birth Year:	1897
Birth Place:	Don Region, Russia
Private Address:	East Broadway, 1025, house 5
Known to:	Mr. E.V. Levitsky, SGT. S.M.P, Bubbl Well P.St.
Report Title:	D.N. Choodovsky, applicant for enlistment in the Russian Regiment, S.V.C.
Report date:	August 5, 1939
Report number:	302
External archival references to this person:	SH/21638

Dimitry Nikolaevitch Choodovsky, Russian, was born on January 27, 1897, in Don Region, Russia. He is reported to have left Russia in 1922 and to have subsequently resided in Harbin, Manchuria. In 1925 he joined Marshal Chang Chung Chang Army and served in it until 1928 when it was disbanded. From 1928 to 1930 he resided in Tientsin. In October 1930, he arrived in Shanghai from Tientsin and resided here until 1932, after which he left for Mukden. He returned here in March, 1939.

Full Name in English:	Rouchieff Ivan Pavlovitch
Full Name in Russian:	Ручьев Иван Павлович
Birth Year:	1915
Birth Place:	Omsk Region, Siberia
Private Address:	Route Vallon, 176, house 5
Known to:	Mr. A.G. Domojiroff, Sgt. in S.M.P.
Report Title:	I.P. Rouchieff, V.S. Griakalo and P.K. Straut, applicants for enlistment in the Russian Regiment, S.V.C.
Report date:	August 5, 1939
Report number:	303

External archival references to this person: SH/101612

Ivan Pavlovitch Rouchieff, Russian, was born on May 15, 1915, in Omsk Region, Siberia. According to his own statement he left Russia together with his parents in 1920 and subsequently resided in Harbin, Manchuria. In September, 1933, he arrived in Shanghai. On January 1, 1934, he joined the Russian Regiment, S.V.C. On August 1, 1936, he left the Regiment of his own accord. He worked casually until December 1937 when he joined the Auxiliary Detachment, French Police. On April 14, 1938, he resigned from that Detachment. Later he worked with the Campbell Paints factory and also with "Olma" Paints Factory. For the past six months he was employed as a trainer with the Columbia and Great Western Riding Academy.

Full Name in English:	Griakalo Vladimir Sergeyevitch
Full Name in Russian:	Грякало Владимир Сергеевич
Birth Year:	1921
Birth Place:	Harbin, Manchuria
Private Address:	Yangtszepoo Rd, 1001, house 20
Report Title:	I.P. Rouchieff, V.S. Griakalo and P.K. Straut, applicants for enlistment in the Russian Regiment, S.V.C.
Report date:	August 5, 1939
Report number:	303

External archival references to this person: SH/41249

Vladimir Sergeyevitch Griakalo, Russian, was born on March 1, 1921, in Harbin, Manchuria. In September, 1933, he arrived in Shanghai and resided together with

Mr. Epifanoff, an employee of the Shanghai Water Works Co., Ltd. In the beginning of 1934, he entered the St. Francis Xavier's College and studied in it until 1939.

Full Name in English:	Straut Pavel Karlovitch
Full Name in Russian:	Страут Павел Карлович
Birth Year:	1914
Birth Place:	Harbin, Manchuria
Report Title:	I.P. Rouchieff, V.S. Griakalo and P.K. Straut, applicants for enlistment in the Russian Regiment, S.V.C.
Report date:	August 5, 1939
Report number:	303

Pavel Karlovitch Straut, Russian of Latvian origin, was born on May 20, 1914, in Harbin, Manchuria. From 1933 to 1935 he served as a Railway guard on the Mukden-Shanhaikuan Railway. From March 1935 to April 1939 he was employed with the Political Section of the Police at Manchouli and Harbin. On June 5, 1939, he, together with several Japanese, left Harbin for Tientsin and later proceeded to Nanking where, according to his own statement, he was offered employment in one of the local cinemas. However, upon their arrival in Nanking, neither the Japanese nor the applicants were permitted to remain there and he proceeded to Shanghai, arriving here on July 25, 1939.

Full Name in English:	Fominih Boris Ilytch
Full Name in Russian:	Фоминых Борис Ильич
Birth Year:	1917
Birth Place:	Harbin, Manchuria
Private Address:	Route De Grouchy, 114
Known to:	Mr. A.S. Mossol, 114 Route De Grouchy
Report Title:	B.I. Fominih, applicant for enlistment in the Russian Regiment, S.V.C
Report date:	August, 15, 1939
Report number:	305
External archival references to this person:	SH/31749

Boris Ilytch Fominih, Russian, was born on June 11, 1917, in Harbin, Manchuria. In February, 1937, he arrived in Shanghai from Harbin. In August of the same year he joined the Auxiliary Detachment of the French Police. On July 24, 1939, he resigned from the Detachment of his own accord,

Full Name in English:	Krassoolia Victor Pavlovitch
Full Name in Russian:	Красуля Виктор Павлович
Birth Year:	1921
Birth Place:	Nikolsk-Ussuryisk, Siberia
Private Address:	Route Say Zoong, 42/7
Known to:	Mr. V.I. Karpoff, 786, Apt 5, Rue Bourgeat
Report Title:	V.P. Krassoolia and V.L. Koshmann, applicants for enlistment in the Russian Regiment, S.V.C
Report date:	August 5, 1939
Report number:	304

External archival references to this person: SH/61702

Victor Pavlovitch Krassoolia, Russian, was born on May 9, 1921, in Nikolsk-Ussuryisk, Siberia. He is reported to have left Russia together with his parents in 1922 and to have subsequently resided in Harbin, Manchuria. In October, 1936, he arrived in shanghai and in December of the same year entered the Commercial School of the Russian Orthodox Confraternity. He left the school in May, 1939.

Full Name in English:	Koshmann Vitaly Loossianvitch
Full Name in Russian:	Кошман Виталий Луссианович (Люцианович)
Birth Year:	1921
Birth Place:	Harkov Province, Russia
Private Address:	Av. Joffre, 905 Flat 3
Known to:	Mr. N.B. Ramsay, EWO Brewery
Report Title:	V.P. Krassoolia and V.L. Koshmann, applicants for enlistment in the Russian Regiment, S.V.C
Report date:	August 5, 1939
Report number:	304

External archival references to this person: SH/61092

Vitaly Loossianvitch Koshmann, Russian, was born on March 19, 1921, in Harkov Province, Russia. In 1924 he arrived in Shanghai from Harbin. From September, 1933 to December, 1938 he studied in the public and Thomas Hanbury School for Boys.

Full Name in English:	Aumann Pavel Leopoldovitch
Full Name in Russian:	Ауман Павел Леопольдович
Birth Year:	1916
Birth Place:	Habarovsk, Siberia

Report Title:	P.L. Aumann, applicant for enrolment in the American Machine-Gun Co., S.V.C.
Report date:	August 16, 1939
Report number:	306
External archival references to this person:	SH/10945. Он же Ауман-Яхно SH/10949

Pavel Leopoldovitch Aumann, Russian, was born on June 29, 1916, in Habarovsk, Siberia. According to his own statement, he left Russia together with his parents in 1925 and subsequently resided in Harbin, Manchuria. He first arrived in Shanghai on May 6, 1939, and after a short stay in this city returned to Harbin. On August 3, 1939, he returned to Shanghai and has since been employed as a supervisor with H.B. Campbell oil and paints Factory, Route Tenant de la Tour.

Applicant's brother, E. Aumann, a musician by occupation, has for the past three years been employed with the Park Hotel orchestra.

Full Name in English:	Sosnovsky Constantin Mihailovitch
Full Name in Russian:	Сосновский Константин Михайлович
Birth Year:	1914
Birth Place:	Odessa, Russia
Private Address:	Route Lorton, 35
Known to:	Mr. A.A. Dimitrieff, 713 Av. Joffre
Report Title:	C.M. Sosnovsky, applicant for enlistment in the Russian Regiment, S.V.C.
Report date:	August 14, 1939
Report number:	307
External archival references to this person:	SH/120385. В карточке опечатка - вместо 1939 указан 1937 г.

Constantin Mihailovitch Sosnovsky, Russian, was born on March 1, 1914 in Odessa, Russia. He is reported to have left Russia together with his parents in 1922 and to have subsequently resided in Harbin, Manchuria.

In February 1934 he arrived in Shanghai from Harbin. Here he worked casually until 1937 when he proceeded to Dairen. Returning to Shanghai in the beginning of 1938, he was unable to secure any fixed employment here.

Applicant's three brothers are at present serving with the Russian Regiment, S.V.C.

Full Name in English:	Brizgin Oleg Valentinovitch
Full Name in Russian:	Брызгин Олег Валентинович
Birth Year:	1921

Birth Place:	Chefoo, China
Private Address:	Kungping Rd, 225
Known to:	Mr. M.N. Choovstvin, Fire Brigade, French Bund
Report Title:	O.V. Brizgin, I.G. Starikoff, V.V. Makedonsky, N.G. Belotzerkovetz and I.A. Stepanoff, applicants for enlistment in the Russian Regiment, S.V.C.
Report date:	September 1, 1939
Report number:	308

External archival references to this person: SH/20824

Oleg Valentinovitch Brizgin, Russian, was born on March 7, 1921, in Chefoo, China. From 1926 he resided in Harbin, where in December 1938 he graduated from a local high school.

He arrived in Shanghai from Harbin on August 17, 1936, in the s.s "Dairen" Maru.

Being a new arrival here, he is not known locally.

Full Name in English:	Starikoff Ivan Gavrilovitch
Full Name in Russian:	Стариков Иван Гаврилович
Birth Year:	1906
Birth Place:	Maritime Province, Russia
Private Address:	Alcock Rd, 154, house 7
Known to:	Capt. N.M. Stepanischeff, Rus Regt S.V.C. no 6 The Bund
Report Title:	O.V. Brizgin, I.G. Starikoff, V.V. Makedonsky, N.G. Belotzerkovetz and I.A. Stepanoff, applicants for enlistment in the Russian Regiment, S.V.C.
Report date:	September 1, 1939
Report number:	308

External archival references to this person: SH/120590

Ivan Gavrilovitch Starikoff, Russian, was born on April 25, 1906, in the Maritime Province, Russia. He is reported to have left Russia in 1921 and to have subsequently resided in Harbin until August 1933, afterwards coming to Shanghai.

On July 26, 1934, he was charged with Larceny at the Shanghai Second Special District Court and sentenced to 10 days' imprisonment. On September 13, 1934, he joined the Russian Regiment, S.V.C. and served in it until April 12, 1938, when he resigned of his own accord. Later he worked casually as a chauffeur-mechanic and from September 1938, to August 1939 was employed in the same capacity with Mr. M. Zeilig, 1248 Rue Lafayette House 2.

Full Name in English:	Makedonsky Vasily Vasilievitch
Full Name in Russian:	Македонский Василий Васильевич
Birth Year:	1914
Birth Place:	Boorea Station, Amur Railway, Siberia
Private Address:	Av Roi Albert, 569
Known to:	Lt. R.A. Chernosvitoff Rus Regt S.V.C. No. 6 The Bund
Report Title:	O.V. Brizgin, I.G. Starikoff, V.V. Makedonsky, N.G. Belotzerkovetz and I.A. Stepanoff, applicants for enlistment in the Russian Regiment, S.V.C.
Report date:	September 1, 1939
Report number:	308
External archival references to this person:	SH/81337

Vasily Vasilievitch Makedonsky, Russian, was born on February 28, 1914, at the Boorea Station, Amur Railway, Siberia. From 1922 to May 1934 he resided in Harbin, after which he came to Shanghai. On June 1, 1934, he joined the Russia Regiment, S.V.C. He resigned from the Regiment of his own accord on June 30, 1939.

Full Name in English:	Belotzerkovetz Nikolai Germogenovitch
Full Name in Russian:	Белоцерковец Николай Гермогенович
Birth Year:	1919
Birth Place:	Maritime Province, Russia
Private Address:	Av. Joffre, 695
Report Title:	O.V. Brizgin, I.G. Starikoff, V.V. Makedonsky, N.G. Belotzerkovetz and I.A. Stepanoff, applicants for enlistment in the Russian Regiment, S.V.C.
Report date:	September 1, 1939
Report number:	308

Nikolai Germogenovitch Belotzerkovetz, Russian, was born on February 7, 1919, in the Maritime Province, Russia. According to his own statement, he left Russia together with his parents in 1924 and proceeded to Brazil where they resided until 1929, afterwards returning to Harbin, and for the following ten years he worked as a chauffeur with various Japanese Military and private concerns in different parts of Manchoukuo, including the Manchoukuo - U.S.S.R. border along the Amur River.

He arrived in Shanghai on July 11, 1939, together with his mother.

Full Name in English:	Stepanoff Igor Alexeyevitch
Full Name in Russian:	Степанов Игорь Алексеевич
Birth Year:	1914
Birth Place:	Harbin, Manchuria
Private Address:	Av. Joffre, 697
Report Title:	O.V. Brizgin, I.G. Starikoff, V.V. Makedonsky, N.G. Belotzerkovetz and I.A. Stepanoff, applicants for enlistment in the Russian Regiment, S.V.C.
Report date:	September 1, 1939
Report number:	308

Igor Alexeyevitch Stepanoff, Russian, was born on August 17, 1914, in Harbin, Manchuria. He first arrived in Shanghai from Harbin in 1930. During 1932 he served with Russian Regiment, S.V.C. for two short periods, having been dismissed on both occasions. Later he proceeded to Tientsin and then Moukden where he was employed as a Railway Guard on Mukden-Kirin Railway. He reappeared in Shanghai in 1934, but having failed to secure any employment here, returned to Harbin after a short stay in this city.

During his stay in Manchoukuo he worked as a chauffeur with Japanese military and private concerns in various cities of Manchoukuo including the Manchoukuo – U.S.S.R. border along Amur River. On August 8, 1939, he arrived in Shanghai and resided together with the 4th applicant at 697 Avenue Joffre.

Full Name in English:	Yakoonin Dmitry Feodorovitch
Full Name in Russian:	Якунин Дмитрий Федорович
Birth Year:	1905
Birth Place:	Blagoveshchensk, Siberia
Private Address:	Chusan Rd, 14
Known to:	Dr. A.A. Givrey, Denis Appt. 42, Bubbling Well Rd
Report Title:	D.G. Yakoonin, B.T. Froloff, G.D. Kochneff and B.A. Limonnikoff, applicant for enlistment in the Russian Regiment, S.V.C.
Report date:	September 1, 1939
Report number:	309
External archival references to this person:	SH/132049

Dmitry Feodorovitch Yakoonin, Russian, was born on November 8, 1905 at Blagoveshchensk, Siberia. According to His own statement, he resided in Harbin, Manchuria, from 1920 to 1934, afterwards coming to Shanghai. From 1920 to 1934, afterwards coming to Shanghai from July 1934 to September 1935 he served in the Auxiliary Detachment, French Police. From September of the same year until March 1939 he was employed as a stocker with the Shanghai Power Company, Riverside Station.

Full Name in English:	Froloff Boris Trofimovitch
Full Name in Russian:	Фролов Борис Трофимович
Birth Year:	1917
Birth Place:	Veishahe Station, Chinese Eastern Railway
Private Address:	Av. Joffre, 1222
Known to:	Mr. G. A. Polinsky, 1222 Av. Joffre
Report Title:	D.G. Yakoonin, B.T. Froloff, G.D. Kochneff and B.A. Limonnikoff, applicant for enlistment in the Russian Regiment, S.V.C.
Report date:	September 1, 1939
Report number:	309

External archival references to this person: SH/31869

Boris Trofimovitch Froloff, Russian, was born on October 1, 1917, at Veishahe Station, Chinese Eastern Railway. He arrived in Shanghai from Harbin on July 31, 1939 and resided together with his sister, Mrs. H. Opalinsky, 1222 Avenue Joffre.

Full Name in English:	Kochneff Georgy Dmitrievitch
Full Name in Russian:	Кочнев Георгий Дмитриевич
Birth Year:	1921
Birth Place:	Sinkiang Province, China
Private Address:	Baikal Rd, 150
Known to:	Mr. P.L. Vdovkin 587 Av. Foch
Report Title:	D.G. Yakoonin, B.T. Froloff, G.D. Kochneff and B.A. Limonnikoff, applicant for enlistment in the Russian Regiment, S.V.C.
Report date:	September 1, 1939
Report number:	309

External archival references to this person: SH/60227

Georgy Dmitrievitch Kochneff, Russian, was born on September 20, 1921, in Sinkiang Province, China. He arrived in Shanghai from Hankow in 1928 together with his parents. His father, Mr. D. Kochneff, is at present chairman of the Cossack Union in Shanghai and hid mother is employed with Yee Tsoong Tobacco Company.

In December 1938, the applicant and other two youths stowed themselves away with the intention to proceed to Mexico, but were discovered upon arrival at Kobe, Japan, and subsequently returned to Shanghai on December 12, 1938.

This applicant participated in the Anti Kuomintang demonstration which was staged north of the Soochow Creek on August 13, 1939. He explained that he was forced to do so by the notorious M. Tretiakoff, Chairman of the "Anti-Communist Union" in Shanghai.

Full Name in English:	Limonnikoff Boris Alexandrovitch
Full Name in Russian:	Лимонников Борис Александрович
Birth Year:	1910
Birth Place:	Harbin, Manchuria
Private Address:	Tongshan Rd., 559/25
Known to:	Mr. P.P. Salicheff, 559/25 Tongshan Rd
Report Title:	D.G. Yakoonin, B.T. Froloff, G.D. Kochneff and B.A. Limonnikoff, applicant for enlistment in the Russian Regiment, S.V.C.
Report date:	September 1, 1939
Report number:	309
External archival references to this person:	SH/80634

Boris Alexandrovitch Limonnikoff, Russian, was born on October 23, 1910, in Harbin, Manchuria. He first arrived in Shanghai in September 1931. In January 1932 he showed himself away in the s.s. "Empress of Russia" and subsequently Landed at Manila, P.I. He returned to Shanghai in 1934 and after a short stay here proceeded to Harbin. From 1936 to December 1938 he resided in Tientsin, after which he came to Shanghai.

Full Name in English:	Golik Konstantin Terentievitch
Full Name in Russian:	Голик Константин Терентьевич
Birth Year:	1915
Birth Place:	Harbin, Manchuria
Private Address:	Route Pere Robert, 33
Known to:	Mrs. A.T. Yates, 216 Seymour Rd. "Fleur-De-Lys"

Report Title:	K.T. Golik, M.V. Nikolseff and K.A. Yakovleff, applicants for enlistment in the Russian Regiment, S.V.C
Report date:	September 7, 1939
Report number:	310

External archival references to this person: SH/40638

Konstantin Terentievtch Golik, Russian, was born on July 3, 1915 in Harbin, Manchuria. He arrived in Shanghai from Harbin on August 16, 1939 in the B.E. "Tsingtao Maru". His sister, Mrs. A.T. Yates, is employed as a manageress with the "Fleur-de-Lys" Milliners, 216 Seymour Road.

Full Name in English:	Nikolaeff Michail Vitalievitch
Full Name in Russian:	Николаев Михаил Витальевич
Birth Year:	1921
Birth Place:	Vladivostok, Maritime Province, Russia
Private Address:	Route Vallon, 516
Known to:	Mr. G.V. Radetsky-Mikoolich 635, Rue Ratard
Report Title:	K.T. Golik, M.V. Nikolaeff and K.A. Yakovleff, applicants for enlistment in the Russian Regiment, S.V.C
Report date:	September 7, 1939
Report number:	310

External archival references to this person: SH/81910

Michail Vitalievitch Nikolaeff, Russia, was born on September 18, 1921 in Vladivostok, Maritime Province, Russia. He arrived in Shanghai from Vladivostok together with his parents in 1922. From 1931 to 1936 he attended the lat. Russian School (now A.S. Poushkin Memorial School). From April 11, 1939 to September 11, 1939 he was employed as an apprentice with the Medical Analysis Laboratory, 3 Ezra Road.

His father is at present employed as a watchman with Andersen, Meyer & Co., Ltd.

Full Name in English:	Yakovleff Konstantin Alexandrovitch
Full Name in Russian:	Яковлев Константин Александрович
Birth Year:	1921
Birth Place:	Dairen
Private Address:	Changping Rd, 675
Known to:	Mr. V.V. Zimin 355 Rue Cardinal Mercieur

Report Title:	K.T. Golik, M.V. Nikolaeff and K.A. Yakovleff, applicants for enlistment in the Russian Regiment, S.V.C
Report date:	September 7, 1939
Report number:	310

External archival references to this person: SH/131993

Konstantin Alexandrovitch Yakovleff, Russian, was born on October 31, 1921 in Dairen. He arrived in Shanghai from Dairen together with his parents IN 1927. From 1931 to 1934 he attended the Public & Thomas Hanbury School for Boys. In November 1936 he obtained employment as a mechanic-apprentice with the China General Omnibus Company. In September 1938 he left that company of his own accord. From February 1939 to September 1939 he was employed as a kennel man with the Canidrome.

Applicant's sister is married to Mr. J.W. Robb of the Revenue Department, S.M.C.

Full Name in English:	Caplan Alexander Lvovitch
Full Name in Russian:	Каплан Александр Львович
Birth Year:	1910
Birth Place:	Harbin
Report Title:	A.L. Caplan, applicant for enrolment in the American Troop, S.V.C
Report date:	September 18, 1939
Report number:	311

External archival references to this person: SH/21142

Alexander Lvovitch Caplan, Russian Jew, was born on April 13, 1910 Harbin together with his parents. From 1915 to 1921 he attended the Thomas Hanbury School. After which he entered the St. Francis Xsavier's College, graduating from in 1926.

From 1927 to 1929 he was employed as a clerk with the Shanghai Water Works Company, Ltd. Leaving that company of his own accord he worked as a salesman with the Office Appliance Company, Ltd, for a period In November 1930 he secured a position as an assistant manager with the Fox lime corporation, 142 museum Rd. In March 1931 he was transferred to the Hongkong branch of the same company. Returning to Shanghai in January 1936 he has since been employed as a general manager with Warner Bros. First National Picture Inc., 142 Museum Road.

Full Name in English:	Shestakoff Georgy Vassilievitch
Full Name in Russian:	Шестаков Георгий Васильевич

Birth Year:	1895
Birth Place:	Altai Province, Russia
Report Title:	G.V. Shestakoff, applicant for enrolment in the American Troop S.V.C.
Report date:	September 13, 1939
Report number:	312

External archival references to this person: SH/110879

Georgy Vassilievitch Shestakoff, Russian, was born on My 29, 1895 in Altai Province, Russia. According to his own statement, he left Russia for China via Mongolia in 1923 and subsequently resided in Hankow until 1930, after which he arrived in Shanghai. Here he worked casually until May 1934 when he secured a position as a chemist with the China Industrial Laboratory Fed, Inc. U.S.A., I56/II-1 Liaoyung Road.

At present he holds a post of manager and chief chemist in the same company and is also reported to have 10% share in the business.

Full Name in English:	Pahomoff Boris Konstantinovitch
Full Name in Russian:	Пахомов Борис Константинович
Birth Year:	1908
Birth Place:	Vladivostok, Maritime Province, Russia
Private Address:	Rue Lorton, 66/27
Known to:	Mr. J.C. Williams 12 The Bund (Texaco)
Report Title:	B.K. Pahomoff and I.I. Sokoloff, applicants for enlistment in the Russia Regiment, S.V.C.
Report date:	September 20, 1939
Report number:	313

External archival references to this person: SH/90621

Boris Konstantinovitch Pahomoff, Russian, was born on November 1, 1908, at Vladivostok, Maritime Province, Russia. He is reported to have left Russia in 1926 and to have subsequently resided in Harbin, Manchuria. In 1927 he left Harbin for Tientsin and in 1928 arrived in Shanghai from the latter city. Here he worked casually until July, 1929 when he joined the Russia Regiment, S.V.C., on June 1, 1930; he left the Regiment of his own accord. On January 1932 he obtained a position as a chauffeur with the Asiatic Petroleum Co. (North China) Ltd. Leaving that company of his own accord in November 1935; he proceeded to Chefoo, where soon afterwards he was engaged as a chauffeur by Mr. S.G. Beare of H.B.M. Consulate-General. He returned to Shanghai in June 1937 together with his employer and continued to work for him until May 2, 1939, the Date of Mr. Beare's departure to England.

From May 20, 1939 to September 8, 1939 he worked in the same capacity with Mr. J.C. Willams of Texaco Company, 12 The Bund.

Full Name in English:	Sokoloff Igor Ivanovitch
Full Name in Russian:	Соколов Игорь Иванович
Birth Year:	1920
Birth Place:	Harbin, Manchuria
Private Address:	Av. Joffre, 804
Report Title:	B.K. Pahomoff and I.I. Sokoloff, applicants for enlistment in the Russia Regiment, S.V.C.
Report date:	September 20, 1939
Report number:	313

Igor Ivanovitch Sokoloff, Russian, was born on June 5, 1920 in Harbin, Manchuria. He arrived in Shanghai from Harbin on September 5, 1939 and is not known locally.

Full Name in English:	Popoff Innokenty Vladimirovitch
Full Name in Russian:	Попов Иннокентий Владимирович
Birth Year:	1920
Birth Place:	Harbin, Manchuria
Private Address:	Yuencnang Rd, 9
Report Title:	I.V. Popoff and K.M. Filipoff, applicants for enlistment in the Russian Regiment, S.V.C
Report date:	September 29, 1939
Report number:	314
External archival references to this person:	SH/100039. В карточке опечатка, указан 1937 год вместо 1939.

Innokenty Vladimirovitch Popoff, Russian, was born on December 15, 1920 in Harbin, Manchuria. He arrived in Shanghai from Harbin together with his mother and sister on September 8, 1939 in the s.s. "Tsingtao Maru"

Being a new arrival in Shanghai he is not known locally.

Full Name in English:	Filipoff Konstantin Maximovitch
Full Name in Russian:	Филиппов Константин Максимович
Birth Year:	1920
Birth Place:	Blagoveschensk, Siberia
Private Address:	Route Vallon, 180
Known to:	Mr. L.V. Arnoldoff, 774 Av. Joffre
Report Title:	I.V. Popoff and K.M. Filipoff, applicants for enlistment in the Russian Regiment, S.V.C

Report date: September 29, 1939
Report number: 314
External archival references to this person: SH/31604

Konstantin Maximovitch Filipoff, Russian, was born on June 5, 1920 in Blagoveschensk, Siberia. He is reported to have left Russian together with his parents in 1922 and to have subsequently resided in Harbin, Manchuria. He arrived in Shanghai from Harbin in 1933. In June 1934 he secured an employment with the Isako Circus and left for the south (India, Malaya, etc.) with the circus. He worked in the company until June 1939 when he returned to Shanghai. On June 15, 1939 he joined the Auxiliary Detachment, French Police in which he served until August 8, 1939 when he resigned of his own accord.

Full Name in English:	Markizoff Anatoly Alexeyevitch
Full Name in Russian:	Маркизов Анатолий Алексеевич
Birth Year:	1921
Birth Place:	Harbin, Manchuria
Private Address:	Route Lorton, Pass. 66 House 2
Known to:	Mr. P.I. Zaitzeff 232/19 Av. Du Roi Albert
Report Title:	A.A. Markizoff, A.S. Anisimoff and I.I. Korkoonoff, applicants for enlistment in the Russia Regiment, S.V.C.
Report date:	September 26, 1939
Report number:	315

External archival references to this person: SH/70775

Anatoly Alexeyevitch Markizoff, Russian, was born on April 12, 1921 in the Harbin, Manchuria. He arrived in Shanghai from Harbin together with his parents in 1928. In 1934 he entered the Commercial School of the Russia Orthodox Confraternity, graduating from same in 1939. His father, a barber by occupation, is at present employed with the U.S.A. Navy Club in Tsingtao.

Full Name in English:	Anisimoff Alexander Stepanovitch
Full Name in Russian:	Анисимов Александр Степанович
Birth Year:	1897
Birth Place:	Kazan, Russia
Private Address:	Broadway, 642/21
Known to:	Mr. B.S. Maklaevsky s/insp S.M.P. Bubbling Well.St

Report Title:	A.A, Markizoff, A.S. Anisimoff and I.I. Korkoonoff, applicants for enlistment in the Russia Regiment, S.V.C.
Report date:	September 26, 1939
Report number:	315

External archival references to this person: SH/10603

Alexander Stepanovitch Anisimoff, Russian, was born on June 2, 1897 in Kazan, Russia. He is reported to have left Russia in 1922 and to have subsequently resided in Hankow for a period and later in Tientsin. In 1925 he arrived in Shanghai from Tientsin. From March 6, 1927 to May 9, 1928 he served with the Russian Regiment, S.V.C. Later he worked as a watchman with the Russian newspaper "Vremia" (now defunct). In September 1930 he was engaged as a bodyguard by Mr. Zia Kuh Ming, 237 Canton Road. He left that place of employment in September 1935 and proceeded to Harbin. He returned to Shanghai in November 1936 and has since been without fixed employment.

Full Name in English:	Korkoonoff Ilia Iliytch
Full Name in Russian:	Коркунов Илья Ильич
Birth Year:	1911
Birth Place:	Transbaikal Province, Russia
Private Address:	Rue Bourgeat, 686
Known to:	Mr. M.A. Ahmatoff, China General Omnibus Co.
Report Title:	A.A. Markizoff, A.S. Anisimoff and I.I. Korkoonoff, applicants for enlistment in the Russia Regiment, S.V.C.
Report date:	September 26, 1939
Report number:	315

External archival references to this person: SH/60894

Ilia Iliytch Korkoonoff, Russian, was born on July 20, 1911 in Transbaikal Province, Russia. He is reported to have left Russia together with his parents in 1922 and to have subsequently resided in Mukden until 1931, after which he proceeded to Tientsin He arrived in Shanghai from Tientsin. In 1933 and in July of the sane year obtained a position as a driver with the China General Omnibus Company. On September 17, 1939 he resigned from the company of his own accord.

Full Name in English:	Ushakoff Victor Alexandrovitch
Full Name in Russian:	Ушаков Виктор Александрович
Birth Year:	1921

Birth Place:	Shanghai
Report Title:	V.A. Ushakoff, applicant for enrolment in No. 3 (Vol) Company, S.V.C.
Report date:	September 28, 1939
Report number:	316

External archival references to this person: SH/130502

Victor Alexandrovitch Ushakoff, Russia, was born on September 29, 1921 in Shanghai. From 1929 to 1932 he attended the French Municipal College and from 1933 to 1935 the Ecole Remi. In May 1935 he left Shanghai for TienTsin together with his mother and returned here in 1936. In December 1936 he obtained employment as apprentice photographer with Vasserman Photo Studio, 861 Avenue Joffre. Leaving that studio in February 1939 has since been working as an assistant photographer with Josepho Photo Studio, 937 Avenue Joffre.

Applicant's mother is cohabiting with one V.L. Dreiling alias V. Yazykoff who forms the subject of criminal record no. F, 2718, the particulars of which are as follows:-

1st. S.S.D. Court	Gambling	$100.00 fine.	12.5.37.
1st. S.S.D. Court	Fraud	4 months imprisonment.	3.9.37.

Full Name in English:	Schekin Victor Vladimirovich
Full Name in Russian:	Щекин Виктор Владимирович
Birth Year:	1920
Birth Place:	Harbin
Private Address:	Avenue du Roi Albert, 345/6
Report Title:	V.V. Shick, applicant to join the American Troop, S.V.C.
Report date:	October 2, 1939
Report number:	317

External archival references to this person: SH/60894 на карточке с фамилией Шик

Victor Vladimirovich Schekin, Russian, born on March 16, 1920 at Harbin. It appears that his mother married one B.M. Shik and that from 1926 to 1931 the family resided in Tientsin, where the applicant attended the Grammar School for four year. Some time towards the end of 1931 they arrived in Shanghai and here since been residing in this city. In 1938 Schekin graduated from the Public & Thomas Hanbury School. From March, 1939 he has been employed in the Public Health Department, S.M.C., as a sanitary overseer.

On 28-1-39 he was formally adopted by his step father and is now known as V.V, Shick.

He is registered with the Russian Emigrants Committee, 118/1 Moulmein Road, and resides at 345/6 Avenue du Roi Albert together with his parents, Mr. and Mrs B.V. Shick, proprietors of the Josepho Photo Studios, 937-939 Avenue Joffre and 61 Nanking Road.

His sister is the wife of Mr. H.D. Rogers, 336 Amherst Avenue.

Full Name in English:	Roboostoff Vadim Alexandrovitch
Full Name in Russian:	Робустов Вадим Александрович
Birth Year:	1917
Birth Place:	Hailar, Manchuria
Report Title:	V.A. Roboostoff, applicant for enrolment in the Signals Company, S.V.C.
Report date:	October 3, 1939.
Report number:	318
External archival references to this person:	SH/101127

Vadim Alexandrovitch Roboostoff, Russian, was born on November 23, 1917 in Hailar, Manchuria. From 1921 to 1936 he resided at Tongehan, near Tientsin where his father is still employed as a veterinary surgeon with the Kailan Mining Administration. From 1930 to 1935 the applicant attended the St. Louis' College in Tientsin.

He first arrived in Shanghai in September 1936 and entered the Henry Lester Institute for Technical Education where he studied until June 1937, after which he proceeded to Tongdhan. In September 1938 he returned to Shanghai and again entered the same Institute, where he is still studying at present, From June 1939 he has also been working as an apprentice engineer with Shanghai Power Company.

His brother, Mr. V. Roboostoff, is employed with the French Municipal Police.

Full Name in English:	Agafonoff Evgeny Vladimirovitch
Full Name in Russian:	Агафонов Евгений Владимирович
Birth Year:	1921
Birth Place:	Vladivostok, Maritime Province, Russia
Report Title:	E.V. Agafonoff, applicant for enrolment in the signals Company, S.V.C.
Report date:	October 3, 1939
Report number:	319
External archival references to this person:	SH/10177

Evgeny Vladimirovitch Agafonoff, Russian, was born on February 7, 1921 in Vladivostok, Maritime Province, Russia. He arrived in Shanghai from Vladivostok together with parents in 1922. From 1931 to 1934 he attended the St. Joan of Arc College, 18 Route Doumer. In 1935 he entered the Lester School and at present is studying in Henry Lester Institute for Technical Education, 505 Seward Road.

His father is employed as an overseer at the Embankment Building and his mother is a care taker in the Foreign Y.M.C.A. grill room.

Full Name in English:	Efremoff Ilia Grigorievitch
Full Name in Russian:	Ефремов Илья Григорьевич
Birth Year:	1902
Birth Place:	Tomsk Province, Siberia
Private Address:	Rue Bourgeat, Pass, 475 House 15
Known to:	Mr. N.A. Alexandroff S/insp. S.M.P.
Report Title:	I.G. Efremoff, O.K. Znamensky, V.N. Chikaloff and A.A. Gladchenko, applicants for enlistment in the Russian Regiment, S.V.C.
Report date:	October 5, 1939
Report number:	320
External archival references to this person: SH/30808	

Ilia Grigorievitch Efremoff, Russia, was born on July 20, 1902 in Tomsk Province, Siberia. He first arrived in Shanghai from Vladivostok in 1923 and resided here until 1925 when left Shanghai for Mukden where he joined Marshal Chang Chung Chang's Army, leaving that service in 1928, he returned to Shanghai. On April 16, 1929 he joined the Russian Regiment, S.V.C. Leaving the regiment of his own accord on August 1, 1929 he soon afterwards obtained a position as a Police watchman with Mr. F.A. Hsi, 153 Darroch Road. In August 1937 his services were dispensed with following which he worked casually until September 1, 1938 when he was engaged as an anti-piracy Guard on the China Import and Export Lumber Company's s.s. "Taangtan". On April 30, 1939 his services were dispensed with and he has since been unemployed.

Full Name in English:	Zhamensky Oleg Konstantinovitch
Full Name in Russian:	Знаменский Олег Константинович
Birth Year:	1920
Birth Place:	Harbin, Manchuria
Private Address:	Baikal Rd, 133, House 3
Known to:	Mr. M.G. Yakovkin, 118/1 Mulmein Rd

Report Title:	I.G. Efremoff, O.K. Znamensky, V.N. Chikaloff and A.A. Gladchenko, applicants for enlistment in the Russian Regiment, S.V.C.
Report date:	October 5, 1939
Report number:	320

External archival references to this person: SH/140657

Oleg Konstantinovitch Zhamensky, Russian, was born on April 16, 1920 in Harbin, Manchuria. He arrived in Shanghai from Japan together with his parents on March 11, 1934. On August 12, 1937 he joined the Auxiliary Detachment, French Police, in which he served until April 9, 1938 when he was dismissed for his wish to resign before the expiration of his contract.

Full Name in English:	Chikaloff Veniamin Nikolaevitch
Full Name in Russian:	Чикалов Вениамин Николаевич
Birth Year:	1908
Birth Place:	Harbin, Manchuria
Private Address:	Route Pere Robert, 67, House 10
Known to:	Mr. G.P. Tkachenko, GSA Rue Pere Robert
Report Title:	I.G. Efremoff, O.K. Znamensky, V.N. Chikaloff and A.A. Gladchenko, applicants for enlistment in the Russian Regiment, S.V.C.
Report date:	October 5, 1939
Report number:	320

External archival references to this person: SH/21533

Veniamin Nikolaevitch Chikaloff, Russian, was born on August 22, 1908 in Harbin, Manchuria. From 1926 to 1928 he served in Marshal Chang Chung Chang's Army in shantung and after the army had been disbanded, again resided in Harbin until February 1930, after which he came to Shanghai. From 1931 to 1934 he was employed with Tkachenko's Restaurant, Avenue Joffre. He left Shanghai for Hankow in 1934 in 1934 and following his return here on August 12, 1937 joined the Auxiliary Detachment, French Police. He was discharged on January 12, 1938 for drunkenness and being late for duty. Upon leaving the Detachment he was employed for a short period with the Arcadia Restaurant, 291 Rue Admiral Courbet, on January 6, 1938 he was charged with gambling but was found not guilty by the 1st. Shanghai Special District Court.

Full Name in English:	Gladchenko Afanasy Anisimovitch
Full Name in Russian:	Гладченко Афанасий Анисимович
Birth Year:	1910

Birth Place:	Harbin, Manchuria
Private Address:	Av. Joffre, 713
Known to:	Mrs A.M. Kabatoff 713 Av. Joffre
Report Title:	I.G. Efremoff, O.K. Znamensky, V.N. Chikaloff and A.A. Gladchenko, applicants for enlistment in the Russian Regiment, S.V.C.
Report date:	October 5, 1939
Report number:	320

External archival references to this person: SH/40399

Afanasy Anisimovitch Gladchenko, Russian, was born on November 11, 1910 in Harbin, Manchuria. He first arrived in Shanghai from Harbin in June, 1932, and in September of the same year joined the Russian Regiment, S.V.C., He left the Regiment of his own accord on April 30, 1935 and proceeded to Harbin. In September, 1938 he joined the troupe of Air Devils and the organizer of which was his uncle, Mr. A.N. Gladchenko-Martini. He performed with this troupe at various towns in Manchoukuo and on February 20, 1939 arrived in Shanghai from Tsingtao. In May 1938 he severed his connections with the troupe and his since been casually working as a painter and carpenter.

Full Name in English:	Peshkoff Viatcheslav Hrisanfovitch
Full Name in Russian:	Пешков Вячеслав Хрисанфович
Birth Year:	1916
Birth Place:	Blagoveschensk, Siberia
Report Title:	V.H. Peshkoff, applicants for enrolment in the Transport Company, S.V.C
Report date:	October 7, 1939
Report number:	321

External archival references to this person: SH/91177

Viatcheslav Hrisanfovitch Peshkoff, Russian, was born on May 15, 1916 in Blagoveschensk, Siberia. He is reported to have left Russia together with his parents in 1925 and to have subsequently resided in Harbin. He arrived in Shanghai from Harbin in October 1936 and during the same month obtained employment as a painter with the Commercial Art Studio. He left that place of employment in March 1937 and soon afterwards secured a position as a ticket inspection with the China General Omnibus Company. In May 1938 he was transferred to the Statistics Office of the same company, where he is at present employed as a draughtsman. He also conduct a small advertising business of his.

Full Name in English:	Pogoodin Evgeny Vasilievich
Full Name in Russian:	Погудин Евгений Васильевич
Birth Year:	1914
Birth Place:	Krasnoyarsk, Siberia
Private Address:	Rue Cardinal Mercieur, 377
Known to:	Mr. B.A. Slossman, 24 The Bund, SK. Paper Induster. Cr.
Report Title:	E.V. Pogoodin, A.F. Medvikus and Golovkin-Postrih applicants for enlistment in the Russian Regiment S.V.C.
Report date:	October 13, 1939
Report number:	322

External archival references to this person: SH/91889 (нет отдельной карточки).

Evgeny Vasilievich Pogoodin, Russian was born on November 24, 1914 at Krasnoyarsk, Siberia. He is reported to have left Russia together with his parents in 1916 and to have subsequently resided in Harbin, Manchuria. On June 23, 1938 he arrived in Shanghai form Harbin and in September of the same year joined the Auxiliary Detachment, French Police. On February 9, 1939 he was dismissed from the Detachment for being absent without leave.

While at in Harbin, the applicant became a Soviet citizen, but prior to his departure to Shanghai he applied for emigrant papers to the Bureau for the Affairs of Russian Emigrants in Manchukuo and 6-6-38 was issued by the latter institution with Provisional Certificate No.304, which he still holds.

His father, Mr. V. Pogoodin, Russian emigrant, is the proprietor of a licensed boarding house at 1166 Broadway East.

Full Name in English:	Medvirus Anatoly Feofanovich
Full Name in Russian:	Медвирус Анатолий Феофанович
Birth Year:	1920
Birth Place:	Irkutsk, Siberia
Private Address:	Av. Joffre, 116 Joffre Terrace
Known to:	Mr. N.N. Kolpinsky Pass 737. House 1, Av Petain
Report Title:	E.V. Pogoodin, A.F. Medvikus and Golovkin-Postrih applicants for enlistment in the Russian Regiment S.V.C.
Report date:	October 13, 1939

Report number: 322
External archival references to this person: SH/71261

Anatoly Feofanovich Medvirus, Russian was born on January 1, 1920 at Irkutsk, Siberia. From 1920 to 1929 he resided in Tientsin together with his parents. He arrived to Shanghai from the latter city in 1929 and in 1930 entered the Commercial School of the Russian Orthodox Confraternity. In 1936 he left that school and later studied in the First Russian School (now A.S. Poushkin Memorial School) graduating from same in 1938. On August 1, 1938 he joined the Auxiliary Detachment, French Police, in which he served until January 12, 1939 when he was dismissed for disobedience of orders.

Full Name in English:	Golovkin-Postrih Yury Konstantinovich
Full Name in Russian:	Головкин Постриг Юрий Константинович
Birth Year:	1920
Birth Place:	Harbin, Manchuria
Private Address:	Route Vallon, 515
Known to:	Mr. G.V. Radetsky-Mikoolich, 1260 Rue Lafayette
Report Title:	E.V. Pogoodin, A.F. Medvikus and Golovkin-Postrih applicants for enlistment in the Russian Regiment S.V.C.
Report date:	October 13, 1939
Report number:	322

External archival references to this person: SH/40731

Yury Konstantinovich Golovkin-Postrih, Russian, was born on June 23, 1920 at Harbin, Manchuria, in 1929 he proceeded to Tientsin where he resided until 1931, after which he came to Shanghai. In 1933 he entered the First Russian School (now A.S. Poushkin Memorial School) graduating from same in 1938. His father is employed as a waiter in the Russian Restaurant "Constantinople", 11011 Avenue Joffre.

Full Name in English:	Baramidze Levan Georgievich
Full Name in Russian:	Барамидзе Леван Георгиевич
Birth Year:	1917
Birth Place:	Harbin
Private Address:	Route Vallon, 505, Room 15
Known to:	Mr. A.E. Shimanovsky 869/1 Rue Bourgeat
Report Title:	L.O. Baramidze, C.I. Shoogin, G.I. Proodnikoff-candidates for enrolment in the Russain Regiment, S.V.C.

Report date: October 17, 1939
Report number: 323
External archival references to this person: SH/11232

Levan Georgievich Baramidze, Russian, was born on October 24, 1917 at Harbin in Shanghai from Harbin on 1-4-38 and in May of the same year secured employment as an assistant chemist in the "Concordia Mineral Water Company", Avenue du Roi Albert (now defunct). During July and August, 1939, he was employed as a ticket inspector with the China General Omnibus Co. His brother is employed with the service department of the X.M.H.A. Radio Broadcasting Station, Race Course Road.

Full Name in English: Shoolgin Constantin Ivanovitch
Full Name in Russian: Шульгин Константин Иванович
Birth Year: 1916
Birth Place: Irkutsk, Siberia
Private Address: House 5 Route Des Soeurs, 241
Known to: Mr. V.I. Yakovleff, 275 Route Tenant De Tour
Report Title: L.O. Baramidze, C.I. Shoolgin, G.I. Proodnikoff-candidates for enrolment in the Russian Regiment, S.V.C.
Report date: October 17, 1939
Report number: 323
External archival references to this person: SH/111334

Constantin Ivanovitch Shoolgin, Russian was born on May 21, 1916 at Irkutsk, Siberia. According to his own statement, he left Russia together with his parents in 1921 and subsequently resided at Jalainor Chinese Eastern Railway, where his father was employed as a supervisor. The applicants arrived in Shanghai in July 1932 and soon afterwards obtained employment as an assistant mechanic in the "Shelco", 958 Avenue Foch Leaving that place of employment of his own accord some time towards the end of 1938, he was engaged in January 1939 by the Press Wireless, 103 Kiukiang Road as a mechanic. His services with this company were dispensed with on 9-3-39 owing to a reduction in staff.

Full Name in English: Proodnikoff Georgy Ivanovich
Full Name in Russian: Прудников Георгий Иванович
Birth Year: 1921
Birth Place: Harbin
Private Address: Rue Du Roi Albert, 222
Known to: Mr. J. Grabovsky, Reserve Unit, S.M.P

Report Title:	L.O. Baramidze, C.I. Shoolgin, G.I. Prood-nikoff-candidates for enrolment in the Russian Regiment, S.V.C.
Report date:	October 17, 1939
Report number:	323

External archival references to this person: SH/100471

Georgy Ivanovich Proodnikoff, Russian was born on August 1, 1921 at Harbin. He arrived in Shanghai from Harbin on September 25, 1939. One of his cousins, named Grabovsky, is at present serving in the Russian Regiment, S.V.C., and another, J. Grabovsky, is a member of the Reserve Unit, S.M.Police

Full Name in English:	Fokin Leonid Vassilievich
Full Name in Russian:	Фокин Леонид Васильевич
Birth Year:	1916
Birth Place:	Cheremhovo, Irkutsk Province, Siberia
Private Address:	Av. Roi Albert, 350
Known to:	Rev. Mother Ariadna 350 Av. du Roi Albert
Report Title:	L.V. Fokin and A.M. Arshakuni, candidate for enrolment in the Russian Regiment, S.V.C.
Report date:	October 18, 1939
Report number:	324

External archival references to this person: SH/31713

Leonid Vassilievich Fokin, Russian, was born on July 2, 1916 at Cheremhovo, Irkutsk Province, Siberia. He is reported to have left Russia for China in 1929 and to have resided in Harbin together with his parents until May, 1935 when he left for Shanghai. On June of the same year he joined the Russian Volunteer Company attached to the French Police, in which he served until June 18, 1936 when he resigned of his own accord. On November 16, 1936 he joined the Russian Regiment, S.V.C. from which he resigned on December 15, 1938. From 24-12-38 to 7-9-39 he was employed as a Anti-Piracy Guard with Jardine Matheson Co., Ltd. He resigned from this service of his own wish.

Full Name in English:	Arshakuni Andronik Mikitovich
Full Name in Russian:	Аршакуни Андроник Микитович
Birth Year:	1920
Birth Place:	Blagoveschensk, Amur Province, Siberia
Private Address:	Tongshan Rd, 725/17
Known to:	Mr. N.G. Gladkoff, Mills Dept. Jardine Matheson Co.

Report Title:	L.V. Fokin and A.M. Arshakuni, candidate for enrolment in the Russian Regiment, S.V.C.
Report date:	October 18, 1939
Report number:	324

External archival references to this person: SH/10818 (Мкрытович)

Andronik Mikitovich Arshakuni, Russian of Armenian origin, born on September 28, 1920 at Blagoveschensk, Amur Province, Siberia. He is reported to have left Russia together resided in Changehun and from 1924 – in Harbin. He first arrived in Shanghai in 1933 and until March 1938 attended the St. Francis Xavier's College, after which he proceeded to Tsingtao. On 28-9-39 he returned to Shanghai.

Full Name in English:	Prosvirnin Igor Ivanovich
Full Name in Russian:	Просвирнин Игорь Иванович
Birth Year:	1921
Birth Place:	Harbin
Private Address:	Cathay Flats, 836
Known to:	Mr. P.S. Romanoff, Av. Petain, 737/1
Report Title:	I.I. Prosvirnin, candidate for enrolment in the Russian Regiment, S.V.C.
Report date:	October 19, 1939.
Report number:	325

Igor Ivanovich Prosvirnin (or Prosvirnin-Platonoff), Russian, born on November 7, 1921 at Harbin. He is reported to have arrived in Shanghai from Harbin in 1932 together with his parents. From 1933 to 1937 he attended the Commercial School of the Russian Orthodox Confraternity, following which he worked as an apprentice in Jeny's Motors, 177 Rue Amiral Courbet, for two months (in 1938) and later in the victor's Vulcanizing Co., 396 Rue Bourgeat, for own accord in June, 1938. In September, 1939 he applied for enrolment in the Russian Auxiliary Detachment, French Police. His application was turned down as he is under the minimum age required by regulations of the detachment (18 years).

The applicant's brother, U.I. Prosvirnin-Platonoff is serving in the Auxiliary Detachment, French Police.

Their father, I.N. Prosvirnin-Platonoff, former employee of the Chinese Eastern Railway, has for the past six years been employed with the "Shanghai Zaria" and resides at 166 Route Vallon. It appears that he was divorced from his wife in 1935 who at present is either married to or cohabiting with a certain American named McCorfney and resides at 836-c Cathay Flats, Avenue Joffre.

Full Name in English:	Lutoff George
Full Name in Russian:	Лютов Георгий
Birth Year:	1921
Birth Place:	Nickolsk-Ussurisk
Private Address:	Embankment Building, North Soochow Road, 328
Report Title:	George Lutoff, applicant for enrolment in the American Machine Gun Company, S.V.C.
Report date:	October 25, 1939.
Report number:	326

External archival references to this person: SH/81154

George Lutoff, Russian, was born on January 28th, 1921 in Nickolsk-Ussurisk, Siberia.

He was brought by his parents to Harbin in 1922 and had lived there until 1929 when his mother took him with her to Shanghai.

Upon his arrival in Shanghai he first entered the French Municipal School and then Public and Thomas Hanbury School at which school he is still studying.

He resides with his mother at Apartment 328, Embankment Building, North Soochow Road. He is registered with the Russian Emigrants' Committee at 118/1 Moulmein Road.

Full Name in English:	Gromoff Fedor Ermolaevitch
Full Name in Russian:	Громов Федор Ермолаевич
Birth Year:	1918
Birth Place:	Chita, Siberia
Private Address:	Av. Roi Albert, 561
Known to:	Mr. E.K. Makaroff, 303 Ave Mercier
Report Title:	F.E. Gromoff, V.E. Kopitoff, V.A. Farafontoff, G.I. Siminiutin and G.A. Tzvetkoff, applicants for enlistment in the Russian Regiment, S.V.C.
Report date:	October 27, 1939.
Report number:	327

External archival references to this person: SH/41413

Fedor Ermolaevitch Gromoff, Russian, was born on January 20, 1918 at Chita, Siberia. He is reported to have left Russian together with his parents in 1918 and to have subsequently resided in Manchouli for a period and later in Harbin. In June 1939 he left Harbin for Tientsin and on latter city in the S.S. "Hoten Maru". Here he resided together with his sister at 561, avenue du Roi Albert.

Full Name in English:	Kopitoff Vladimir Fedorovitch
Full Name in Russian:	Копытов Владимир Федорович
Birth Year:	1917
Birth Place:	Vladivostok, Maritime Province, Russia
Private Address:	Gordon Rd, 645
Known to:	Mr. G. Muhametzianoff, 645 Gordon Rd.
Report Title:	F.E. Gromoff, V.E. Kopitoff, V.A. Farafontoff, G.I. Siminiutin and G.A. Tzvetkoff, applicants for enlistment in the Russian Regiment, S.V.C.
Report date:	October 27, 1939.
Report number:	327

External archival references to this person: SH/60832

Vladimir Fedorovitch Kopitoff, Russian, was born on September 5, 1917 in Vladivostok, Maritime Province, Russia. He arrived in Shanghai from Manchuria in 1925 together with his parents. From 1930 to 1933 he attended the Commercial School of the Russian Orthodox Confraternity. In February, 1933 he secured a position as a kennel man with his Canidrome. He left that place of employment in July, 1938 and on August 30, 1938 proceeded to Hongkong in the S.S. "Aramis", where, according to his own statement, he secured a position with the Hongkong Dairy Farm. In November of the same year his services were dispensed with owing to a reduction in staff and he returned to Shanghai on December 8, 1938. From January 1939 to June 1939 he worked as an apprentice barber with the Chernoff's Beauty Parlour, Route Say Zoong.

His step father, Mr. Mouhamedzianoff, is employed as a supervisor with Keylock & Pratt, 645 Gordon Road.

Full Name in English:	Farafontoff Valentin Alexandrovitch
Full Name in Russian:	Фарафонтов Валентин Александрович
Birth Year:	1915
Birth Place:	Bouhedu station, Chinese Eastern Railway
Private Address:	Route Lorton, 137
Known to:	Mr. P.I. Kozoolin, 43 Park Apts
Report Title:	F.E. Gromoff, V.E. Kopitoff, V.A. Farafontoff, G.I. Siminiutin and G.A. Tzvetkoff, applicants for enlistment in the Russian Regiment, S.V.C.
Report date:	October 27, 1939.
Report number:	327

External archival references to this person: SH/31234

Valentin Alexandrovitch Farafontoff, Russian, was born on May 5, 1915 at Bouhedu station, Chinese Eastern Railway. He arrived in Shanghai in May 1932 and during the same month joined the Russian regiment, S.V.C. He left the regiment of his own accord on May 1, 1938 in order to take up a position with the Bill's Motors, Fed. Inc. U.S.A. in their Tyre Re-treading Department. He left that place of employment of his own accord on October 1, 1939. Applicant's uncle, Mr. N.P. Farafontoff, owns a small grocery store at 1568 Avenue Joffre.

Full Name in English:	Siminiutin Georgy Ivanovitch
Full Name in Russian:	Симинютин Георгий Иванович
Birth Year:	1921
Birth Place:	Harbin, Manchuria
Private Address:	Av. Joffre, 1200/6
Report Title:	F.E. Gromoff, V.E. Kopitoff, V.A. Farafontoff, G.I. Siminiutin and G.A. Tzvetkoff, applicants for enlistment in the Russian Regiment, S.V.C.
Report date:	October 27, 1939.
Report number:	327

Siminiutin Georgy Ivanovitch, Russian, was born on December 17, 1921 in Harbin, Manchuria.

He arrived from Harbin on June 25, 1939 and resided together with his step father, Mr. I.N. Morozoff at 1200/51 Avenue Joffre.

Full Name in English:	Tsvetkoff Georgy Alexandrovitch
Full Name in Russian:	Цветков Георгий Александрович
Birth Year:	1916
Birth Place:	Samara, Russia
Private Address:	Rue Lafayette, 1252/6
Known to:	Mr G.A. Pogibin, 265/30 Av. Haig
Report Title:	F.E. Gromoff, V.E. Kopitoff, V.A. Farafontoff, G.I. Siminiutin and G.A. Tzvetkoff, applicants for enlistment in the Russian Regiment, S.V.C.
Report date:	October 27, 1939.
Report number:	327
External archival references to this person:	SH/130220

Georgy Alexandrovitch Tsvetkoff, Russian, was born on July 24, 1916 in Samara, Russia. He arrived in Shanghai from Harbin on September 24, 1939.

It is believed that this applicant has already resigned from the Russian Regiment, S.V.C.

Full Name in English:	Mihaleff Georgy Nikolaevitch
Full Name in Russian:	Михалев Георгий Николаевич
Birth Year:	1921
Birth Place:	Manchouli Station, Chinese Eastern Railway.
Private Address:	Route Vallon, 132
Report Title:	G.N. Mihaleff and P.M. Okoojnoff, applicants for enlistment in the Russian Regiment, S.V.C.
Report date:	November 1, 1939
Report number:	328

External archival references to this person: SH/71630

Georgy Nikolaevitch Mihaleff, Russian, was born on April 14, 1921 at Manchouli Station, Chinese Eastern Railway. He resided for a period at Hailar and later at Harbin, where his father Dr. N. Mihaleff, practiced medicine. In June 1938 he left Harbin for Tsingtao and after about one year's residence in that city proceeded to Shanghai, arriving here on October 17, 1939 in the S.S. "Hoten Maru".

Full Name in English:	Okroojnoff Pavel Mihailovitch
Full Name in Russian:	Окружнов Павел Михайлович
Birth Year:	1903
Birth Place:	St. Petersburg
Private Address:	Rue Lorton, 66 /48
Known to:	Mr. I.S. Chijoff 13 Av.Haig
Report Title:	G.N. Mihaleff and P.M. Okoojnoff, applicants for enlistment in the Russian Regiment, S.V.C.
Report date:	November 1, 1939
Report number:	328

External archival references to this person: SH/90124

Pavel Mihailovitch Okroojnoff, Russian, was born on December 22, 1903 at St. Petersburg. According to his own statement, he left Russia in 1917 and subsequently resided in Harbin until 1925, after which he proceeded to Japan. He arrived in Shanghai from Japan on October 15, 1939 and is not known in the local Russian community.

Full Name in English:	Shirokoff Vladimir Victorovitch
Full Name in Russian:	Широков Владимир Викторович
Birth Year:	1915

Birth Place:	Irkutsk, Siberia
Private Address:	Rue Chu Pao San, 7
Report Title:	V.V. Shirokoff, applicant for enrolment in the American Machine-Gun Company. S.V.C.
Report date:	November 6, 1939.
Report number:	330

External archival references to this person: SH/111095

Vladmir Victorovitch Shirokoff, Russian, was born on June 23, 1915 at Irkutsk, Siberia. According to his own statement, he left Russian together with his family in 1919 and for the following two years resided at Harbin. Later the family moved to Hankow, in 1925 the applicant came to Shanghai and until 1931 attended the St. Francis Xavier's College. During the same year his family consisting of mother and three sisters came to Shanghai from Hankow. For the following five years he resided together with them without fixed employment, being provided by his two elder sisters, who at that time were married to Mr. G.A. Warring, British, and Mr. L.A. Blackburn, Britian, respectively. In 1936, the applicant made a trip to Tientsin and in 1937 to Hankow, returning to Shanghai from the latter city in January, 1938. Still being supported by his sisters he did not bother himself with securing any employment except casual work until May, 1939, when he was engaged by the Globe Wireless Company, Ltd., 51, Canton Road. In July of the same year his services were dispensed with owing to his inefficiency and laziness.

At present he is still unemployed and resides together with his sisters, who conduct the "International Kitchen Bar", 7, Rue Chu Pao San.

He is in possession of passport No. 288, issued on September 11, 1937, by the Hankow Police.

He is not registered with the Russian Emigrants' Committee or any other Russian Public Organization.

Full Name in English:	Choopikoff Mihail Alexeyevitch
Full Name in Russian:	Чуйков Михаил Алексеевич
Birth Year:	1908
Birth Place:	Harbin, Manchuria
Private Address:	Av. du Roi Albert, 359/2
Known to:	Mr. N.A. Yakovleff, 359/2 Av. du. Roi Albert
Report Title:	M.A. Chooikoff, B.I. Chernih and E.I. Griboff, applicants for enlistment in the Russian Regiment, S.V.C.
Report date:	November 13, 1939

Report number: 332
External archival references to this person: SH/21656

Mihail Alexeyevitch Choopikoff, Russian, was born on April 23, 1908 at Harbin, Manchuria. He arrived in Shanghai from Harbin in February 1934. Being a barber by occupation he worked in his professional capacity at various barber shops locally. In February 1938 he left Shanghai for Tsingtao, where according to his own statement he also worked in the same capacity. On October 6, 1939 he returned to Shanghai.

Full Name in English:	Chernih Boris Ivanovitch
Full Name in Russian:	Черных Борис Иванович
Birth Year:	1921
Birth Place:	Maritime Province, Russia
Private Address:	Bubbling Well Rd, 86, Majestic Appt 317
Known to:	Mr. S.G. Nadeef, Sgt of S.M.P
Report Title:	M.A. Chooikoff, B.I. Chernih and E.I. Griboff, applicants for enlistment in the Russian Regiment, S.V.C.
Report date:	November 13, 1939
Report number:	332

External archival references to this person: SH/21308

Boris Ivanovitch Chernih, Russian, was born on April 4, 1921 in Maritime Province, Russia. According to his own statement, he escaped from the U.S.S.R in 1928 together with his sister and subsequently resided at Mukden. In 1931 he left Mukden for Tientsin where he entered the St. Louis College, graduating from same in 1938. He arrived in Shanghai on November 1, 1939 in the S.S. "Dairen Maru" and resided together with F.S. Nadeyeff of the Shanghai Municipal Police.

Full Name in English:	Griboff Evgeny Ivanovitch
Full Name in Russian:	Грибов Евгений Иванович
Birth Year:	1920
Birth Place:	Nikolsk-Ussuriisk, Siberia
Private Address:	Route Des Soeurs, 118/15, FE.2,.
Known to:	Mr. F.L. Denisoff, 225 Rungfine Rd.
Report Title:	M.A. Chooikoff, B.I. Chernih and E.I. Griboff, applicants for enlistment in the Russian Regiment, S.V.C.
Report date:	November 13, 1939

Report number: 332
External archival references to this person: SH/41270

Evgeny Ivanovitch Griboff, Russian, was born on November 20, 1920 at Nikolsk-Ussuriisk, Siberia. He is reported to have left Russia together with his parents in 1921 and to have subsequently resided at Harbin, Manchuria. He arrived in Shanghai from Harbin on October 29, 1939. Being a new arrival here he is little known in the local Russian Community.

Full Name in English:	Zapolsky (Ogneff) Iosif Alexeyevitch,
Full Name in Russian:	Запольский (Огнев) Иосиф Алексеевич
Birth Year:	1921
Birth Place:	Vladivostok, Maritime Province, Russia
Private Address:	Rue Bourgeat, 770
Report Title:	I.A. Zapolsky, M.V. Zaboeff and P.I. Cheshkin, applicants for enlistment in the Russian Regiment, S.V.C.
Report date:	November 4, 1939
Report number:	329

External archival references to this person: SH/140327

Iosif Alexeyevitch Zapolsky (Ogneff), Russian, was born on September 9, 1921 at Vladivostok, Maritime Province, Russia. He is reported to have left Russia together with his parents in 1922 and to have subsequently resided in Mukden.

His father, Mr. Ogneff, died in 1925 in Mukden, and in 1926 his mother married one Mr. A. Zapolsky who, it is said, officially adopted the applicant.

From 1935 the applicant resided at the St. Tichon's Orphanage and from 1936 to 1939 attended the First Russian High School (now A.S. Poushkin Memorial School).

Full Name in English:	Zaboeff Mihail Victorovitch
Full Name in Russian:	Забоев Михаил Викторович
Birth Year:	1904
Birth Place:	Irkutsk, Siberia
Private Address:	Rue Mollier, 48
Report Title:	I.A. Zapolsky, M.V. Zaboeff and P.I. Cheshkin, applicants for enlistment in the Russian Regiment, S.V.C.
Report date:	November 4, 1939.
Report number:	329

SMP D.917 file

External archival references to this person: SH/140072

Mihail Victorovitch Zaboeff, Russian, was born on November 8, 1904 at Irkutsk, Siberia. According to his own statement, he escaped from U.S.S.R. to Manchuria in 1927 and subsequently resided at Harbin, where from 1929 to 1939 he was employed as a billiard marker with the Hotel Modern Billiard Saloon. He arrived in Shanghai in June 1939 and until present was unemployed.

Full Name in English:	Cheshkin Pavel Ivanovitch
Full Name in Russian:	Чешкин Павел Иванович
Birth Year:	1908
Birth Place:	Maritime Province, Russia
Private Address:	Great Western Rd, 61
Known to:	Mr. G.C. Bologoff, 27 The Bund.
Report Title:	I.A. Zapolsky, M.V. Zaboeff and P.I. Cheshkin, applicants for enlistment in the Russian Regiment, S.V.C.
Report date:	November 4, 1939.
Report number:	332

External archival references to this person: SH/21351

Pavel Ivanovitch Cheshkin, Russian, was born on May 31, 1908 in Maritime Province, Russia. He left Russia in 1920 and resided at the Yaomin Station, Chinese Eastern Railway for a period and later in Harbin. He arrived in Shanghai from Harbin in October, 1930. On May 28, 1931, he joined the Russian Regiment S.V.C. where prior to his resignation on December 1, 1937 he held the rank of Sergeant. Upon leaving the Regiment he worked casually as a driver until January, 1939 when he joined the Labour Company of the Royal Army Service Corps. He left that place of employment in October 1939 in order to rejoin the Russian Regiment, S.V.C.

Full Name in English:	Boobeloff Alexander Maximovitch
Full Name in Russian:	Бубелов Александр Максимович
Birth Year:	1917
Birth Place:	Harbin, Manchuria
Private Address:	Route Vallon, 133
Known to:	Mrs. H.S. Babooshkin, 133 Route Vallon
Report Title:	A.M. Boobeloff, F.E. Bolotnenko, V.G. Chernisheff and H.M. Outusheff, applicants for enlistment in the Russian Regiment, S.V.C.
Report date:	November, 9, 1939.
Report number:	331

Alexander Maximovitch Boobeloff, Russian, was born on December 12, 1917, at Harbin, Manchuria. He first arrived in Shanghai in December, 1938, and resided together with his aunt, Mrs. H.S. Babooshkin, 133 Route Vallon. In February 1939 he proceeded to Harbin and, in March of the same year returned to Shanghai. In May 1939 he joined the Russian Auxiliary Detachment of the French Police, but after about one week's service received a telegram from Harbin informing him of his father's illness, following which he resigned and proceeded to Harbin. His father, who was chief of The Harbin Fire Bridge, died on September 4, 1939. On October 29, 1939 the applicant returned to Shanghai in the S.S. "Tsingtao Maru".

Full Name in English:	Bolotnenko Feodor Eremeyevitch
Full Name in Russian:	Болотненко Федор Еремеевич
Birth Year:	1918
Birth Place:	Maritime Province, Russia
Private Address:	Av. Joffre, 682/10
Known to:	Mr. V.V. Roodenko, 682/10, av. Joffre
Report Title:	A.M. Boobeloff, F.E. Bolotnenko, V.G. Chernisheff and H.M. Cutusheff, applicants for enlistment in the Russian Regiment, S.V.C.
Report date:	November, 9, 1939.
Report number:	331

Feodor Eremeyevitch Bolotnenko, Russian, was born on September 16, 1918, in Maritime Province, Russia. According to his own statement, he escaped from the U.S.S.R. to Manchuria in 1932 and subsequently resided in Harbin. He arrived in Shanghai from Harbin in October 26, 1939 in the S.S. "Hoten Maru" and is not known locally.

Full Name in English:	Chernysheff Vassily Georgievitch
Full Name in Russian:	Чернышов Василий Георгиевич
Birth Year:	1921
Birth Place:	Tokyo, Japan
Private Address:	Hsian Rd., 202
Known to:	Mr. P. Yankovsky
Report Title:	A.M. Boobeloff, F.E. Bolotnenko, V.G. Chernisheff and H.M. Cutusheff, applicants for enlistment in the Russian Regiment, S.V.C.
Report date:	November, 9, 1939.

Report number: 331
External archival references to this person: SH/21319

Vassily Georgievitch Chernysheff, Russian, was born on January 1, 1921 at Tokyo, Japan. He arrived in Shanghai from Korea together with his mother in 1931 and resided here until 1933, after which he proceeded to Peking. In 1935 he returned to Shanghai and resided together with his mother who was employed as a cook with Mr. P. Yankovsky of the French Municipal Police.

Full Name in English:	Outusheff Hamsia Mohametjanovitch
Full Name in Russian:	Утишев Хамсия Мухаметжанович
Birth Year:	1920
Birth Place:	Hailar, Manchuria.
Private Address:	Rue Lafayette,1248, House 6,
Known to:	Mr. S. Duseeff, 1248 house 6, Rue Lafayette
Report Title:	A.M. Boobeloff, F.E. Bolotnenko, V.G. Chernisheff and H.M. Outusheff, applicants for enlistment in the Russian Regiment, S.V.C.
Report date:	November, 9, 1939.
Report number:	331

External archival references to this person: SH/21351

Hamsia Mohametjanovitch Outusheff, Russian of Tartar origin, was born on February 1, 1920 at Hailar, Manchuria. In 1934 he left Hailer for Tientsin. On October 26, 1939 he arrived in Shanghai from Tientsin and resided with Mr. S. Duzeyeff, 1248/6 Rue Lafayette.

Full Name in English:	Ivanoff Boris Nikolaevitch
Full Name in Russian:	Иванов Борис Николаевич
Birth Year:	1913
Birth Place:	Samara Province, Russia
Private Address:	Av. Dubail, 169/34
Known to:	Mr. P.I. Malinovsky, 169/3y av. Bubhil
Report Title:	B.N. Ivanoff and G.D. Ivanzoff, applicants for enlistment in the Russian Regiment, S.V.C.
Report date:	November 17, 1939.
Report number:	333

External archival references to this person: SH/50448

Boris Nikolaevitch Ivanoff, Russian, was born on July 19, 1913 in Samara Province, Russia. He is reported to have left Russia together with his parents in 1919 and to have subsequently resided at Manchouli Station, Chinese Eastern Railway until 1929 and later at Harbin. In May 1939 he left Harbin for Dairen and on November 12, 1939 arrived in Shanghai from the later city.

Full Name in English:	Ivanzoff Georgy Dmitrievitch
Full Name in Russian:	Иванцов Георгий Дмитриевич
Birth Year:	1921
Birth Place:	Harbin, Manchuria
Private Address:	Route Vallon, 162-C
Known to:	Mr. G.V. Vasilieff 1432, Sinza rd (Bakerite co).
Report Title:	B.N. Ivanoff and G.D. Ivanzoff, applicants for enlistment in the Russian Regiment, S.V.C.
Report date:	November 17, 1939.
Report number:	333

External archival references to this person: SH/50587

Georgy Dmitrievitch Ivanzoff, Russian, was born on August 30, 1921 at Harbin, Manchuria. He arrived in Shanghai from Harbin on November 9, 1939 and resided at 162 C. Route Vallon, together with his brother A.D. Ivanoff, an employee of Bakerite Company.

Full Name in English:	Pioulsky Lev Vladislavovitch
Full Name in Russian:	Пиульский Лев Владиславович
Birth Year:	1905
Birth Place:	Mogilev, Russia
Private Address:	Route Vallon, 162/B
Known to:	Mr. E.G. Ivanoff, French Munic Police
Report Title:	L.V. Pioulsky and V.A. Velgous, applicants for enlistment in the Russian Regiment, S.V.C.
Report date:	November 17, 1939.
Report number:	334

External archival references to this person: SH/91601

Lev Vladislavovitch Pioulsky, Russian, was born on October 25, 1905 at Mogilev, Russia. According to his own statement, he left Russia in 1923 and subsequently resided in Harbin. In 1925 he joined Marshal Chang Chung Chang's Army in which he served until 1927 when the army was disbanded. In 1927 he arrived in Shanghai from Tsingtao and in March of the same year joined the Russian Regiment, S.V.C. On March 31, 1929 he left the Regiment of his own accord and later worked casually until March 1930 when he was engaged as a chauffeur by Mr. B. Julien, proprietor of the pharmacie Generale, 949 - 951 Avenue Joffre. In November 1938 his services were dispensed with owing to Mr. Julien's departure for France. In May 1939 the applicant secured a position as an Anti-Piracy Guard with Jardine, Matheson & Company, Ltd., but was dismissed on November 3, 1939 for neglect of duty.

Full Name in English:	Velgous Victor Andreevitch
Full Name in Russian:	Вельгус Виктор Андреевич
Birth Year:	1921
Birth Place:	Moscow
Private Address:	Av. Joffre, 697/1
Known to:	Mr. G.V. Radetsky Mikoolich 1260 Rue Lafayette
Report Title:	L.V. Pioulsky and V.A. Velgous, applicants for enlistment in the Russian Regiment, S.V.C.
Report date:	November 17, 1939
Report number:	334
External archival references to this person:	SH/130999

Victor Andreevitch Velgous, Russian, was born on September 5, 1921 at Moscow. He is reported to have escaped from the U.S.S.R. to Manchuria in 1928 together with his mother and step-father, who is of the Chinese nationality. The family proceeded to Chefoo where the applicant resided until 1934 after which he came to Shanghai. From 1934 to 1938 he studied in the First Russian School (now A.S. Poushkin Memorial School) and later attended the Pirogoff Memorial School, 249 Avenue Haig. His mother and step-father, who are reported to be unemployed at present, are residing at 697/1 Avenue Joffre.

Full Name in English:	Antropoff Vladimir Andreyevitch
Full Name in Russian:	Антропов Владимир Андреевич
Birth Year:	1919
Birth Place:	Moscow
Report Title:	V.A. Antropoff, applicant for enrolment in the Signals Company, S.V.C.
Report date:	November 18, 1939
Report number:	335
External archival references to this person:	SH/10690

Vladimir Andreyevitch Antropoff, Russian, was born on April 23, 1919 at Moscow. He is reported to have left Russia together with his parents in 1922 and to have subsequently resided in Harbin. In 1926 he left Harbin for Tientsin where his father, a musician by occupation, was employed in his professional capacity. In 1930 the family proceeded to Java. In the beginning of 1931 they arrived In Shanghai. In

1933 the applicant entered the St. Francis Xavier's College graduating from same in 1936. During 1937 he studied in the Shanghai Business College, Arnhold Building, Szechuen Road. From November 1938 to April 1939 he attended the Radio Technical Centre, Avenue Haig, after which he secured his present employment as an office assistant with J.A. Thompson, Real Estate Agents, 57 Broadway.

His father is at present employed as a musician in the French Police Brass and also at the Weida Hotel, 993 Avenue Joffre.

Full Name in English:	Batalin Evgeny Vladimirovitch
Full Name in Russian:	Баталин Евгений Владимирович
Birth Year:	1921
Birth Place:	Maritime province, Russia.
Private Address:	Avenue Joffre, 913
Report Title:	K. Batalin, applicant for enrolment in the American Machine Gun Company, S.V.C.
Report date:	November 21, 1939
Report number:	336
External archival references to this person:	SH/11430

Evgeny Vladimirovitch Batalin, Russian, was born on December 13, 1921 in Maritime province, Russia. According to his own statement, he left Russia together with his mother in 1922 and subsequently resided at Enda Station, Chinese Eastern Railway. In 1932 he arrived in Shanghai from Harbin. From 1933 to 1936 he attended the ecole Remi after which he entered the St. Francis Xavier's College, where he is still studying.

Applicant's mother, Mrs. Batalin, is a mid-wife by occupation and resides together with him at 913 Avenue Joffre.

Full Name in English:	Gavriloff Serafim Gavrilovitch
Full Name in Russian:	Гаврилов Серафим Гаврилович
Birth Year:	1909
Birth Place:	Viatka province, Russia
Report Title:	S.G. Gavriloff, applicant for enrolment in No 3(vol.) Company, S.V.C.
Report date:	November 21, 1939
Report number:	336

Serafim Gavrilovitch Gavriloff, Russian, was born on November 25, 1909 in Viatka province, Russia. According to his own statement, he left Russia in 1920 and subsequently resided in Harbin, Manchuria. Upon graduating from a local high school he entered the Harbin polytechnic Institute, graduating from same in June 1939. He arrived in Shanghai from Harbin on September 11, 1939 travelling on passport No. 1839 issued on 20-7-39 by the Harbin Police. Since his arrival here he been working as an engraver with Lisick Co. (Jewellers), 241/4 Route des Soeurs.

The applicant is not registered with the Russian Emigrants' Committee or any Russian public organization.

Full Name in English:	Gecker Mark Grigorievitch
Full Name in Russian:	Геккер Марк Григорьевич
Birth Year:	1917
Birth Place:	Melitople, South Russia
Report Title:	M. Gecker, applicant for enrolment in the Transport Company, S.V.C.
Report date:	November 24, 1939
Report number:	337
External archival references to this person:	SH/40109 (на карточке Гиршевич)

Mark Grigorievitch Gecker, Russian Jew, was born on January 17, 1917 at Melitople, South Russia. He is reported to have left Russia with his parents in 1919 and to have subsequently resided at Harbin. He arrived in Shanghai in 1924 and soon afterwards entered the Shanghai Jewish School, graduating from same in 1936. In March 1938, he left Shanghai for Yokohama, Japan, where he secured employment with Captain Victory, Import & Exports. In December of the year, he left that place of employment of his own accord and subsequently returned to Shanghai. From January 1939 till May of the same year, he was employed with the press Wireless Inc. 103, Kiukiang Road. In September 1939 he secured his present position with the China General Omnibus Co.

Full Name in English:	Meshkoff Ury Alexandrovitch
Full Name in Russian:	Мешков Юрий Александрович
Birth Year:	1899
Birth Place:	Ekaterinoslav Province, Russia
Private Address:	Chaoufoong Rd., 241
Known to:	P.A. Vedeniapin, 163/44 Route De Grouchy
Report Title:	U.A. Meshkoff, D.D. Kireevsky, V.D. Minaeff, G.N. Pavlovsky, P.V. Poluhoff and A.Z. Mosol, applicants for enlistment in the Russian Regiment, S.V.C.
Report date:	December 4, 1939

Report number: 338
External archival references to this person: SH/ 70885 (Гурий)

Ury Alexandrovitch Meshkoff, Russian, was born on September 21, 1899 in Ekaterinoslav Province, Russia. According to his own statement he left Russia for China in 1920 and subsequently resided in Tientsin. In Tientsin he was engaged in the fur business and later worked as a pianist at various hotels and cabarets in that city. After the applicant was an active member of the Anti-Communist Committee, for some time being a commander of the Officers Company of Russian Volunteers.

In May 1939 he was arrested for some unknown reason, and after being kept prisoner at the so- called "White House" for about 30 days, was subsequently deported to Shanghai, arriving at this port in the beginning of June, 1939. Here he again worked in his professional capacity as a pianist until September, since which he has been unemployed.

Full Name in English:	Kireevsky Dmitry Dmitrievitch
Full Name in Russian:	Киреевский Дмитрий Дмитриевич
Birth Year:	1919
Birth Place:	Blagoveschensk Maritime Province, Russia
Private Address:	Rue Bourgeat, 332/11
Known to:	Rev. Father P. Triodin, 236 Av. du Roi Albert.
Report Title:	U.A. Meshkoff, D.D. Kireevsky, V.D. Minaeff, G.N. Pavlovsky, P.V. Poluhoff and A.Z. Mosol, applicants for enlistment in the Russian Regiment, S.V.C.
Report date:	December 4, 1939
Report number:	338

Dmitry Dmitrievitch Kireevsky, Russian, was born on October 21, 1919 at Blagoveschensk Maritime Province, Russia. He left Russia together with his parents in 1920 and subsequently resided in Harbin, Manchuria. He arrived in Shanghai from Harbin on November 17, 1939 and is not known locally.

Full Name in English:	Minaeff Valentin Dmitrievitch
Full Name in Russian:	Минаев Валентин Дмитриевич
Birth Year:	1921
Birth Place:	Blagoveschensk, Maritime Province, Russia.
Private Address:	Av. Joffre, 1251A
Known to:	Mr. V.N. Sodvorin, 184-185 Av. Dubail

Report Title:	U.A. Meshkoff, D.D. Kireevsky, V.D. Minaeff, G.N. Pavlovsky, P.V. Poluhoff and A.Z. Mosol, applicants for enlistment in the Russian Regiment, S.V.C.
Report date:	December 4, 1939
Report number:	338

External archival references to this person: SH/71761

Valentin Dmitrievitch Minaeff, Russian, was born on December 31, 1921 at Blagoveschensk, Maritime Province, Russia. He is reported to have escaped from the U.S.S.R. to Manchuria together with his parents in 1925 and to have subsequently resided in Harbin. He arrived in Shanghai from Harbin on November 3, 1939.

Full Name in English:	Pavlovsky Georgy Nikolaevitch
Full Name in Russian:	Павловский Георгий Николаевич
Birth Year:	1920
Birth Place:	Harbin, Manchuria
Private Address:	Embankment Buildings, 711
Known to:	Mrs A.F. Pavloff, 263 Av. Haig
Report Title:	U.A. Meshkoff, D.D. Kireevsky, V.D. Minaeff, G.N. Pavlovsky, P.V. Poluhoff and A.Z. Mosol, applicants for enlistment in the Russian Regiment, S.V.C.
Report date:	December 4, 1939
Report number:	338

External archival references to this person: SH/90959

Georgy Nikolaevitch Pavlovsky, Russian, was born on October 5, 1920 at Harbin, Manchuria. He arrived in Shanghai from Harbin on November 9, 1939 and resided together with his cousin Mrs. R. Unger at 711 Embankment Buildings.

Full Name in English:	Poluhoff Peter Vassilievitch
Full Name in Russian:	Полюхов Петр Васильевич
Birth Year:	1913
Birth Place:	Manchouli
Private Address:	Av Du Roi Albert, 101/9
Known to:	Mr. G.I. Lavrinenko 101/9 Av. du Roi Albert
Report Title:	U.A. Meshkoff, D.D. Kireevsky, V.D. Minaeff, G.N. Pavlovsky, P.V. Poluhoff and A.Z. Mosol, applicants for enlistment in the Russian Regiment, S.V.C.

Report date: December 4, 1939
Report number: 338
External archival references to this person: SH/92112

Peter Vassilievitch Poluhoff, Russian, was born on June 10, 1913 at Manchouli. He resided at that town until 1936 after which he proceeded to Harbin. He arrived in Shanghai from Harbin on November 17, 1939 and is not known locality.

Full Name in English:	Masol Alexander Zaharovitch
Full Name in Russian:	Масол Александр Захарович
Private Address:	Route Crouchy,1148
Known to:	Mr. E.M. Buyanover, 177 Rue Amiral Gourbet
Report Title:	U.A. Meshkoff, D.D. Kireevsky, V.D. Minaeff, G.N. Pavlovsky, P.V. Poluhoff and A.Z. Mosol, applicants for enlistment in the Russian Regiment, S.V.C.
Report date:	December 4, 1939
Report number:	338

External archival references to this person: SH/80014

Alexander Zaharovitch Masol Harbin, Manchuria. From his early childhood he resided at Changchun in 1931. Here he worked as an apprentice at various garages until November 1936 when he was engaged as a mechanic by Jenny's Motors, 177 Rue Amiral Courbet. He left that place of employment of his own accord in the beginning of November 1939.

Full Name in English:	Shikaloff Victor Ivanovitch
Full Name in Russian:	Шикалов Виктор Иванович
Birth Year:	1920
Birth Place:	Blagoveschensk, Maritime Province, Russia.
Private Address:	Route Vallon, 505/13
Known to:	Mr I.C. Pensen, 637 Av. Joffre
Report Title:	V.I. Shikhloff, applicant for enlistment in the Russian Regiment, S.V.C.
Report date:	December 4, 1939
Report number:	339

External archival references to this person: SH/111013

Victor Ivanovitch Shikaloff, Russian, was born on August 26, 1920 at Blagoveschensk, Maritime Province, Russia. He is reported to have escaped from the U.S.S.R. to Manchuria in 1925 and to have subsequently resided in Harbin. He arrived in Shanghai from Harbin on November 9, 1939 and resided at 20 Route de Grouchy, together with his brother, an employee of N.S. Petroff & Company, 856 Avenue Joffre.

Full Name in English:	Konovets Anatoly Anatolievitch
Full Name in Russian:	Коновец Анатолий Анатольевич
Birth Year:	1921
Birth Place:	Pogranichnaya Station, Chinese Eastern Railway.
Private Address:	Av. Dubail, 256/5
Known to:	Mr. Radetsky Mikoolich, 635/5 Rue Ratard.
Report Title:	A.A. Konvets and M.V. Miroshnichenko, applicants for enlistment in the Russian Regiment, S.V.C.
Report date:	December 7, 1939
Report number:	340

External archival references to this person: SH/60662

Anatoly Anatolievitch Konovets, Russian, was born on September 24, 1921 at Pogranichnaya Station, Chinese Eastern Railway. In 1925 he proceeded to Tientain, together with his   parents and from 1935 to 1938 studied at the St. Loui's College in that city. He arrived in Shanghai on September 8, 1939 and soon afterwards obtained employment with "Modern Women" magazine, 597 Avenue Joffre. On December 1, 1939 he left that place of employment of his own accord.

Full Name in English:	Miroshnichenko Mihail Vassilievitch
Full Name in Russian:	Мирошниченко Михаил Васильевич
Birth Year:	1920
Birth Place:	Hailar station, Chinese Eastern Railway.
Private Address:	Connaught Rd., 385
Known to:	Mrs M.Y. Meyer, 385 Connaught Rd.
Report Title:	A.A. Konvets and M.V. Miroshnichenko, applicants for enlistment in the Russian Regiment, S.V.C.
Report date:	December 7, 1939
Report number:	340

External archival references to this person: SH/71833

Mihail Vassilievitch Miroshnichenko, Russian, was born on September 11, 1920 at Hailar station, Chinese Eastern Railway. He arrived in Shanghai from Harbin on

November 1, 1939 and took up residence with Mrs. M.Y. Meyer, 385, Connaught Road. Being a new arrival in Shanghai he is not known locally.

Full Name in English:	Velissoff Victor Vassilevitch
Full Name in Russian:	Велисов Виктор Васильевич
Birth Year:	1921
Birth Place:	Harbin, Manchuria
Private Address:	Route Des Soeurs, 118 House, App. 3
Known to:	Mrs K.I. Ellis. 118, House, app.3, Route Des Soeurs.
Report Title:	V.V. Velissoff, N.P. Schoolgin, B.M. Mousalevsky and V.M. Mezavtzeff, applicants for enlistment in the Russian Regiment, S.V.C.
Report date:	December 18, 1939
Report number:	341

External archival references to this person: SH/131028

Victor Vassilevitch Velissoff, Russian, was born on October 10, 1921 in Harbin, Manchuria. In 1923 he left Harbin for Tientsin together with his parents. In 1929 he entered the St. Loui's College on that city, graduating from same in 1935. In December 1938 he proceeded to Swatow where he resided together with his aunt Mrs. H. Hills, wife of Mr. H. Hills of the Chinese, maritime customs. On September 29, 1939 the applicant arrived in Shanghai together with his aunt and resided at 118/1 Route de Soeurs, Apartment 3.

Full Name in English:	Shoolgin Nicolai Pavlovitch
Full Name in Russian:	Шульгин Николай Павлович
Birth Year:	1921
Birth Place:	Pogranichnaya station, Chinese Eastern Railway.
Private Address:	Route Vallon, 508
Known to:	Mrs. V.N. Popoff 508 Route Vallon
Report Title:	V.V. Velissoff, N.P. Schoolgin, B.M. Mousalevsky and V.M. Mezavtzeff, applicants for enlistment in the Russian Regiment, S.V.C.
Report date:	December 18, 1939
Report number:	341

External archival references to this person: SH/111420

Nicolai Pavlovitch Shoolgin, Russian, was born on November 19, 1921 at Pogranichnaya station, Chinese Eastern Railway. He arrived in shanghai from Harbin on December 10, 1939 and is not known locally.

Full Name in English:	Mousalevsky Boris Mihailovitch
Full Name in Russian:	Мусалевский Борис Михайлович
Birth Year:	1906
Birth Place:	Harbin, Manchuria
Private Address:	Rue Bourgeat, 297
Known to:	Mr. N.N. Nikolaeff, 68 Rue Paul Henry.
Report Title:	V.V. Velissoff, N.P. Schoolgin, B.M. Mousalevsky and V.M. Mezavtzeff, applicants for enlistment in the Russian Regiment, S.V.C.
Report date:	December 18, 1939
Report number:	341

Boris Mihailovitch Mousalevsky, Russian, was born on October 14, 1906 in Harbin, Manchuria. He arrived in shanghai in January 1930 and in June of the same year obtained employment as a clerk with the Tkachenko Restaurant, Avenue Joffre. In March 1933 he left that place of employment his own accord and on May 1, 1939 joined the Russian Auxiliary Detachment of the French police. On June 4, 1934 he left the Detachment of his own accord and on June 15, 1934 was engaged as a ticket inspector by the China General Omnibus Co. He was employed in that capacity until December 11, 1939, when he resigned in order to join the Russian Regiment, S.V.C.

Full Name in English:	Mezavitzeff Victor Mihailovitch
Full Name in Russian:	Мезавицев Виктор Михайлович
Birth Year:	1920
Birth Place:	Manchouli Station, Chinese Eastern Railway.
Private Address:	Rue Bourgeat, 398
Known to:	Mr. A.N. Philippoff Ph.D. S.M.C
Report Title:	V.V. Velissoff, N.P. Schoolgin, B.M. Mousalevsky and V.M. Mezavtzeff, applicants for enlistment in the Russian Regiment, S.V.C.
Report date:	December 18, 1939
Report number:	341
External archival references to this person:	SH/71454

Victor Mihailovitch Mezavitzeff, Russian, was born on January 22, 1920 at Manchouli Station, Chinese Eastern Railway. On November 9, 1939 he arrived in Shanghai from Harbin and is not known locally.

Full Name in English:	Kraizelman Boris Naumovich
Full Name in Russian:	Крейзельман Бина (Борис) Наумович
Birth Year:	1919
Birth Place:	Harbin, Manchuria
Report Title:	B. Kraizelman, applicant for enrolment in the Transport Company, S.V.C.
Report date:	December 27, 1939
Report number:	342

External archival references to this person: SH/61596

Boris Naumovitch Kraizelman, Russian Jew, was born on December 4, 1919 in Harbin, Manchuria. In 1924 he arrived in Shanghai together with his parents. In 1927 he entered the French Municipal College, graduating from the same in 1937. Later he assisted his mother, who owns a haberdashery store, "Vigoda", 693 Avenue Joffre. On December 5, 1939 he secured his present position as an office assistant with N.J. Sbath & Company, 49 Szechuen Road.

Full Name in English:	Leonoff Georgy Alexandrovitch
Full Name in Russian:	Леонов Георгий Александрович
Birth Year:	1913
Birth Place:	Changchung, South Manchuria
Report Title:	G.A. Leonoff, applicant for enrolment in the American Troop, S.V.C.
Report date:	December 27, 1939
Report number:	342

External archival references to this person: SH/80335

Georgy Alexandrovitch Leonoff, Russian Jew, was born on November 1, 1913 in Changchung, South Manchuria. In 1926 he arrived in Shanghai from Tientsin and during the same year entered the Public and Thomas Hanbury School for Boys, graduating from same in December 1930. Later he worked casually until October 1932 when he secured his present position as a reporter with the China Press.

This applicant is not registered with the Russian Emigrants' Committee, or any other Russian Public Association.

Full Name in English:	Briansky Nikolai Nikolaevitch
Full Name in Russian:	Брянский Николай Николаевич

Birth Year:	1920
Birth Place:	Harbin, Manchuria
Private Address:	Route Delastre, 2
Report Title:	N. Briansky, applicant for enrolment in Signals Company, S.V.C.
Report date:	Dec 27th 1939
Report number:	343

External archival references to this person: SH/20804

Nikolai Nikolaevitch Briansky, Russian, was born on April 20, 1920 in Harbin, Manchuria. He arrived in Shanghai from Harbin in November 1937. In January 1938 he entered the St. Francis Xavier's College, graduating from same in January 1939.

In September 1939 he entered the Henry Lester Institute for Technical Education, where he is still studying.

He has a sister, Miss I. Briansky, who is employed as a stenotypist with the Shanghai Land Investment Company, and resides together with the applicant at 2 Route Delastre.

Full Name in English:	Sokoloff Mihail Anfinogenovitch
Full Name in Russian:	Соколов Михаил Афиногенович
Birth Year:	1920
Birth Place:	Tientsin, North China
Report Title:	M. Sokoloff, applicant for enrolment in Signals Company, S.V.C.
Report date:	Dec 27 1939
Report number:	343

External archival references to this person: SH/120017 (в карточке Александрович).

Mihail Anfinogenovitch Sokoloff, Russian, was born on December 6, 1920 in Tientsin, North China. In 1937 he graduated from the Tientsin Grammar School. He arrived in Shanghai on October 29, 1939 and entered the Henry Lester Institute for Technical Education. He left Shanghai for Tientsin on December 17, 1939 and is expected to return here in the beginning of 1940.

Full Name in English:	Novgorodoff Evgeny Maksimovitch
Full Name in Russian:	Новгородов Евгений Максимович
Birth Year:	1919
Birth Place:	Harbin, Manchuria

Report Title:	K. Novgorodoff, applicant for enrolment in Signals Company, S.V.C.
Report date:	December 27, 1939.
Report number:	343
External archival references to this person:	SH/82085

Evgeny Maksimovitch Novgorodoff, Russian, was born on January 6, 1919 in Harbin, Manchuria. In 1924 he arrived in Shanghai from Vladivostok together with his parents. In 1927 he entered the Public and Thomas Hanbury School for Boys, graduating from same in December 1935. Later he was unemployed until November 1937, when he was engaged as a Supervisor by the Economic Transport Company, 150 Kiukiang Road. On December 31, 1938, he left the place of employment of his own accord and in January 1939, obtained his present position with the public Works Department, Shanghai Municipal Council.

Full Name in English:	Petroff Igor Alexeyevitch
Full Name in Russian:	Петров Игорь Алексеевич
Birth Year:	1920
Birth Place:	Hailar, Chinese Eastern Railway
Report Title:	I. Petroff, applicant for enrolment in Signals Company, S.V.C
Report date:	December 27, 1939
Report number:	343
External archival references to this person:	SH/91325

Igor Alexeyevitch Petroff, Russian, was born on April 23, 1920 in Hailar, Chinese Eastern Railway. He arrived in Shanghai from Harbin early in 1937 and towards the end of the same year entered the St. Francis Xavier's College, graduation from same in 1938.

In January 1939 he obtained employment as a clerk with the Asiatic Credit company, 303 Route Cardinal Mercier, in which company his father holds a post of the chief accountant.

From September 1939 the applicant has been attending the Center Technique Superieur, 200 Route Remi.

Full Name in English:	Dengin Boris Pavlovitch
Full Name in Russian:	Деньгин Борис Павлович
Birth Year:	1920
Birth Place:	Chita, Siberia

Report Title:	B.P. Dengin, applicant for enrolment in American Troop, S.V.C
Report date:	December 29, 1939
Report number:	344

External archival references to this person: SH/22038

Boris Pavlovitch Dengin, Russian, Was born on October 19, 1920 in Chita, Siberia. He is reported to have left Russia together with his parents in 1922 and to have subsequently resided in Harbin.

In 1927 he arrived in Shanghai from Harbin. From 1928 to 1931 he attended the Commercial School of the Russian Orthodox Confraternity. Later he studied in the Ecole Remi. Leaving that School in 1937 he was unemployed until June 1938 when he was engaged as an apprentice by the Shanghai Dockyards ltd., 640 Yanngtszepoo Road.

Full Name in English:	Primortzeff Alexey Lvovitch
Full Name in Russian:	Приморцев Алексей Львович
Birth Year:	1921
Birth Place:	Hailar, Manchuria
Private Address:	Route Remi, Pass 146, House 26
Known to:	Mr. P.T. Konovaloff Sub Inspector S.M.P.
Report Title:	A.L. Primortzeff, A.I. Osadchy and A.A. Alexeyeff, applicants for enlistment in the Russian Regiment, S.V.C.
Report date:	December 29, 1939
Report number:	345

External archival references to this person: SH/100394

Alexey Lvovitch Primortzeff, Russian, was born on August 25, 1921 in Hailar, Manchuria. In 1937 he arrived in Shanghai together with his parents. Here he attended the Commercial School of the Russian Orthodox Confraternity for one year and later studied in the First Russian High School (now, A.S. Pushkin Memorial School). Applicant's father, Mr. L. Primortzeff forms the subjects of a criminal record no. 3123, the contents of which read as follows:-

1st. Shanghai Special District Court.	Fraud.
One year imprisonment.	15-12-38.
Released on Bail for Employment.	15-9-39.

Applicant's mother and the younger brother are known to be members of the Repatriation Union, a pro-Soviet organization, 105, Love Lane. However, the applicant denies having any connection with the above organization.

Full Name in English:	Osadchy Alexander Iosifovitch
Full Name in Russian:	Осадчий Александр Иосифович
Birth Year:	1919
Birth Place:	Harbin, Manchuria
Private Address:	Szechuen Rd., 625
Known to:	Mrs P.I. Manakoff, 625 Szechuen RD
Report Title:	A.L. Primortzeff, A.I. Osadchy and A.A. Alex-eyeff, applicants for enlistment in the Russian Regiment, S.V.C.
Report date:	December 29, 1939
Report number:	345

External archival references to this person: SH/90445

Alexander Iosifovitch Osadchy, Russian, was born on July 23, 1919 in Harbin, Manchuria. On December 18, 1939 he arrived in Shanghai from Harbin and took up residence at 625 Szechuen Road, together with his sisters Mrs. P.I. Manakova, a paramour of a foreign member of the Chinese Maritime Customs.

Full Name in English:	Alexeyeff Anatoly Alexeyevitch
Full Name in Russian:	Алексеев Анатолий Алексеевич
Birth Year:	1918
Birth Place:	Blagoveschensk, Maritime Province, Russia.
Private Address:	Szechuen Rd., 625
Known to:	Mr. D. Yanchevsky Res. Unit. S.M.P.
Report Title:	A.L. Primortzeff, A.I. Osadchy and A.A. Alex-eyeff, applicants for enlistment in the Russian Regiment, S.V.C.
Report date:	December 29, 1939
Report number:	345

External archival references to this person: SH/10369

Anatoly Alexeyevitch Alexeyeff, Russian, was born on September 27, 1918 in Blagoveschensk, Maritime Province, Russia. He is reported to have left Russia together with his parents in 1922 and to have subsequently resided in Harbin. On December 18, 1939 he arrived in Shanghai from Harbin and took up residence together with the second applicant at 625, Szechuen Road. Being a new arrival in Shanghai he is not known locally.

Full Name in English:	Lev Nicolaevich Primortsev
Full Name in Russian:	Приморцев Лев Николаевич
Report Title:	L.N. Primortsev

Report date:	30-07-1951

Lev Nicolaevich Primortsev/ late/ father of Pavel Lvovich Primortsev Transbaikal cossack arrived in China in 1921-2 with remnants of White Army. It is known that he resided at Hailar, Manchuria near Mongolia from 1921-29 it is known that he had doubtful reputation and was strongly suspected in horse stealing.

Later he resided with his family consisting of the wife S.A. Primortsev nee Potissova (illiterate), son P.L. Primortseff (mentioned in attached Question List if RSO), daughter G.L. Primortseff born on 21 April 1921 and son Alexey Lvovich Primortsev (subject of SMP File D.917/348 born on 25.VIII. 1921 at Hailer, son Fedor Lvovich Primortsev, born on 27 April 1925

From 1921 to 1929 he resided at Hailer.

From 1929 to 1935 at Harbin

From 1935 to 1936 at Peking

From 1937 to 1946(1) at Shanghai

It is known that before his departure from Shanghai he owned a small bar 96 Rte Grouchy together with his son Pavel Lvovich Primortsev.

According to SMP File D 9171345 Mrs. E.A. Primortsev and her young son Fedor were members of Repatriation Union already in 1939. Nothing is mentioned re Pavel Lvovich Primortsev in this report?

Primortsev's family father mother, P.L. Primortsev with his wife Helena (Yelena) Primortseff and some other members were repatriated to USSR in 1946-7

In 1949 it was discovered by different Intelligences that Pavel Lvovich Primortsev and his wife returned back to Shanghai. He was questioned by the member of Chinese Intelligence including one Marcel Kao Deputy of the Chief of Investigation Office of Ministry of Interior. P.L. Lojnikoff stated that he was sent together with other former Russian emigrants repatriated to USSR first to Port Nahodoka near Vladivostok. Later he was residing in Sverdlovsk Areas, Ural. He as soon disappointed

Soon after his arrival in condition in USSR By bribing a doctor he was exempt from labor as suffering from T.B.

Once pretending to go on hunting trip he boarded a train at other station and left to Far East. At Iriarbuk he succeed to bribe a member of Control Guard which check all passenger going in both direction and proceeded to (invisible) Region.

He crossed according to him near river with his wife and left to Harbin travelling from one town to the other. He was in possession of USSR passport and besides has very good knowledge of Chinese Language.

After staying for a period at Harbin B.L. Primortseff and his wife left to Kirin (?) where they were detained by Intelligence Service of Chinese Nationalist Government. Probably at that time they were questioned by USA officers attached to Chinese Army.

Some time later P.L. Primortseff arrived to Shanghai. At Shanghai he was very reserved regarding his adventures in USSR and refused to give information to "Sino Chinese Newspaper" Kuomintang daily in Russian language. However few articles describing his case with anti communist commentary appeared at above daily. P.L. Primortsev objected, stating that he like to be out of politic. It should be mentioned that he was known as a member of Shanghai "underworld" consisting of criminals, "Black Maricot operators and different study characters many of them obtained USSR citizenship after termination of the 2nd Great War as "socially close" elements.

P.L. Primortsev maintained friendly relation with his former friends and it seems returned only owing purely personal reason to Shanghai where he had an "easy life" in his past.

It should be mentioned, that P.L. Primortsev from Sverdlovsk, Ural sent to his aunt residing at wayside District (ManGregor Rd?) some of personal photos before he started his journey to Shanghai. His wife Helena (Yelena) Primortsev is a young, alternative, smart woman.

It was strongly rumored that P.L. Primortseff invented all his story and that he actually was at Peking or some other place in North China. But Chinese authorities verified his statement and disclosed the fnot, that he correspondent with his aunt from USSR and sent above mentioned photos.

To escape from USSR is not easy and amny were surprised, that he could escape together with his wife. But it should be noted, that P.L. Primortsev a member of "underworld" who was close to Soviet and criminal circles at Shanghai and has good knowledge of Chinese was just a type for this adventure.

Date: 30 July 1951

Report Date: 30 July 1951

Subject: TRANSLATION

RUSSIAN EMIGRANTS COMMITTEE IN SHANGHAI
QUESTION LIST

FAMILY NAME, NAME, FATHER'S NAME PRIMORTSEV Pavel Lvovich (AGETEV)

Date of birth - 16 February 1919

Place of birth - Verhneudinsk. (Transbaikal Province, Soberia)

Religion, nationality - Orthodox, Russian.

Education - At Harbin from 1930 to 1933- Towns school (Primary)

Family status - Single (married to Helen (Yelena)? /)

What position, employment had in Russia

When and from where arrived to China, Where resided since. - In 1920 from Verhnoudinsk via Station Manchuria to Hailar in 1920 to 1929 until Sino Soviet conflict, at Harbin. Arrived in 1929 until 1957 was employed at Japanese guard at Toinikar.

In possession of what document arrived to China With Manchukyo passport, changed to Chinese registration at Tiantsin No 3474.

What document at present- Chinese registration No 3474 is issued at Tiantsin by Chinese Government in 1957

Remarks of REC Cort D.D.6747 dated 12, 6.41 Reg Dn Dao No 6747 18.VIII.42.

In 1937 to October from Kalgun. At Kalgun was solling covers (blankets?)   Repaired radios.

Did you been or are member of social or political organisations - No

Did you been charged or under investigation - No

Your attitude towards Soviet Power, Communism and Comintern - I have no notion.

Where are residing your close relatives, their names addresses - At Shanghai at 1254 Rue Lafayette father L.N. Primortsev, E/L.Primortsev

Your membership fee $0.50

P.L. PRIMORTSEV

Your profession and knowledge of foreign languages - Driver, radio mechanic, English, Chinese.

Permanent address - 96, Rte Grouchy.

Guarantor names D.N. Suhopluieff 804 Av Joffre.

P.Utia........314 rue Deintour.

Pavel NEKRASOFF 992 Rte de Zikawei.

24 march 1939

Signature P.L. Primortsoff.

NOTES OF REC

27./IXX.39 Cortif for regist.

21. XI.39 to Russian Hospital

14 Aug 1941 to the Bus Co.

Attached to his application form in an article from Novoe Vremia (New Time)

TRANSLATION. CASE OF PRIMORTSEV

In 7th chamber of the 2nd District Court took place hearing of the case regarding re-cover of $ 1000 from P.L. Primortsev which he took under receipt from P.M. Grinberg. Primortsev did not denied that he took money, but stated to the Court that the money were taken from Mr Levov.

Lawyer of Mr Grinberg, legal advisor Pichahohi produced receipt signed by Primortsev, that he took money from Grinberg and explained to the Court that Levov is only an employee of Mr Grinberg's enterprise.

After that judge asked could prosecuted to repay his debts during one month, but Mr Primortsev to cover his debts by monthly payment OD $20

Lawyer of plaintiff did not agree and judge announced that resolution on above would be made on 15 June.

Full Name in English:	Kibireff Kuzma Mefodievitch
Full Name in Russian:	Кибирев Кузьма Мефодиевич
Birth Year:	1920
Birth Place:	Transbaikal Province, Russia
Private Address:	Av Joffre, 804
Known to:	Father A. Filimonoff
Report Title:	K.M. Kibireff and A. Garifoolin, applicants for enlistment in the Russian Regiment, S.V.C
Report date:	January 4, 1940
Report number:	346

External archival references to this person: SH/51781

Kuzma Mefodievitch Kibireff, Russian was born on October 12, 1920 in Transbaikal Province, Russian. According to his own his own statement, he escaped from the U.S.S.R. together with his mother in 1929 and subsequently resided in Harbin. On November 15, 1939 he arrived in Shanghai from Harbin. On 21-11-39 he joined the Auxiliary Detachment. French Police, however, on 23-11-39 he absented himself without leave and was consequently discharged for that reason.

Full Name in English:	Garifoolin Abdurahman
Full Name in Russian:	Гарифулин Абдурахман
Birth Year:	1903
Birth Place:	Ufimsk Province, Russian
Private Address:	Av. Joffre, 918/5
Known to:	Mr. A. Domojiroff Sgt S.M.P.
Report Title:	K.M. Kibireff and A. Garifoolin, applicants for enlistment in the Russian Regiment, S.V.C
Report date:	January 4, 1940
Report number:	346

External archival references to this person: SH/32057

Abdurahman Garifoolin, Russian of Tartar origin, was born on February 14, 1903 in Ufimsk Province, Russian. He is reported to have left Russia in 1922 and to have subsequently resided in Mukden. From 1924 to 1927 he served in Marchall's Chang Chung Chang Army and later again resided in Mukden, where he worked as a chauffeur, In April 1929 he arrived in Shanghai and soon afterwards was engages as a chauffeur by the China General Omnibus Company. He worked in that capacity until December 20, 1939 when he resigned on his own accord.

Full Name in English:	Alexandroff Boris Victorovitch
Full Name in Russian:	Александров Борис Викторович
Birth Year:	1920
Birth Place:	Habarovsk, Siberia
Report Title:	B.A. Alexandroff, applicant for enrolment in No.3 (Vol) Company, S.V.C.
Report date:	January 9, 1940
Report number:	347

External archival references to this person: SH/10304

Note:	applied twice.

Boris Victorovitch Alexandroff, Russian, was born on August 21, 1920 in Habarovsk, Siberia. He is reported to have left Russia in 1921 together with his parents and to have subsequently resided in Harbin until 1934, after which he came to Shanghai. Here he attended the First Russian High School during 1935 and 1936. In September 1937 he joined the Auxiliary Detachment, French Police in which he served until February, 1938 when he resigned of his own accord. Later he worked together with his father at the Alcohol Distilling Works of Liddell Bros. & Co., Ltd., 1140, Yangtszepoo Road. In October 1939, applicant's father established a business of his own, Asiatic Alcohol Distilling Works, 941, Ward Road, and the applicant is at present assisting his father in conducting the same.

Full Name in English:	Korenevsky Vadim Fedorovitch
Full Name in Russian:	Кореневский Вадим Фёдорович
Birth Year:	1912
Birth Place:	Handaohedzi Station, Chinese Eastern Railway
Report Title:	V.F. Korenevsky, applicant for enrolment in No.3 (Vol) Company, S.V.C.
Report date:	January 9, 1940
Report number:	347
External archival references to this person:	SH/60870

Vadim Fedorovitch Korenevsky, Russian, was born on December 16, 1912 in Handaohedzi Station, Chinese Eastern Railway. Upon graduating from a high school in Harbin in 1930 he entered the Harbin Polytechnic Institute, graduating from same in 1935. In March 1936 he arrived in Shanghai from Harbin and in May of the same year obtained employed as a draughtman with the Wegon-Lits Company. His services were dispensed with in August 1937, owing to the outbreak of the local hostilities. In December 1937 he secured his present position as a paper maker with the China Fiber Company, 273 Haichow Road.

Full Name in English:	Cherniatieff Nikolai Semenovitch
Full Name in Russian:	Чернятьев Николай Семенович
Birth Year:	1910
Birth Place:	Harbin, Manchuria
Private Address:	Kiukiang Rd, 50
Known to:	N.V. Pinaeff 50 Kiukiang Rd
Report Title:	N.S. Cherniatieff, applicant for enlistment in the Russian Regiment, S.V.C
Report date:	Jan 13th 1940
Report number:	349

External archival references to this person: SH/21406

Nikolai Semenovitch Cherniatieff, Russian, was born on July 4, 1910 in Harbin, Manchuria. According to his own statement, he resided in Harbin until December 27, 1939, after which he proceeded to Shanghai, arriving in this port on December 30, 1939 in the s.s. "Dairen Maru".

Being a new arrival in Shanghai he is not known locally.

Full Name in English:	Sokoloff Boris Vladimirovtich
Full Name in Russian:	Соколов Борис Владимирович
Birth Year:	1915
Birth Place:	Transbaikal Province, Russia
Report Title:	B.V. Sokoloff, applicants for enrolment in Signals Company, S.V.C
Report date:	January 11, 1940
Report number:	348

Boris Vladimirovtich Sokoloff, Soviet citizen, was born on November 5, 1915 in Transbaikal Province, Russia. From 1921 to February 1936 he resided in Harbin, where his father was employed with the Chinese Eastern Railway. He arrived in Shanghai from Harbin in February 1936 and during the name month entered the St. John's University, graduating from same in June 1939. On November 15, 1939 he secured his present position with the Southeastern Architectural & Engineering Company, 113 KiuKieng Road.

The applicant is in Possession of Soviet passport No.010979, issued by the Soviet Consulate General in Harbin on January 29, 1936.

Full Name in English:	Alexeyeff Igor Mihailovitch
Full Name in Russian:	Алексеев Игорь Михайлович
Birth Year:	1914
Birth Place:	Vitebsk, Russia
Report Title:	I.M. Alexeyeff, applicant for enrolment in the transport Company, S.V.C.
Report date:	January 16th 1940.
Report number:	350

Igor Mihailovitch Alexeyeff, Russian, was born on September 13, 1914 in Vitebsk, Russia. He is reported to have left Russian together with his parents in 1921 and to have subsequently resided in Harbin. On March 6, 1938 he arrived in Shanghai from Harbin. On March 10, 1938 he joined the Russian Regiment, S.V.C. in which he served until June 9, 1939 when he resigned of his own accord. On August 20,

1939 he secured his present position as a building inspector with E.D. Sassoon & Co., Ltd.

Full Name in English:	Borodin Daniil Ivanovitch
Full Name in Russian:	Бородин Даниил Иванович
Birth Year:	1920
Birth Place:	Vladivostok, Maritime Province, Russia
Report Title:	D.I. Borodin, applicant for enrolment in the Signals Company, S.V.C.
Report date:	January 19, 1940
Report number:	351

Daniil Ivanovitch Borodin, Russian, was born on October 19, 1920 in Vladivostok, Maritime Province, Russia. According to his own statement, he left the U.S.S.R. together with his mother in 1929 and subsequently resided in Harbin. He arrived in Shanghai from Harbin in 1932 and took up residence together with his grandfather, Mr. A. Feldman, 328 Route Cardinal Mercier. In 1932 he entered the Public and Thomas Hanbury School for Boys, graduating from same in December 1937. In March 1938 he proceeded to Harbin, returning to this city in September of the same year. Upon his return here, he entered the Henry Lester institute for Technical Education, where he is still studying.

Full Name in English:	Ignatenko Boris Vassilievitch
Full Name in Russian:	Игнатенко Борис Васильевич
Birth Year:	1921
Birth Place:	Harbin, Manchuria
Private Address:	Av Du Roi Albert, 384 Apt 6
Known to:	Mr. N.E. Malikoff S Kelmscott Gardens, Av Du Roi Albert
Report Title:	B.V. Ignatenko and B.G. Sesko – applicants for enlistment in the Russian Regiment, S.V.C.
Report date:	January 25, 1940
Report number:	352
External archival references to this person: SH/50121	

Boris Vassilievitch Ignatenko, Russian, was born on March 27, 1921 in Harbin, Manchuria. He arrived in Shanghai from Harbin, Manchuria. He arrived in Shanghai from Harbin on December 30, 1939 and took up residence together with his sister, Miss A.V. Ignatenko, at 384/6 Avenue du Roi Albert. His second sister is married to Mr. L. Spunt and resides at 303/42 Avenue Petain. Applicant's father, who from 1909 to 1934 was employed with the Chinese Eastern Railway, at present, resides in Harbin.

Full Name in English:	Sesko Boris Georgievitch
Full Name in Russian:	Сеська Борис Георгиевич
Birth Year:	1917
Birth Place:	Harbin, Manchuria
Private Address:	Rue Bourgeat, 613, House 17
Known to:	Mr. A.P. Krootikoff 613,House 17, Rue Bourgeat
Report Title:	B.V. Ignatenko and B.G. Sesko – applicants for enlistment in the Russian Regiment, S.V.C.
Report date:	January 25, 1940
Report number:	352
External archival references to this person:	SH/110467

Boris Georgievitch Sesko, Russian, was born on July 24, 1917 in Harbin, Manchuria. In 1929, the applicant proceeded to Tientsin, together with his parents and for the following four years attended the St. Louis College in that city. Later he worked casually until January 2, 1940 when he arrived in Shanghai. He has a sister in Shanghai who is married to Mr. A.P. Krootikoff, who is employed as an Anti-Piracy Guard with the China Navigation Company.

Full Name in English:	Koodriavtzeff Georgy Nikitich
Full Name in Russian:	Кудрявцев Георгий Никитич
Birth Year:	1922
Birth Place:	Harbin, Manchuria
Private Address:	Tongshan Rd, 696/31
Known to:	Mrs O.I. Groozdeff 696/31 Tongshan Rd
Report Title:	G.N. Koodriavtzeff, U.M. Buikis and L.A. Sanotsky, applicants for enlistment in the Russian Regiment, S.V.C.
Report date:	1/2/1940
Report number:	353
External archival references to this person:	SH/62161

Georgy Nikitich Koodriavtzeff, Russian, was born on April 22, 1922 in Harbin, Manchuria. He arrived on January 8, 1940 in Shanghai from Harbin and took up residence together with his aunt, Mrs. O.I. Groozdeva, 696/31 Tongshan Road. His brother is at present serving in the Russian Regiment, S.V.C.

Full Name in English:	Buikis Ury Mihailovitch
Full Name in Russian:	Буйкис Юрий Михайлович
Birth Year:	1905
Birth Place:	Vitebsk Province, Russia
Private Address:	Baikal Rd, 152
Known to:	Mr. G.S. Stolitza, Msin. Franchise, Division Voie Publique.
Report Title:	G.N. Koodriavtzeff, U.M. Buikis and L.A. Sanotsky, applicants for enlistment in the Russian Regiment, S.V.C.
Report date:	1/2/1940
Report number:	353
External archival references to this person:	SH/20555

Ury Mihailovitch Buikis, Russian, was born on February 14, 1905 in Vitebsk Province, Russia. He is reported to have left Russia in 1923 and to have subsequently resided in Harbin. In May 1930 he was engaged as chauffeur by the China General Omnibus Company, in which capacity he worked until January 1932 when he resigned of his own accord. During the same month he obtained employment with the Taylor Garage. In February 1935 his services were dispensed with owing to a reduction of staff. For the following two years, until August 1937 he employed with the French Fire Brigade. He afterwards worked as a driver in the employ of various owners of private trucks.

Full Name in English:	Sanotsky Leonid Antonovitch
Full Name in Russian:	Санотский Леонид Антонович
Birth Year:	1921
Birth Place:	Vladivostok, Maritime Province, Russia
Private Address:	Lirga Rd., 31
Known to:	G.A. Stephanoff, 800 Av. Joffre.
Report Title:	G.N. Koodriavtzeff, U.M. Buikis and L.A. Sanotsky, applicants for enlistment in the Russian Regiment, S.V.C.
Report date:	1/2/1940
Report number:	353

Leonid Antonovitch Sanotsky, Russian, was born on December 29, 1921 in Vladivostok, Maritime Province, Russia. According to his own statement, he left Russia together with his parents in 1923 and subsequently resided in Harbin. On December 30, 1939 he arrived in Shanghai from Harbin. He is known to several members of the local Russian community who speak favourably of him.

Full Name in English:	Skreitul Alfred C.
Full Name in Russian:	Скрейтул Альфред
Birth Year:	1922
Birth Place:	Vladivostok, Maritime Province, Russia
Report Title:	A.C. Skreitul- applicant for enrolment in American Machine Gun Company, S.V.C.
Report date:	13/2/1940
Report number:	354

Alfred C. Skreitul, Latvian, was born on April 23, 1922 at Vladivostok, Maritime Province, Russia. In 1923 he arrived in Shanghai from Vladivostok, together with his family. From 1933 to 1937 he studied in the St. Joan D'Arc College. In July 1938 he entered the Y.M.C.A. Matriculation Classes, graduating from same in January 1940.

The applicant's brother has been in the employ of the Shanghai Municipal Police (Gaol Branch) since August 1937.

The applicant is registered with the local Finnish Consulate (in charge of Latvian interests in Shanghai) and holds passport No. 006390 R, issued on May 20, 1939.

Full Name in English:	Roussett Constantine Constantinovitch
Full Name in Russian:	Руссет Константин Константинович
Birth Year:	1921
Birth Place:	Shanghai
Report Title:	C. Roussett, applicant for enrolment in American Machine Gun Company, S.V.C.
Report date:	13/2/1940
Report number:	354
External archival references to this person:	SH/101500

Constantine Constantinovitch Roussett, Russian, was born on December 7, 1921 in Shanghai. During 1936 and 1937 he attended the Senior Lester School of Technical Education. In July 1938 he left Shanghai for Chefoo, returning to this city in September 1939. Upon his return here he entered the Y.M.C.A. Matriculation Classes, where he is still studying.

His father, Mr. C. Roussett, is employed as a ship's captain with Moller & Co.

Full Name in English:	Kolpachnikoff Enver Stepanovitch
Full Name in Russian:	Колпачников Энвер Степанович
Birth Year:	1921
Birth Place:	Harbin, Manchuria

Report Title:	E. Kolpachnikoff, applicant for enrolment in American Machine Gun Company, S.V.C.
Report date:	13/2/1940
Report number:	354

Enver Stepanovitch Kolpachnikoff, Russian, was born on December 17, 1921 in Harbin, Manchuria. He resided in Harbin until 1933 after which he proceed to Tsingtao together with his mother. In October 1935 he arrived in Shanghai from Tsingtao. From January 1936 to January 1938 he attended the Public and Thomas Hanbury School for Boys. In September 1938 he entered the Senior Lester School of Technical Education. In August 1939 he secured his present position as an apprentice with Anderson, Meyer & Co., Ltd.

Full Name in English:	Froloff Victor Nikolaevitch
Full Name in Russian:	Фролов Виктор Николаевич
Birth Year:	1921
Birth Place:	Pogranichnaya station, Chinese Eastern Railway
Private Address:	Tongshan Rd., 599 House 72
Known to:	Mrs L.M. Tsicritsi Gig Av. Joffre
Report Title:	V.N. Froloff and M.N. Tretiakoff – candidates for enlistment in the Russian Regiment, S.V.C.
Report date:	20/2/1940
Report number:	355

External archival references to this person: SH/31871

Victor Nikolaevitch Froloff, Russian, born on June 7, 1921 at Pogranichnaya station, Chinese Eastern Railway. According to his own statement, he graduated from a middle school at Harbin in 1934 and later studied in the Y.M.C.A. College (Commercial Section) until 1940, after which he proceeded to Shanghai, arriving in this city on 22-1/40 in the S.S. "Tsingtao Maru". Here he resided with his sister who is married to Mr. Ivanoff- Eumjieff, a corporal in the Russian Regiment, attached to Headquarters as interpreter. Mrs. L.M. Tsicritsi, 616 Avenue Joffre, is applicant's aunt.

Froloff stated that his parents were divorced some years ago at Harbin. His mother later married another Russian and resides in Harbin at present, while his father, Mr. N. Froloff, has been residing in Shanghai for the past five or six years and at one time worked as a teacher at first Russian School, Tulin Road.

Full Name in English:	Tretiakoff Mihail Nikiforovich
Full Name in Russian:	Третьяков Михаил Никифорович

Birth Year:	1921
Birth Place:	Manchouli Station, Chinese Eastern Railway
Private Address:	Rue De Kahn,13
Known to:	M.G. Yakovkin, 118/1 Mulmein Rd.
Report Title:	V.N. Froloff and M.N. Tretiakoff – candidates for enlistment in the Russian Regiment, S.V.C.
Report date:	20/2/1940
Report number:	355

External archival references to this person: SH/122109 (Митрофан Никитич)

Mihail Nikiforovich Tretiakoff, Russian, born on November 8, 1921 at Manchouli Station, Chinese Eastern Railway. He arrived in Shanghai from Mukden in 1931 to-gether with his parents. His father, a Transbaikal Cossack died at Shanghai in 1936, and his mother, three sisters and two brothers reside at 13 Rue Gaston Kahn. Mrs. Tretiakoff has been casually working as a char-woman etc.

In Shanghai the applicant attended St. Andrew's elementary school for a short peri-od, after which he studied in the Russian Orthodox Confraternity's School, Avenue Petain, and lived at St. Tichon's Orphanage. Upon leaving school in 1939 he was employed at the Alliance Bakery, 60 Rue Pere Robert for about one year, leaving this place in order to join the Regiment.

He is the nephew of M.N. Tretiakoff, notorious because of his connection with the so-called "Anti-Communist Union at Shanghai".

Full Name in English:	Terehoff Vladimir Ivanovitch
Full Name in Russian:	Терехов Владимир Иванович
Birth Year:	1909
Birth Place:	Omsk, Siberia
Private Address:	Route Paul Henry, 72
Report Title:	V.I. Terehoff, applicant for enrolment in No. 3 (Vol.) Company, S.V.C.
Report date:	26/2/1940
Report number:	356

Vladimir Ivanovitch Terehoff, Russian, was born on July 28, 1909 in Omsk, Siberia. He is reported to have left Russia together with his parents in 1919 and to have sub-sequently resided in Harbin. He first came to Shanghai in November, 1929 but after a short stay in this city returned to Harbin in February, 1929. In Harbin he worked for his father who is the owner of a small shop dealing in furs and skins. It is also rumoured that after the Japanese occupation of Manchuria and until his departure

---

to Shanghai in August, 1938, the applicant was employed as a agent by the Japanese Gendarmerie in Harbin.

The applicant returned to Shanghai in the s.s. "Dairen Maru" on August, 30, 1938 and took up residence at 72, Route Paul Henry, where he is still living.

On October 1, 1938 he joined the Russian Regiment, S.V.C. in which he served until January 31, 1940, when he resigned of his own accord. Since then he has been connected with the Ayurvedic Hall, 651 Weihaiwei Road, where he is employed as an expert in electrotherapy treatment.

While in Harbin, the applicant became a naturalized Chinese citizen. In September, 1938 in Shanghai he renounced his allegiance to the Chinese Government and registered with the Council of the United Russian Organizations (SORO) as a Russian Emigrant.

Full Name in English:	Kovikin Victor Dmitrievitch
Full Name in Russian:	Ковыкин Виктор Дмитриевич
Birth Year:	1909
Birth Place:	Transbaikal Province, Siberia
Private Address:	Rungping Rd., 220/1
Known to:	Mrs. E.K. Popoff, 82/1A, Cathay Flats. Av. Joffre
Report Title:	V. Kovikin, P. Lejenin, N. Zorenko and P. Ivanoff, applicants for enlistment in the Russian Regiment, S.V.C.
Report date:	27/2/1940
Report number:	357

External archival references to this person: SH/ 61463

Victor Dmitrievitch Kovikin, Russian, was born on February 2, 1909 in Transbaikal Province, Siberia. He arrived in Harbin from Vladivostok in 1919 and resided there until his departure to Shanghai. Upon leaving school he casually worked in that city until 1932 when he was engaged by I.I. Tchurin & Co., as a shop assistant. Leaving that firm of his own accord in 1936 he proceeded to Sui-Hua City where he was employed as a railway guard. He arrived in Shanghai from Harbin in October 1938 and on November 18, 1938 joined the Russian regiment, S.V.C. on December 12, 1939 he left the Regiment of his own accord and on January 7, 1940 proceeded to Harbin in order to marry. On returning to Shanghai on February 1, 1940, he rejoined the Regiment and again resigned on February 25th.

Full Name in English:	Lejenin Peter Ivanovitch
Full Name in Russian:	Леженин Петр Иванович

Birth Year:	1910
Birth Place:	Voronej, Russia
Private Address:	Route Winling, 197
Known to:	Mr. D. Sokolovsky. 197 Winling Rd
Report Title:	V. Kovikin, P. Lejenin, N. Zorenko and P. Ivanoff, applicants for enlistment in the Russian Regiment, S.V.C.
Report date:	27/2/1940
Report number:	357

External archival references to this person: SH/ 80286

Peter Ivanovitch Lejenin, Russian, was born on September 13, 1910 in Voronej, Russia. During the same year he arrived in Harbin, where his father was employed with the Chinese Eastern Railway. He arrived in Shanghai from Harbin on January 27, 1940 and took up residence at 197 route Winling. His brother, A. Lejenin, has been a member of the Russian Regiment, S.V.C. since July 1, 1936.

Full Name in English:	Zorenko Nikolai Kirillovitch
Full Name in Russian:	Зоренко Николай Кириллович
Birth Year:	1922
Birth Place:	Imianpo Station, Chinese Eastern Railway.
Private Address:	Av. Joffre, 606
Known to:	Mr. A. Zavalin, 606 Av. Joffre
Report Title:	V. Kovikin, P. Lejenin, N. Zorenko and P. Ivanoff, applicants for enlistment in the Russian Regiment, S.V.C.
Report date:	27/2/1940
Report number:	357

External archival references to this person: SH/140726

Nikolai Kirillovitch Zorenko, Russian, was born on January 1, 1922 at Imianpo Station, Chinese Eastern Railway. For the last ten years he resided in Harbin and arrived in Shanghai Eastern Railway. For the last ten years he resided in Harbin and arrived in Shanghai from that city on February 4, 1940. His brother, H. Zorenko has been serving with the Russian Regiment, S.V.C. since July 1, 1937 and at present holds the rank of a Corporal.

Full Name in English:	Ivanoff Peter Trofimovitch
Full Name in Russian:	Иванов Петр Трофимович
Birth Year:	1908
Birth Place:	Ekaterinoslav, Russia

Private Address:	Av. Joffre., 785/1
Known to:	Mr. A.A. Dmitrief, 713 Av. Joffre.
Report Title:	V. Kovikin, P. Lejenin, N. Zorenko and P. Ivanoff, applicants for enlistment in the Russian Regiment, S.V.C.
Report date:	27/2/1940
Report number:	357

External archival references to this person: SH/500446

Peter Trofimovitch Ivanoff, Russian, was born on May 27, 1908 in Ekaterinoslav, Russia. According to his own statement, he escaped from the U.S.S.R. to Harbin in 1930 and in September of the same year arrived in Shanghai from that city.

Here, on two occasions he worked as a splicer with the Shanghai Telephone Company, first between January 1931 and July 1931 and again between August 1937 and September 1938, leaving that company on both occasions of his accord.

He also worked an as acrobat with various acrobatic companies, appearing in local theatres, cabarets etc.

This applicant made several attempts to travel around the world, in the company of another Russian, N. Kouznetzoff, first in 1931, again in 1934 and in 1935, all attempts proved to be a failure and after a short absence from Shanghai they returned on earth occasion. His last attempt to travel around the world was made in company of three Poles, namely V. Koudel, S. Franchik and I. Sikora and two Russians, N. Kouznetzoff and K. Depoutatoff when on October 16, 1938 they sailed from Shanghai on a small sailing boat called "Visla" heading for Philippine Islands.

Owing to bad weather they were forced to enter a Formosan port and were arrested by the Japanese authorities on a charge of espionage. They were detained for about 4 months, after which they were permitted to go, and eventually they reached Manila P.I. in that city the party broke up and the applicant returned to Shanghai in August 1939.

It is learned that he has already resigned from the Russian Regiment, S.V.C. with the intention of joining the French Foreign Legion.

Full Name in English:	Soorinoff Alexander Nikolaevitch
Full Name in Russian:	Суринов Александр Николаевич
Birth Year:	1919
Birth Place:	Kazan Province, Russia
Private Address:	Tongshan Rd., 599/70
Known to:	A. Ipatoff, 599/70 Tongshan Rd.

Report Title:	A.N. Soorinoff, V.N. Socoloff and M.A. Osipoff, applicants for enlistment in the Russian Regiment, S.V.C.
Report date:	27/2/1940
Report number:	358

External archival references to this person: SH/121103

Alexander Nikolaevitch Soorinoff, Russian, was born on August 20, 1919 in Kazan Province, Russia. According to his own statement, he escaped from the U.S.S.R. together with his mother in 1926 and subsequently resided in Harbin. He arrived in Shanghai from Harbin on February 10, 1940 and is not known locally.

Full Name in English:	Socoloff Vladimir Mihailovitch
Full Name in Russian:	Соколов Владимир Михайлович
Birth Year:	1922
Birth Place:	Shanghai
Private Address:	Route Vallon, 175
Known to:	Mr. A.A. Dmitrieff, 713 Av. Joffre.
Report Title:	A.N. Soorinoff, V.N. Socoloff and M.A. Osipoff, applicants for enlistment in the Russian Regiment, S.V.C.
Report date:	27/2/1940
Report number:	358

External archival references to this person: SH/120037

Vladimir Mihailovitch Socoloff, Russian, was born on February 22, 1922 in Shanghai. From 1935 to December 1939 he studied in the St. Joan D'Arc College. His father is employed as a stoker with the Shanghai Power Company.

Full Name in English:	Osipoff Mihail Artemievitch
Full Name in Russian:	Осипов Михаил Артемьевич
Birth Year:	1911
Birth Place:	Harbin, Manchuria
Private Address:	Route Vallon, 510
Known to:	V.A. Jilochkin, S.M.P, Reserve Unit.
Report Title:	A.N. Soorinoff, V.N. Socoloff and M.A. Osipoff, applicants for enlistment in the Russian Regiment, S.V.C.
Report date:	27/2/1940
Report number:	358

Mihail Artemievitch Osipoff, Russian, was born on August 12, 1911 in Harbin, Manchuria. For the past ten years he has been employed as an assistant shop manager with Vorontzoff Brothers, a well known firm in Harbin. On February 7, 1940 he arrived in Shanghai from Harbin and took up residence together with his God mother, Mrs. A.A. Krichevtzova at 510 Route Vallon.

Full Name in English:	Brozdounoff Vladimir Feodorovitch
Full Name in Russian:	Бруздунов Владимир Федорович
Birth Year:	1917
Birth Place:	Vladivostok, Maritime Province, Russia
Report Title:	V.F. Brozdounoff, applicant for enrolment in No.3 (Vol.) Company, S.V.C.
Report date:	December 21, 1939
Report number:	359

External archival references to this person: SH/20883

Vladimir Feodorovitch Brozdounoff, Russian, was born on July 28, 1917 in Vladivostok, Maritime Province, Russia. He is reported to have escaped from U.S.S.R. together with his parents in 1930 and to have subsequently resided at Harbin. In 1932 he arrived in Shanghai from Harbin. In 1933 he entered the Public & Thomas Hanoury School for Boys, graduating from same in December 1938. Since then he has been assisting his father, who conducts a Second Hand Store, 364 Rue Bourgeat.

Full Name in English:	Beloff Constantin Millianovitch
Full Name in Russian:	Белов Константин Миллианович
Birth Year:	1920
Birth Place:	Harbin, Manchuria
Private Address:	Riangse Rd, Hamilton House,
Known to:	I.T. Aksenoff, 58E, S.M.P, Central Pol, St.
Report Title:	C.E. Beloff, I.F. Golovenko, E.F. Malahovsky and V.N. Maltzeff, applicants for enlistment in the Russian Regiment, S.V.C
Report date:	December 13, 1939
Report number:	360

Constantin Millianovitch Beloff, Russian, was born on September 2, 1920 in Harbin, Manchuria. He arrived in Shanghai from Harbin on December 1, 1939 and took up residence at 501 Hamilton House, together with his brother-in-law, Mr. I.T. Aksenoff, Sergeant of the Shanghai Municipal Police.

Full Name in English:	Golovenko Ivan Fillipovitch
Full Name in Russian:	Головенко Иван Филипович
Birth Year:	1919
Birth Place:	Vladivostok, Maritime Province, Russia
Private Address:	Urga Rd, 41
Known to:	Mrs E.A. Kotchan, 627 Av. Foch
Report Title:	C.E. Beloff, I.F. Golovenko, E.F. Malahovsky and V.N. Maltzeff, applicants for enlistment in the Russian Regiment, S.V.C.
Report date:	December 13, 1939
Report number:	360

External archival references to this person: SH/40719

Ivan Fillipovitoh Golovenko, Russian, was born on January 19, 1919 in Vladivostok, Maritime Province, Russia. He is reported to have escaped from the U.S.S.R to Manchuria in 1925 and to have subsequently resided at Harbin. He arrived in Shanghai from Harbin on November 15, 1939. He has a Godmother in Shanghai, Mrs. E.A. Katchan, 627 Avenue Foch, whose son is employed with the Reserve Unit, Shanghai Municipal Police.

Full Name in English:	Malahovsky Mihail Fedotovitch
Full Name in Russian:	Малаховский Михаил Федотович
Birth Year:	1908
Birth Place:	Kiev, South Russia
Private Address:	Rue Bourgeat, 310
Known to:	Mrs M.E. Mason 141 Av. Haig
Report Title:	C.E. Beloff, I.F. Golovenco, E.F. Malahovsky and V.N. Maltzeff, applicants for enlistment in the Russian Regiment, S.V.C.
Report date:	December 13, 1939
Report number:	360

External archival references to this person: SH/70496

Mihail Fedotovitch Malahovsky, Russian, was born on November 21, 1908 in Kiev, South Russia. According to his own statement he escaped from the U.S.S.R. in 1931 and subsequently resided in Harbin, Manchuria. He arrived in Shanghai from Harbin on December 1, 1939.

Full Name in English:	Maltzeff Vitaly Nikolaevitch
Full Name in Russian:	Мальцев Виталий Николаевич
Birth Year:	1919

Birth Place:	Petropavlovsk, Akmolinsk Region, Siberia
Private Address:	Rue Bourgeat, 310
Known to:	Mrs P.A. Petelin, 118/25 Route Des Soers.
Report Title:	C.E. Beloff, I.F. Golovenco, E.F. Malahovsky and V.N. Maltzeff, applicants for enlistment in the Russian Regiment, S.V.C.
Report date:	December 13, 1939
Report number:	360
External archival references to this person: SH/70608	

Vitaly Nikolaevitch Maltzeff, Russian, was born on March 11 1919 in Petropavlovsk, Akmolinsk Region, Siberia. He is reported to have left Russia together with his parents in 1919 and to live subsequently resided in Harbin. He arrived in Shanghai from Harbin on December 1, 1939 and is not known locally.

Full Name in English:	Sokoloff Georgy Alexeyevich
Full Name in Russian:	Соколов Георгий Алексеевич
Birth Year:	1906
Birth Place:	Amur Province, Siberia
Private Address:	Avenue du Roi Albert, 427, Garage No 4.
Report Title:	G.A. Sokoloff, applicant for enrolment in No 3 (Vol) Company, "C" Battalion, S.V.C.
Report date:	March 9, 1940
Report number:	361

Georgy Alexeyevich Sokoloff, Russian, born on 13-5-1906 at Blagoveschensk, Amur Province, Siberia. According to his own statement, he left Russia for China 1921 together with parents and for the following 13 years resided in Harbin where he graduated from a Russian Middle School in 1925 and later worked as a mechanic. From 1934 to 1938 he resided at Tientsin. He holds a testimonial from Frazer Automotive and Industrial Engineers and Importers, to the effect that he was employed by thin firm for a year as a refrigerator and radio mechanic. On behalf of this company he visited Netherlands East Indies in 1938, after which he arrived in Shanghai.

Here he worked independently at his home as a mechanic until November, 1938 when he secured his present employment with Andersen Meyer Co., Ltd, at their Yangtszepoo works.

He is registered with the Russian Emigrants committee, Moulmein Road, and with the French Police (Register No. 9960 of 23-11-38).

At present he resides at 427 Avenue du Roi Albert, Garage No 4.

Full Name in English:	Shoolygin Leonid Maximilianovich
Full Name in Russian:	Шулигин Леонид Максимилианович
Birth Year:	1916
Birth Place:	Tientsin
Private Address:	Seymour Road, 159/4
Report Title:	L.M. Shoolygin, applicant for enrolment in the American Troop, S.V.C.
Report date:	March 9, 1940
Report number:	361

External archival references to this person: SH/111289

Leonid Maximilianovich Shoolyngin, Russian, born on 23-10-1916 at Tientsin. According to his own statement, he attended the Tientsin Grammar School from 1924 to 1929 and later studied in the German School in that city graduating in 1933.

He arrived in Shanghai from Tientsin in February, 1935 and until June of the same year attended the preparatory school of the Aurora University. From September, 1935 to June, 1937 he studied medicine in the same university and from 1937 to January, 1940 – in St. John's University.

He is registered with the Russian Emigrants Committee and at present resides at 159/4 Seymour Road.

He has a brother in Shanghai, N.M. Shoolyngin, Attorney and counselor-at-law. Their parents reside at Tientsin.

Full Name in English:	Mrochkovsky Ivan Konstantinovich
Full Name in Russian:	Мрочковский Иван Константинович
Birth Year:	1896
Birth Place:	Nijny Novgorod, Russia
Private Address:	Rue Lafayette, 599 – D.
Report Title:	I.K. Mrochkovsky, V.A. Willer, I.F. Lemann, V.N. Steher, F.I. Skopin and B.D. Dmitrieff – application for enrolment in the "C" (M. G.) Coy, S.V.C.
Report date:	March 8, 1940
Report number:	362

External archival references to this person: SH/80078

Ivan Konstantinovich Mrochkovsky, Russian, born 28-3-1896 at Nijny Novgorod, Russia. A graduate of the Military Cadets School in that city (1914) and of the Odessa School for Artillery Officers (1915) he served in the Russian army during the Great War from 1915 to 1918 and later fought against the Bolsheviks in the ranks of the "White" army in Siberia from 1918 to 1922. He arrived in china from Vladivostok in November, 1922. In 1925 he joined the Russian Detachment of Marshal Chang Chung Chang's army in Shantung (Armoured Trains Division). In 1929 he was taken prisoner by the Nationalist army and later was engaged to serve in that army as a instructor. According to his own statement he was connected as an advisor with the 2nd Department of the General Staff of the Chinese Army, Nanking, until the outbreak of the Sino-Japanese hostilities in 1937, after which he claims to have been working in Shanghai as a journalist. In Shanghai ha has been generally known as an agent of the Chinese military intelligence service.

At Present he resides at 599 – D. Rue Lafayette.

Full Name in English:	Willer Vladmir Andreyevich
Full Name in Russian:	Виллер Владимир Андреевич
Birth Year:	1892
Birth Place:	Moscow
Private Address:	Route de Grouchy, 20
Report Title:	I.K. Mrochkovsky, V.A. Willer, I.F. Lemann, V.N. Steher, F.I. Skopin and B.D. Dmitrieff – application for enrolment in the "C" (M. G.) Coy, S.V.C.
Report date:	March 8, 1940
Report number:	362
External archival references to this person:	SH/131879

Vladmir Andreyevich Willer, Russian, born on 18-9-1892 at Moscow. Former officer of the Russian army he saw active service during the Great War from 1914 to 1918 and later served in the ranks of the "White" army in Siberia from 1918-1922. He arrived in china from Vladivostok in November, 1922 together with the remainders of the "White" army. From 1924 to 1927 he served in the Russian Department of Marshal Chang Chung Chang's army in Shantung and from 1928 to the end of 1931 was employed with the Netherlands Harbour Works Co., Hulutao. Arriving in Shanghai some time in 1932 he is reported to have since been working for Mrochkovsky and at times also was engaged in commercial pursuits on a small scale.

From September, 1937 he has been a member of the French Police (Specials) in which he is now a sergeant (No. 195).

At present he resides at 20 Route de Grouchy.

Full Name in English:	Lemann Ivan Fedorovich
Full Name in Russian:	Леман Иван Федорович

Birth Year:	1896
Birth Place:	Kaluga province, Russia
Private Address:	Route Lorton, 66, House 22,
Report Title:	I.K. Mrochkovsky, V.A. Willer, I.F. Lemann, V.N. Steher, F.I. Skopin and B.D. Dmitrieff – application for enrolment in the "C" (M. G.) Coy, S.V.C.
Report date:	March 8, 1940
Report number:	362

External archival references to this person: SH/80296

Ivan Fedorovich Lemann, Russian, born 4-7-1896 in Kaluga province, Russia. According to his own statement, he graduated from the Military Cadets School at Voronej in 1914 and from the Cavalry Officers School at Elisevetgrad in 1916. He served in the ranks of the Russian army during the Great War and later in various "White" armies from 1917 to 1922. He arrived in china from Vladivostok in November, 1922. From 1925 to 1927 he served in the Russian Detachment of Marshal Chang Chung Chang's Army in shantung and from 1927 to 1932 was employed with the International Sleeping Car Co. in Manchuria. Arriving in Shanghai in 1932 he is reported to have since been employed as a ticket inspector at the Canidroms and from 1933 also with Russian newspaper "Slovo" (Advertising Department).

At present he resides at passage 66, Route Lorton, House 22, together with his wife and daughter.

Full Name in English:	Steher Vsevolod Nikolaevich
Full Name in Russian:	Стеер Всеволод Николаевич
Birth Year:	1910
Birth Place:	Petrograd, Russia
Private Address:	Route de Grouchy, Passage 51, House 23
Report Title:	I.K. Mrochkovsky, V.A. Willer, I.F. Lemann, V.N. Steher, F.I. Skopin and B.D. Dmitrieff – application for enrolment in the "C" (M. G.) Coy, S.V.C.
Report date:	March 8, 1940
Report number:	362

Vsevolod Nikolaevich Steher, Russian, born on 29-3-1910 at Petrograd, Russia. He is reported to have left Russia for China in 1920 and for the following 11 years to have resided at Harbin. Upon graduating from a Russian Middle School in that city in 1927 he was employed with the Harbin branch of the National City Bank from

1927 to 1931 first has a guard and later as a clerk. In September, 1931 he arrived in Shanghai. Here he was employed with Palmer & Turner (Property Officer) from 1931 to 1937, after which he has been connected with the Real Estate Agencies, 233 Ranking Road, being in charge of their Rent Department.

Mr. Steher was a member of the Light Battery, S.V.C., from 1932 to 1936 and served in the S.M. Police (Specials) from 1936 to 1939.

His present address is Passage 51, House 23, Route de Grouchy, where he resides together with his wife.

Full Name in English:	Skopin Fedor Ilyich
Full Name in Russian:	Скопин Федор Ильич
Birth Year:	1909
Birth Place:	Irkutsk, Siberia
Private Address:	Rue Ratard, 635/4
Report Title:	I.K. Mrochkovsky, V.A. Willer, I.F. Lemann, V.N. Steher, F.I. Skopin and B.D. Dmitrieff – application for enrolment in the "C" (M. G.) Coy, S.V.C.
Report date:	March 8, 1940
Report number:	362

Fedor Ilyich Skopin, Russian, born 20-4-1909 at Irkutsk, Siberia. According to his own statement, he left Russia for China in 1923 together with parents and subsequently resided at Harbin. In 1926 he graduated from a Russian Middle School and in 1928 – from a Chinese Language School in that city. From 1930 to 1932 he casually worked as a foreman and supervisor in Harbin and Mukden. He also claims to have been employed in 1933-1935 as an interpreter with the Foreign Section of the Police Department of Greater Harbin. In 1926, at the time when he studied in the Chinese Language School mentioned above, he became a naturalized Chinese citizen and at present holds Naturalization Certificate No.195 issued in December, 1937 by the Ministry of Interior.

Skopin arrived in Shanghai from Harbin in April, 1935. Here he was employed as a clerk with the International Savings Society from 20-8-35 to 31-10-36. Leaving this position on account of a reduction in staff and with a good testimonial, he has since been working as a secretary and office assistant with Mr. A.Ya. Slobodchikoff, Russian Lawyer, 101 Verdun Terrace.

He resides at 635/4 Rue Ratard.

Full Name in English:	Dmitrieff Boris Dmitrievich
Full Name in Russian:	Дмитриев Борис Дмитриевич
Birth Year:	1896
Birth Place:	Petrograd, Russia
Private Address:	Avenue Dubail, 256, House 4, Room 5
Report Title:	I.K. Mrochkovsky, V.A. Willer, I.F. Lemann, V.N. Steher, F.I. Skopin and B.D. Dmitrieff – application for enrolment in the "C" (M. G.) Coy, S.V.C.
Report date:	March 8, 1940
Report number:	362

Boris Dmitrievich Dmitrieff, Russian, born on 29-10-1896 at Petrograd, Russia. In 1914 he graduated from the Naval Officers' School at Petrograd, following which he served in the Russian Navy until 1917. During the civil war in Russia he served in the ranks of the "White" army in Siberia from 1918-1920 when he left for China. For the following 9 years he was employed with the Chinese Eastern Railway at Harbin, after which he proceeded to Shanghai. Here he was engaged in commercial pursuits on a small scale and also worked casually in various Russian newspapers etc. until 1938. Since that time he was employed in his professional capacity (marine officer) for various periods with Moller & Co. and Foreign Investments Co. From 24-2-40 he has been employed with Butterfield & Swire as second Officer on the s.s. "Tatung".

In 1927, in order to keep his employment with the C.E. Railway he became a naturalized Chinese citizen and at present holds naturalization Certificate No. 119722 issued in October, 1927 by the Ministry of Interior of the National Government.

At present he resides at 256 Avenue Dubail, House 4, Room 5.

Full Name in English:	Grigorieff Sergey Sergeyevich
Full Name in Russian:	Григорьев Сергей Сергеевич
Birth Year:	1899
Birth Place:	Simbirsk Province, Russia
Private Address:	Bubbling Well Road, 1025, House No 7, Rm 4.
Report Title:	S.S. Grigorieff and A.V. Kalkey, applicants for enrolment in "C" (M. G) Company, S.V.C.
Report date:	March 11, 1940
Report number:	363
External archival references to this person:	SH/41289

Sergey Sergeyevich Grigorieff, Russian, born 16-9-1899 in Simbirsk Province, Russia. In 1916 he graduated from a middle school in Kazan after which he attended the Petrograd Institute for Mining Engineers for two years. Following the outbreak of the civil war in Russia he served in the ranks of the "White" army in Siberia from 1913 to end of 1922. In 1923 he arrived in Shanghai from Vladivostok via Manchuria and shortly afterwards left for Hongkong where as a clerk of works with an American firm from 1924-1927, Returning to Shanghai he worked in the same capacity for various periods with different local firms including F. Berndt (1927-1928), E.J. Muller (1930-1932). From 1934 to 1935 he was employed in the Public Works Department, S.M.C, after which he was connected with the Allied Constructing Co. from 1936 to 1938. For the following two years he worked independently as a general constructor and on 1-1-1940 was re-engaged by E.J. Muller, Norwegian Civil Engineers, 2 Peking Road, his present employers.

In 1934-1938 he served in the 3rd (Vol.) coy, Russian Regiment, S.V.C.

He is one of the prominent members of the Russian Sporting Association "Sokol", 888 Weihaiwei Road.

At present he resides at 1025 Bubbling Well Road, House No 7, Room 4.

Full Name in English:	Kalkey Anatoly Vassilievich
Full Name in Russian:	Калькей Анатолий Васильевич
Birth Year:	1907
Birth Place:	Harbin
Private Address:	Weihaiwei Road, 888
Report Title:	S.S. Grigorieff and A.V. Kalkey, applicants for enrolment in "C" (M. G) Company, S.V.C.
Report date:	March 11, 1940
Report number:	363
External archival references to this person:	SH/51090

Anatoly Vassilievich Kalkey, Russian, born on 22-12-1907 at Harbin. According to his own statement, he escaped from the U.S.S.R to Manchuria in 1934 and later made his way to Shanghai arriving in this city some time towards the end of the same year.

Here he was employed as an office assistant with F. Rayden, 1040 N. Szecheun Road, for about six months in 1935 and from 1936 to 1938 worked as an assistant bookkeeper with Shriro Bros., 123 Canton Road. His next employment was with Vienna Shoe Store, 653 Avenue Joffre, in the capacity of a cashier and general assistant from December, 1938 to July, 1939. He holds good references from his employers.

From September, 1939 he has been studying in the Center Technique Superior (Electric Engineering Dept.), Route Remi. At present he resides at 888 Weihaiwei Road, the premises of the Russian Sporting Association Sokol, of which association he is a member.

Full Name in English:	Boutskoi Vladimir Alexeyevich
Full Name in Russian:	Бутской Владимир Алексеевич
Birth Year:	1891
Birth Place:	Orel province, Russia
Report Title:	V.A. Boutskoi, K.K. Akintievsky – applicants for enlistment in "C" (M.G.) Company, S.V.C.
Report date:	March 12, 1940
Report number:	364
External archival references to this person:	SH/21076

Vladimir Alexeyevich Boutskoi, Russian, born on 7-5-1891 in Orel province, Russia. In 1910 he graduated from the Naval Officers School at Petrograd and subsequently served in the Russian Navy until the outbreak of the revolution in Russia in 1917. During the civil war in Russia he served in the "White" army in South Russia following the defeat of which he made his way to Mesopotamia where he was interned for a period. In 1922 he arrived in Vladivostok. Towards the end of the same year he proceeded to Manila via Shanghai together with Admiral Stark's flotilla. Returning to Shanghai from Manila in July, 1923 he has since been residing in this city since 1924 he has been employed with Butterfield & Swire.

Full Name in English:	Akintievsky Konstantin Konstantinovich
Full Name in Russian:	Акинтиевский Константин Константинович
Birth Year:	1884
Birth Place:	Chernigov province, Russia
Private Address:	Rue Paul Henry, 27/2
Report Title:	V.A. Boutskoi, K.K. Akintievsky – applicants for enlistment in "C" (M.G.) Company, S.V.C.
Report date:	March 12, 1940
Report number:	364

Konstantin Konstantinovich Akintievsky, Russian born 14-10-1884 in Chernigov province, Russia. In 1905 he graduated from an Artillery Officers School at Petrograd and in 1913 from the Petrograd Military Academy. He saw active service in the Russian army during the Great War and also participated in the civil war Siberia until 1920, after which he resided at Harbin for the following 15 years. During this period he is known to have been associated with the monarchist movement amongst

Russian emigrants. In September, 1935 he arrived in Shanghai from Harbin. It is reported that he and several other prominent Russian emigrants were obliged to leave Manchuria because their political convictions were disapproved by the Japanese authorities.

In 1937 he was elected President of the Russian Ex-Office Club, 1250 Rue Lafayette, but had to resign from this post shortly afterwards owing to the unfavourable impression created by one of his lectures on the subject of the "Russian National Union", 720 Avenue Foch, and allegedly contained remarks derogatory to certain leaders of the "White" movement in Russia.

At present he is working in the "Shanghai Zaria" to which paper he contributes military reviews etc.

He resides at 27/2 Rue Paul Henry.

Full Name in English:	Paritsky Serafim Petrovitch
Full Name in Russian:	Парицкий Серафим Петрович
Birth Year:	1905
Birth Place:	Sedletz Province, Russia
Report Title:	S. Paritsky, V. Petroff, and K. Apanaskevitch, applicants for enrolment in "C" (M.G.) Company, S.V.C.
Report date:	March 19, 1940
Report number:	365

External archival references to this person: SH/90856

Serafim Petrovitch Paritsky, Russian, was born on August 26, 1905 in Sedletz Province, Russia. In 1922 he completed his course of study at the Habarovsk Cadet School at Vladivostok. Upon the defeat of "whites" in Vladivostok he left for China via Genzan, arriving in Shanghai in the autumn of 1923. In December of the same year he left for Harbin for the purpose of continuing his education. He remained in that town until 1927 when he joined the Russian Detachment under Marshal Chang Chung Chang and served with this unit until the end of 1928 when Chang's forces were disbanded. In November 1928 he returned to Shanghai and soon afterwards obtained employment with the Shanghai International Greyhounds Ltd. At the Stadium race track, where he worked until the beginning of 1931 when that company was closed down. During the same year he proceeded to Macao where he was engaged as an assistant dog trainer by the Hongkong and Macao Sports Club. He worked in that capacity until October 1936 when the company ceased functioning. Returning to Shanghai during the same month he obtained employment as a watchman with Anderson Mayer & co., Ltd., He left that place of employment of his own accord in March 1937. From 13-10-37 to 31-5-38 he served with the Auxiliary Detachment of the French Police. Between 1-11-38 and 1-1-40 he worked an as Anti-piracy Guard with the China Navigation Company.

On March 1, 1940 he secured his present position as a night watchman with the Metropole Hotel.

This applicant holds good references from his former employers.

Full Name in English:	Petroff Vladimir Vladimirovitch
Full Name in Russian:	Петров Владимир Владимирович
Birth Year:	1895
Birth Place:	Odessa, South Russia
Report Title:	S. Paritsky, V. Petroff, and K. Apanaskevitch, applicants for enrolment in "C" (M.G.) Company, S.V.C.
Report date:	March 19, 1940
Report number:	365

External archival references to this person: SH/91289

Vladimir Vladimirovitch Petroff, Russian, was born on January 12, 1895 in Odessa, South Russia. In 1911 he graduated from the Odessa Military Cadet School and in 1913 from the Irkutsk Military School for Officers. He saw the active service during the Great War in the ranks of 18th Siberian Fusiliers Regiment. During the civil war in Russia he served in the "white" army in Siberia, following the defeat of which he made his way to Harbin, arriving in that city in 1920.

He arrived in Shanghai in May 1933 and in July of the same year joined the Russian Regiment, S.V.C. in which he served until July 1934 when he resigned of his own accord. He later worked casually until September 1936 when he secured his present position with the Russian Daily Newspaper, "Slovo", and 238 Avenue du Roi Albert.

Full Name in English:	Apanaskevitch Konstantin Stepanovitch
Full Name in Russian:	Апанаскевич Константин Степанович
Birth Year:	1909
Birth Place:	Maritime Province, Russia
Report Title:	S. Paritsky, V. Petroff, and K. Apanaskevitch, applicants for enrolment in "C" (M.G.) Company, S.V.C.
Report date:	March 19, 1940
Report number:	365

External archival references to this person: SH/10697

Konstantin Stepanovitch Apanaskevitch, Russian, was born on July 14, 1909 in Maritime Province, Russia. In 1910 he proceeded to Harbin together with his parents, where his father was employed with the Chinese Eastern Railway. In 1932 he graduated from the Harbin Polytechnic Institute. He arrived in Shanghai towards the end of 1934 and in March 1935 joined the Russian Auxiliary Detachment of the French Police. On January 3, 1936 he was dismissed from the Detachment for breach of contract. Since then he has been working as a salesman for various companies dealing in motor cars.

On November 21, 1938 he appeared in the 1st Shanghai District Court on a charge of Driving a Car Without a permit, for which offence he was fined 10 dollars.

Full Name in English:	Raiko Nikolai Konatantinovitch
Full Name in Russian:	Райко Николай Константинович
Birth Year:	1916
Birth Place:	Grodnensk Province, Russia
Private Address:	Chaou Foong Rd, 241/28
Known to:	P.P. Iliyin 241/28 Chaou Foong Rd
Report Title:	N.K. Raiko, applicant for enlistment in the Russian Regiment, S.V.C.
Report date:	March 21, 1940
Report number:	366
External archival references to this person: SH/100685	

Nikolai Konstantinovitch Raiko, Russian, was born on September 22, 1916 in Grodnensk Province, Russia. He is reported to have left Russia together with his parents in 1918 and to have subsequently resided in Manchouli until 1929 after which he proceeded to Harbin. For the Past five years he has been employed as a Railway guard in Harbin. On March in the s.s. "Tsingtao Maru".

Full Name in English:	Nesteroff Vladimir Dmitrievitch
Full Name in Russian:	Нестеров Владимир Дмитриевич
Birth Year:	1913
Birth Place:	Vladivostok, Maritime Province, Russia.
Report Title:	V.D. Nesteroff, applicant for enrolment in Transport Company, S.V.C.
Report date:	March 26, 1940
Report number:	367
External archival references to this person: SH/81721	

Vladimir Dmitrievitch Nesteroff, Russian, was born on November 5, 1913 in Vladivostok, Maritime Province, Russia. In 1926 he arrived in Shanghai from Vladivostok together with his mother and in 1927 entered the Commercial School of the Russian Orthodox Confraternity, graduating from same in 1930. In the beginning of 1931 he obtained employment with the Shanghai Telephone Company. In November of the same year he left that company of his own accord.

In March 1932 he secured his present position with the China General Omnibus Company.

Full Name in English:	Golovan Evgeniy Mihailovitch
Full Name in Russian:	Голован Евгений Михайлович
Birth Year:	1914
Birth Place:	Harbin, Manchuria
Report Title:	E.M. Golovan, applicant for enrolment in No. 3 (vol) Company, S.V.C.
Report date:	March 28, 1940
Report number:	368
External archival references to this person:	SH/100685

Evgeniy Mihailovitch Golovan, Russian, was born on March 15, 1914 in Harbin, Manchuria. In 1933 he graduated from a local high school and for the following year studied in the Harbin Polytechnic Institute. He arrived in Shanghai from Harbin in 1935 and took up residence together with his brother-in-law, Mr. D.N. Smirnoff, an employee of the Chinese Maritime Customs. Here he failed to obtain any fixed employment until January 4, 1940 when he was engaged as an Antipiracy guard with the China Navigation Company. His half-brother, Mr. N.I. Semenoff is also employed with the Chinese Maritime Customs, and residence at Apt. 371 King's Albert Apartments.

Full Name in English:	Mennig Georgy Genrihovitch
Full Name in Russian:	Меннинг Георгий Генрихович
Birth Year:	1917
Birth Place:	Harbin, Manchuria
Private Address:	Rue Poentice, 166
Known to:	A.P. Dobrovolsky, 118 Route Des Soeurs
Report Title:	G. Mennig, E.I. Riashnitzeff and A.S. Sorokin, applicants for enlistment in the Russian Regiment, S.V.C.
Report date:	April 2, 1940
Report number:	369

External archival references to this person: SH/71326

Georgy Genrihovitch Mennig, Russian, was born on July 4, 1917 in Harbin, Manchuria. In 1925 he left Harbin for Mukden together with his parents and resided in this city until 1930 when he returned to Harbin. His father has been employed with the Chinese Eastern Railway from 1905 to1930. On March 10, 1940 the applicants arrived in Shanghai from Harbin. Being a new arrival here he is not known locally.

Full Name in English:	Riashnitzeff Evgeny Ivanovitch
Full Name in Russian:	Ряшницев Евгений Иванович
Birth Year:	1922
Birth Place:	Vladivostok, Maritime Province, Russia
Private Address:	Ward Rd, 397
Report Title:	G. Mennig, E.I. Riashnitzeff and A.S. Sorokin, applicants for enlistment in the Russian Regiment, S.V.C.
Report date:	April 2, 1940
Report number:	369

External archival references to this person: SH/100999

Evgeny Ivanovitch Riashnitzeff, Russian, was born on June 23, 1922 in Vladivostok, Maritime Province, Russia. According to his own statement he left Russia together with his parents in 1923 and subsequently resided at various places in Manchuria. On March 10, 1940 he arrived in Shanghai from Harbin and is not known in the local Russian community.

Full Name in English:	Sorokin Alexander Sergeyevitch
Full Name in Russian:	Сорокин Александр Сергеевич
Birth Year:	1912
Birth Place:	Harbin, Manchuria
Private Address:	Alcock Rd, 144
Known to:	Mr. I.A. Korabloff, 413 Ningpo Rd
Report Title:	G. Mennig, E.I. Riashnitzeff and A.S. Sorokin, applicants for enlistment in the Russian Regiment, S.V.C.
Report date:	April 2, 1940
Report number:	369

External archival references to this person: SH/120353

Alexander Sergeyevitch Sorokin, Russian, was born on August 24, 1912 in Harbin, Manchuria. In 1928 he proceeded to Chefoo, where he entered the Yih Wen Commercial College, graduating from same in 1932. In October, In October 1933 he arrived in Shanghai from Chefoo and on February 1, 1934 joined the Russian Regiment, S.V.C. He served in the Regiment until May 31, 1939 when he resigned of his own accord. In September of the same year he found employment as a kennel man with the Canidrome, however on November 6, 1939 he was dismissed for drunkenness.

On June 17, 1939 he was fined $5.00 by the 1st Shanghai Special District Court on a charge of Drunk and Disorderly.

Full Name in English:	Dunaeff Vladimir Nikolaevich
Full Name in Russian:	Дунаев Владимир Николаевич
Birth Year:	1897
Birth Place:	Warsaw
Private Address:	Avenue du Roi Albert, 569/1
Report Title:	V.N. Dunaeff, V.V. Orloff, O.A. Kosloff and A.C. Ignatieff - applicants for visas to Hongkong
Report date:	April 4, 1940
Report number:	370
External archival references to this person:	SH/30538

Vladimir Nikolaevich Dunaeff, Russian, born on January 9, 1897 at Warsaw. According to his own statement, he left the U.S.S.R. for Manchuria early in 1931 and in March of the same year arrived in Shanghai. From 10-8-31 to 1-9-33 he was employed with Reyer Construction Corporation, 24 The Bund, as a watchman and assistant supervisor. For the following five years he casually worked with various local firms including the Radio Doctor Service, Ellers Construction Co and Graphic Printing Establishment. From 6-8-38 has been employed as a watchman with Shanghai Inland Water Navigation Co, 434 N.Soochow Road. Since 16-7-34 he was been on the S.M.F. list of approved candidates for the position of a police watchman and / or bodyguard.

At present he resided at 569/1 Avenue du Roi Albert.

Full Name in English:	Orloff Victor Vassilievich
Full Name in Russian:	Орлов Виктор Васильевич
Birth Year:	1913
Birth Place:	Pskov Province, Russia
Private Address:	Avenue du Roi Albert, 347, Apt.2.
Report Title:	V.N. Dunaeff, V.V. Orloff, O.A. Kosloff and A.C. Ignatieff - applicants for visas to Hongkong

Report date: April 4, 1940
Report number: 370
External archival references to this person: SH/90310

Victor Vassilievich Orloff, Russian, born on 14-9-1913 in Pskov Province, Russia. He is reported to have left Russia for Manchuria in 1919 and for the following 13 years to have resided at Harbin. In November, 1933 he arrived in Shanghai from Dairen. Here he is known to have worked as a musician (violinist) in various local cabarets and night clubs. On several occasions he was absent from Shanghai to Tsingtao, Chefoo etc. to work there in the same capacity.

His last known address in Shanghai is 347 Avenue du Roi Albert, Apt. 2.

Full Name in English: Kosloff Onufry Andrianovich
Full Name in Russian: Козлов Онуфрий Андрианович
Birth Year: 1913
Birth Place: Harbin
Private Address: Tracey Terrace, 6
Report Title: V.N.N. Dunaeff, V.V. Orloff, O.A. Kosloff and A.C. Ignatieff - applicants for visas to Hongkong
Report date: April 4, 1940
Report number: 370
External archival references to this person: SH/61130

Onufry Andrianovich Kosloff, Russian, born on 12-6-1913 at Harbin. According to his own statement, he attended a school at Harbin until 1930 following which he worked as a typesetter in various printing works and newspapers in that city for several years. In April, 1932 he arrived in Shanghai from Harbin. Here he worked as a musician (drummer and guitar player) in various local cabarets. On 23-3-40 he returned in Shanghai from Tsingtao where he had been employed in his professional capacity for about ten months.

At present he resided at 6 Tracey Terrace together with his wife, Mrs. Nadejda Nikolaevna Kosloff nee Andreyevich-Ivanoff, native of Harbin.

Full Name in English: Ignatieff Arcady Constantinovich
Full Name in Russian: Игнатьев Аркадий Константинович
Birth Year: 1913
Birth Place: Vladivostok
Private Address: Rue Lafayette, 1248, Apt. 6
Report Title: V.N.N. Dunaeff, V.V. Orloff, O.A. Kosloff and A.C. Ignatieff - applicants for visas to Hongkong

Report date: April 4, 1940
Report number: 370
External archival references to this person: SH/50093

Arcady Constantinovich Ignatieff, Russian, born on 14-8-1913 at Vladivostok. He is reported to have left the U.S.S.R. for Manchuria in 1926 and for the following 8 year to have resided at Harbin. In 1932 he graduated from the Y.M.C.A. School in that city. During the same year he renounced his Soviet citizenship and took out emigrant papers. In October, 1934 he arrived in Shanghai from Harbin. Here he is known to have been working as a musician (pianist) in various local cabarets.

At present he resides at 1248 Rue Lafayette, Apt. 6 together with his wife Mrs. Tamara Andreyevna Ignatieff nee Mastaroff, 25, native of Vladivostok.

With the exception of Mrs. N.N. Kosloff who arrived in Shanghai only about two weeks ago, all applicants are registered with the Russian Emigrants Committee Moulmein Road.

Full Name in English:	Kiviking Pavel Mihailovitch
Full Name in Russian:	Кивикинг Павел Михайлович
Birth Year:	1900
Birth Place:	Viljand, Russia (now Estonia)
Report Title:	P.N. Kiviking, applicant for enrolment in No.3 (vol) Company, S.V.C.
Report date:	April 4, 1940
Report number:	371

Pavel Mihailovitch Kiviking, Estonian, was born on June 20, 1900 in Viljand, Russia (now Estonia). Since his boyhood he resided in Vladivostok, until 1926 after which he proceeded to Harbin. In November 1933 he arrived in Shanghai from Harbin.

Here he worked casually as a chauffeur until May 1934 when he secured his presents position with Messrs. Lang & Semin Sausage Factory, 28 Route Dollfus.

This applicant is registered with the local Estonian Consulate and holds passport No. 179 issued on Februrary 1, 1939.

Full Name in English:	Greenberg Meyer
Full Name in Russian:	Гринберг Мейер
Birth Year:	1915
Birth Place:	Shanghai
Report Title:	M. Greenberg, applicant for enrolment in American Troop, S.V.C.

Report date: April 6, 1940
Report number: 372

Meyer Greenberg, Russian Jew, was born on November 10, 1915, at Shanghai. His father, Mr. B. Greenberg, owns a fur store at 978 – 980 Bubbling Well Road. Meyer Greenberg first came to the notice of the Municipal police in 1930 while he was a schoolboy attending the public and Thomas Hanbury School.

During July, 1930, complaints were made to the Tsingtao Authorities concerning thefts of money and jewellery from a bathing hut on the beach which Greenberg was sharing and he was strongly suspected of the thefts. On returning to Shanghai from Tsingtao on July 28, 1930. Information was laid with the Municipal police that Greenberg was wearing the wrist watch which was stolen in Tsingtao. Greenberg was not charged on this occasion and the watch was returned to its owner, but the money totaling 330.00 and the brooch were not recovered.

Meyer Greenberg again came to the notice of the Municipal police in November, 1930 when he was arrested with two young British subjects in connection with the forging and uttering of a cheque for $150.00. All three youths were charged and Greenberg was subsequently arraigned for trial before the 1st Shanghai special District Court and sentenced on November 27, 1930 to three month's imprisonment suspended for three years.

Enquiries at this time also revealed that Greenberg had acquired the habit of hiring public motor cars and signing false names to the motor car chits.

Greenberg is reported to have worked from February, 1932 to April, 1933 with the firm of Heath Importers and Exporters, Tea Merchants, 2 Peking Road. In July 1933 he obtained a position with Reiss Massey and Co. Ltd., Importers and Exporters, 15 Museum Road and was sent to Hongkong in order to learn business routine in connection with the sale of typewriters.

In Hongkong, it came to the notice of his employers that he had a record and he was later dismissed but before leaving the company in Hongkong, a typewriter was found to be missing and Greenberg was suspected of the theft, but no action was taken in the matter.

On August 10, 1933 he again visited Hongkong and after a short stay in that city returned to Shanghai in September of the same year.

In the beginning of 1934, he secured his present position as a general office assistant with S.E. Levy & Company, 113 Kiukiang Road. This applicant is not registered with Russian Emigrants' Committee or any other Russian Public organization.

Full Name in English:	Kosovsky Solomon Iosifovitch
Full Name in Russian:	Косовский Соломон Иосифович
Birth Year:	1901
Birth Place:	Harbin
Report Title:	S.I. Kosovsky, applicant for enrolment in Transport Company, S.V.C.
Report date:	April 9, 1940
Report number:	373

Solomon Iosifovitch Kosovsky, Russian Jew, Soviet citizen, was born on January 29, 1901 in Harbin. Upon graduating from a Harbin High School in 1921 he proceeded to Philadelphia, U.S.A. where he entered the University of Pennsylvania. He graduated from this university in 1925 and returned to Harbin. In Harbin he was engaged in commercial activities, assisting his father who was a big business man in that town.

The applicant arrived in Shanghai from Harbin in December, 1935. In June, 1936 he obtained employment with the China Finance Corporation and at present is employed by the same company as a factory manager of the Crown Aerated Water Company, 413/50 Ningkuo Road.

Applicant's father who is in Shanghai at present owns a men's tailoring shop at 868 Avenue Joffre.

This applicant is registered with the local Soviet Consulate and holds passport No. 011253 issued on December 25, 1935.

Full Name in English:	Yashanoff Boris Alexeyevitch
Full Name in Russian:	Яшанов Борис Алексеевич
Birth Year:	1907
Birth Place:	Harbin, Manchuria
Report Title:	B.A. Yashanoff, applicant for enrolment in American Troop, S.V.C
Report date:	April 9, 1940
Report number:	373
External archival references to this person:	SH/132151

Boris Alexeyevitch Yashanoff, Russian, was born on July 29, 1907 in Harbin, Manchuria. In 1919 he left Harbin for Tientsin, together with his parents and resided in that city until 1927. In 1927 he proceeded to Vancouver, B.C. Canada, where he entered the University of British Columbia. He studied in this university until 1928 after which he proceeded to Seattle, U.S.A. Where in 1931 he graduated from the Seattle University.

He arrived in Shanghai from America in 1932 and early in 1933 secured a position with E.W. Langdon & Company, Import and Export, 417 Avenue Foch. He left that company of his own accord in 1935 in order to take up a position with the National Carbon Company Fed. Inc. U.S.A. in which company he is still employed in the capacity of a purchasing agent.

Full Name in English:	Vassilieff Leonid Iosifovitch
Full Name in Russian:	Васильев Леонид Иосифович
Birth Year:	1920
Birth Place:	Blagoveschensk, Amur Region, Russia
Private Address:	Route Lorton, 66/27
Known to:	Mr. V.D. Narbut, 859 Wei-Hai-Wei Rd.
Report Title:	L.l. Vassilieff, A.P. Romanoff and I.G. Lambiris, applicants for enlistment in the Russian Regiment, S.V.C.
Report date:	April 9, 1940
Report number:	374

External archival references to this person: SH/130790

Leonid Iosifovitch Vassilieff, Russian, was born on May 28, 1920 in Blagoveschensk, Amur Region, Russia. He arrived in shanghai from Vladivostok in 1922 together with his parents. Until 1937 he studied in the Commercial School of the Russian Orthodox Confraternity and later in the First Russian school (now A.S. Poushkin Memorial school), graduating from same in June 1939.

His sister is married to Captain Poronik of the Russian Regiment, S.V.C.

Full Name in English:	Romanoff Alexander Feodorovitch
Full Name in Russian:	Романов Александр Федорович
Birth Year:	1913
Birth Place:	Chita, Siberia
Private Address:	Kung Pine Rd., 220/7
Known to:	Mr. M.F. Polejak, 1161 Bubbling Well Rd.
Report Title:	L.l. Vassilieff, A.P. Romanoff and I.G. Lambiris, applicants for enlistment in the Russian Regiment, S.V.C.
Report date:	April 9, 1940
Report number:	374

External archival references to this person: SH/132

Alexander Feodorovitch Romanoff, Russian, was born on January 23, in Chita, Siberia. He is reported to have left Russia together with his parents in 1919 and to have subsequently resided in Manchouli and later in Harbin. From 1933 to December 1938 he has been employed with the Harbin Railway Police and later worked as a chauffeur of a hire car. He arrived in Shanghai from Harbin on February 21, 1940 and is not known locally.

Full Name in English:	Lambiris Ioann Georgievitch
Full Name in Russian:	Ламбирис Иван Георгиевич
Birth Year:	1920
Birth Place:	Mukden
Private Address:	Av Joffre, 1021.200TH
Known to:	Mr. G.V. Radetzky Mikulitch,635/5 rue Ratard
Report Title:	L.l. Vassilieff, A.P. Romanoff and I.G. Lambiris, applicants for enlistment in the Russian Regiment, S.V.C.
Report date:	April 9, 1940
Report number:	374

External archival references to this person: SH/70211

Ioann Georgievitch Lambiris, Russian, was born on October 13, 1920 in Mukden. In 1930 he proceeded to Tientsin together with his mother. Until 1938 he studied at the St.Loui's College. Until his departure to shanghai he has been employed as a passport Inspector with the Peking- Mukden Railway.

He arrived in shanghai from Tientsin on March 21, 1940.

Being a new arrival here he is not known in the local Russian Community.

Full Name in English:	Bogunsky Sviatoslav Nikolaevitch
Full Name in Russian:	Богунский Святослав Николаевич
Birth Year:	1922
Birth Place:	Kiev Province, Russia
Private Address:	Av. Joffre, 613/29
Known to:	Mr. N.I. Goloschapoff, Reserve Unit, S.M.P
Report Title:	S.N. Bogunsky and L.S. Zivinsky, applicants for enlistment in the Russian Regiment, S.V.C.
Report date:	April 10, 1940
Report number:	375

External archival references to this person: SH/20237

Sviatoslav Nikolaevitch Bogunsky, Russian was born on January 1, 1922 in Kiev Province, Russia. According to his own statement he escaped from the U.S.S.R. together with his mother in 1927 and subsequently resided in Harbin. In 1933 he arrived in Shanghai from Harbin and in 1934 entered the St. Francis Xavier's College in which he studied until June, 1939.

His mother is employed as a housekeeper with Mr. Valejanin, Grosvenor House, Route Cardinal Mercier.

Full Name in English:	Zivinsky Leonid Sergevevitch
Full Name in Russian:	Зивинский Леонид Сергеевич
Birth Year:	1922
Birth Place:	Pogranichnaya Station, Manchuria
Private Address:	Verdun Terrace Av. Du Roi Albert, 88
Known to:	Mrs V.N. Depreradovich, 88 Verdun Terrace. Av. Du Roi Albert.
Report Title:	S.N. Bogunsky and L.S. Zivinsky, applicants for enlistment in the Russian Regiment, S.V.C.
Report date:	April 10, 1940
Report number:	375

Leonid Sergevevitch Zivinsky, Russian was born on February 6, 1922 in Pogranichnaya Station, Manchuria. He later resided at various stations along the Chinese Eastern Railway, as his father been employed with that concern until 1935.

On March 28, 1940 he arrived in Shanghai from Harbin and is not known in the local Russian community.

Full Name in English:	Mosichkin Nikolai Stepanovitch
Full Name in Russian:	Мосичкин Николай Степанович
Birth Year:	1909
Birth Place:	Maritime Province, Russia
Private Address:	Av. Joffre, 1019
Report Title:	N.S. Mosichkin, applicant for enrolment in No.3 (Vol) Company, S.V.C.
Report date:	April 12th 1940
Report number:	376
External archival references to this person:	SH/72191

Nikolai Stepanovitch Mosichkin, Russian, was born on July 20, 1909 in Maritime Province, Russia. He is reported to have escaped from the U.S.S.R. to Manchuria in 1930 and to have subsequently resided in Harbin. A chauffeur mechanic by occupation, he worked in his professional capacity in various garages in Harbin, On December 1, 1939 he arrived in Shanghai from Harbin and took up residence at 1019 Avenue Joffre, together with his brother, an employee of Lang & Semin, Sauaage Factory, 28 Route Dollfus.

On December 11, 1939 he was engaged as a mechanic by Frazer Motors, 36 Great Western Road.

Full Name in English:	Kiriloff Lev Sergeyevitch
Full Name in Russian:	Кирилов Лев Сергеевич
Birth Year:	1915
Birth Place:	Vladivostok, Maritime Province, Russia
Report Title:	L.S. Kiriloff-applicant for enrolment in American Machine Gun Company, S.V.C.
Report date:	April 22, 1940
Report number:	377
External archival references to this person:	SH/51852

Lev Sergeyevitch Kiriloff, Russian, was born on July 26, 1915 in Vladivostok, Maritime Province, Russia. In 1985 he arrived in Shanghai from Vladivostok. In 1927 he left Shanghai for Vancouver, B.C. Canada together with his parents and returned here in October 1933. Here for about one year he attended the Public and Thomas Hanbury School for Boys. From 1935 to August 1937 he worked as a Commercial Artist at the Studio Department of Millington Ltd., 668 Szechuen Road. Later he assisted his father in conducting the latter's business, Pacific Stamp Company, 973 Bubbling Well Road.

In November 1939 he secured his present employment as an office assistant and draughtsman with the United Mechanical Industries, 138 Kiangse Road.

Full Name in English:	Kischkin Lev
Full Name in Russian:	Кишкин Лев
Birth Year:	1920
Birth Place:	Vladivostok, Maritime Province, Russia
Report Title:	L. Kischkin-applicant for enrolment in American Machine Gun Company, S.V.C.
Report date:	April 22 1940
Report number:	377

Lev Kischkin, Russian, was born on September 24, 1920 in Vladivostok, Maritime Province, Russia. According to his own statement, he left Vladivostok together with his mother in 1924 and subsequently resided in Harbin. In 1934 he arrived in Shanghai from Harbin. During the same year he entered the Public and Thomas Hanbury School in which he studied up to 1937. In December 1937 he was engaged as an office assistant by Glatne & Witt, Importers and Exporters, 410 Szechuen Road, where he is still employed.

Full Name in English:	Caro Evgeny Nikolaevitch
Full Name in Russian:	Каро Евгений Николаевич
Birth Year:	1917
Birth Place:	China, Siberia
Report Title:	E.N. Caro, applicant for enrolment in American Machine Gun Company, S.V.C.
Report date:	April 22, 1940
Report number:	377

External archival references to this person: SH/51411

Evgeny Nikolaevitch Caro, Russian, was born on May 28, 1917 at China, Siberia. He is reported to have left the U.S.S.R. together with his mother in 1926 and subsequently resided in Tientsin. He arrived in Shanghai from that city in 1930 and during the same year entered the Junior Public School in which he studied up to 1933 From 1933 to 1935 he studied in the Public and Thomas Hanbury School for Boys.

In May, 1936 he was engaged by Andersen, Meyer & Company, Ltd. As an apprentice and at present holds the position of a supervisor in their Motor and Appliance Shop.

Full Name in English:	Robin (Rabinovich) Edward Josefovich
Full Name in Russian:	Робин (Рабинович) Эдуард Иосифович
Birth Year:	1919
Birth Place:	Harbin
Report Title:	E. Robin, alias Rabinovich-applicant for enrolment in American Machine Gun Company, S.V.C.
Report date:	April 22, 1940
Report number:	377

External archival references to this person: SH/100593

Edward Josefovich Robin, alias Rabinovich, Russian of Jewish origin, was born on March 25th, 1919 in Harbin. In 1932 he went to Tientsin where he joined the Grammar School from which he graduated in 1936. He then obtained a position of a clerk at A.S. Gold Furriers Company with which firm he remained until August, 1938 when he left for Shanghai. Shortly afterwards he joined the staff of the Auto Palace Company, Ltd., as a salesman and is still with this firm.

He is not registered with the Russian Emigrants, Committee or any other Russian Public organization.

Full Name in English:	Petrischeff Efftropy Efftropievitch
Full Name in Russian:	Петрищев Ефтропий Ефтропиевич
Birth Year:	1916
Birth Place:	Habarovsk, Siberia
Private Address:	Bubbling Well Road, 1025/37
Report Title:	E. Petrischeff, applicant for enrolment in American Machine Gun Company, S.V.C
Report date:	April 22, 1940
Report number:	377
External archival references to this person:	SH/91259

Efftropy Efftropievitch Petrischeff, Russian, was born on July 10, 1916 in Habarovsk, Siberia. According to his own statement, he left Russian for China together with his parents during the same year and subsequently resided in Harbin. In August 1925 he arrived in Shanghai from Harbin together with his mother. Here he attended the Public and Thomas Hanbury School for Boys, graduating from same in 1935. Later he worked for a period of about 8 months with the Soviet newspaper China Herald until its closure in 1936.

Since then he failed to obtain any fixed employment and at present resided together with his mother, Mrs. Petrooshevskaya, a boarding house keeper at 1025/37 Bubbling Well Road.

Full Name in English:	Sdobnikoff Ury Andreyevitch
Full Name in Russian:	Сдобников Юрий Андреевич
Birth Year:	1915
Birth Place:	Barnaul, Siberia
Report Title:	U.A. Sdobnikoff-applicant for enrolment in American Machine Gun Company, S.V.C.
Report date:	April 22, 1940
Report number:	377
External archival references to this person:	SH/110169

Ury Andreyevitch Sdobnikoff, Russian, was born on July 21, 1915 at Barnaul, Siberia. According to his own statement, he left Russia for China in 1925 together with his mother and after a short stay in Harbin proceeded to Tientsin where he resided for the following 14 years. In 1934 he graduated from the St. Louis college in that city, after which he is reported to have been employed as an office assistant with the Oriental Trading & Engineering Corporation from January 1935 to November 1937, when the firm was closed. His next employment was with the Concordia, Societe Vehicule, as an accountant (March-November, 1938). Leaving this company of his own accord he joined the American Textile Co., where he worked in the same capacity from November 1938 to May 1939. From May 1939 to August 1939 he worked in the Transport Department of Siemassen & Company, after which he left for Shanghai, arriving in this city on September 3, 1939.

While in the employ of the Oriental Trading & Engineering Company, he was attached to the Shanghai Branch of this firm for about one year, 1236-1937.

On September 25, 1939 he secured his present position with the Accountant Department of Moller Ltd., 30 Foochow Road.

Full Name in English:	Potemkin-Liapoonoff Evgeny Mihailovitch
Full Name in Russian:	Потемкин-Ляпунов Евгений Михайлович
Birth Year:	1920
Birth Place:	Harbin Manchuria
Private Address:	Rue Lafayette, 808 C
Known to:	MR. N.P. Hoodiakoff, 808C. Rue Lafayette
Report Title:	E.M. Potemkin-Liapoonoff and V.E. Starikoff, applicants for enlistment in the Russian Regimental, S.V.C.
Report date:	May 9, 1940
Report number:	378

Evgeny Mihailovitch Potemkin-Liapoonoff, Russian, was born on December 26, 1920 in Harbin Manchuria. After graduating from a Harbin High school in 1937 he worked as a shop assistant at various stores in Harbin. On April 11, 1940 he arrived in Shanghai from Harbin and is not known in the local Russian Community.

Full Name in English:	Starikoff Vassily Eflmovitch
Full Name in Russian:	Стариков Василий Ефимович
Birth Year:	1920
Birth Place:	Manchouli, Manchuria
Private Address:	Rue Lafayette, 808 C
Known to:	Mr. C.S. Malih 66 Route De Sieyes

Report Title:	E.M. Potemkin-Liapoonoff and V.E. Starikoff, applicants for enlistment in the Russian Regimental, S.V.C.
Report date:	May 9, 1940
Report number:	378
External archival references to this person:	SH/120583

Vassily Eflmovitch Starikoff, Russian, was born on April 14, 1920 in Manchouli, Manchuria. According to his own statement, he resided at various stations along the Chinese Eastern Railway and for the past eight years has been resided in Harbin, where his father, an ex-employee of the Chinese Eastern Railway, owns a small dairy farm.

On April 11, 1940 he arrived in Shanghai from Harbin together with the first applicant and is also not a locally.

Full Name in English:	Brayner Evgeny Ivanovitch
Full Name in Russian:	Брайнер Евгений Иванович
Birth Year:	1914
Birth Place:	Petrograd, Russia
Report Title:	E.I. Brayner, applicants for enrolment in American Company, S.V.C.
Report date:	May 15, 1940
Report number:	379
External archival references to this person:	SH/20783 Брейнер

Evgeny Ivenevitch Brayner, Russian, was born on January 27, 1914 in Petrograd, Russia. He is reported to have left Russia together with his parents in 1920 and to have subsequently resided in Harbin. On July 9, 1931 he arrived in Shanghai from Harbin and has since been residing in this city. While here, he has been employed at the following places:- 1932 to 1933 as a mechanic with the Bills Motors, Fed. Inc. U.S.A.; 1933-34 as an electrician with Messrs Arc Welders, 781 Wuting Road; 1935-September 1936 as a mechanic and electrician with Moller's Ltd.; 1936-December 1938, as a shop manager with Beta Shoe Company. In January 1939 he obtained his present position as a masseur with Kortus Orthopedic Institute, 679 Szechuen Road. The applicant is in possession of good references from his former employers.

Full Name in English:	Koptilin Alexander Alexandrovitch
Full Name in Russian:	Коптилин Александр Александрович
Birth Year:	1916

Birth Place:	Habarovsk, Maritime Province, Russia.
Report Title:	A.A. Koptilin, applicant for enrolment in American Company, S.V.C.
Report date:	May 16, 1940
Report number:	379

External archival references to this person: SH/60824

Alexander Alexandrovitch Koptilin, Russian, was born on September 9, 1916 in Habarovsk, Maritime Province, Russia. In 1924 he arrived in Shanghai from Vladivostok together with his parents. In 1925 he entered the First Russian High School (now A.S. Poushkin Memorial School) and graduated from same in 1934. For the following two years he studied at the Centre Technique Superiere. In June, 1936 he secured his present position with the Moister Testing Department of Yee Tsoong Tobacco Company, Ltd., 733 Ward Road.

Applicant's mother, Mrs. N. Borisoff, was charged with Larceny at the 1st Shanghai Special District Court on September 7, 1937, and was sentenced to 3 months imprisonment, suspended for two years.

Full Name in English:	Ginter Evgeny Segeyevitch
Full Name in Russian:	Гинтер Евгений Сергеевич
Birth Year:	1921
Birth Place:	Vladivostok, Maritime Province, Russia
Private Address:	Route De Sieyes, 79 appt2.
Known to:	Mr. V.R. Ginter 1904 Apt S Av. Joffre
Report Title:	B.S. Ginter, applicant for enlistment in the Russian Regiment, S.V.C.
Report date:	May 23, 1940
Report number:	380

External archival references to this person: SH/40368

Evgeny Sergeyevitch Ginter, Russian, was born on March 8, 1921 in Vladivostok, Maritime Province, Russia. In 1923 he arrived in Shanghai from Vladivostok together with his mother. From 1929 to 1935 he attended the St. Joan of Arc's College, 18 Route Doumer. From 1936 to 1938 (invisible) studied at the Public and Thomas Hanbury School for Boys.

He later worked casually until January 3, 1940 when he joined the Russian Auxiliary Detachment of the French Police. On April 18, 1940 he was permitted to resign owing to his poor health.

Full Name in English:	Bousigin Mihail Iosifovitch
Full Name in Russian:	Бусыгин Михаил Иосифович
Birth Year:	1921
Birth Place:	Harbin, Manchuria
Private Address:	Chusan Road, 69
Report Title:	M.I. Bousigin and A.T. Melnik, applicants for enlistment in the Russian Regiment, S.V.C.
Report date:	June 7, 1940
Report number:	381
External archival references to this person: SH/21049	

Mihail Iosifovitch Bousigin, Russian, was born on October 14, 1921, in Harbin, Manchuria. Upon graduation from a Harbin high school in December, 1940, he worked as a chauffeur until May, 1940 after which he proceeded to Shanghai arriving in this port on May 20, 1940.

Being a new arrival here he is not known in the local Russian community.

Full Name in English:	Melnik Alexey Trofimovitch
Full Name in Russian:	Мельник Алексей Трофимович
Birth Year:	1920
Private Address:	Av. Joffre, 582/5
Known to:	E.T. Tomashevsky 582/5 Av. Joffer
Report Title:	M.I. Bousigin and A.T. Melnik, applicants for enlistment in the Russian Regiment, S.V.C.
Report date:	June 7, 1940
Report number:	381
External archival references to this person: SH/71153	

Alexey Trofimovitch Melnik, Russian, was born on October 5, 1940 [*as in original-KC*], in Harbin, Manchuria. He arrived in Shanghai from Harbin May 24, 1940. His sister is married to Private D. Kouznetzoff of the Russian Regiment, S.V.C.

Full Name in English:	Eliseyeff Mihail Nikolaevitch
Full Name in Russian:	Елисеев Михаил Николаевич
Birth Year:	1917
Birth Place:	Petrograd, Russia
Private Address:	Route Tenant de la Tour, 25 fl 3.
Known to:	Skvortzoff A.F. 25, Rte Tenant dela Tour, flat 3.
Report Title:	M.N. Eliseyeff and N.G. Konisheff, applicants for enlistment in the Russian Regiment, S.V.C.

Report date: June 12, 1940
Report number: 382
External archival references to this person: SH/30923

Mihail Nikolaevitch Eliseyeff, Russian, was born on June 5, 1917 in Petrograd, Russia. He is reported to have left Russia together with his parents in 1919 and to have subsequently resided at Manchouli and later at Jalainor Coal Mines, where his father was employed as a mechanic. In 1929 he proceeded to Harbin, where for the past two years he has been employed with the Railway Police. This applicant arrived in Shanghai on May 31, 1940 and is little known locally.

Full Name in English: Konisheff Nikolai Grigorievitch
Full Name in Russian: Конышев Николай Григорьевич
Birth Year: 1911
Birth Place: Harbin, Manchuria
Private Address: Rue Bourgeat N310
Known to: Mr. A. Bagroff Russian Newspaper "Shanghai zaria" 774, Av. Joffre.
Report Title: M.N. Eliseyeff and N.G. Konisheff, applicants for enlistment in the Russian Regiment, S.V.C.
Report date: June 12, 1940
Report number: 382
External archival references to this person: SH/60683

Nikolai Grigorievitch Konisheff, Russian, was born on August 8, 1911 in Harbin, Manchuria. For the past several years he has been employed as a type-setter with various Harbin newspapers. On May 31, 1940 he arrived in Shanghai from Harbin.

Full Name in English: Kukuishko Evgeny Ivanovitch
Full Name in Russian: Кукуишко Евгений Иванович
Birth Year: 1908
Birth Place: Ekaterinoslav Province, Russia
Private Address: Avenue Joffre, 703, room 6.
Known to: G.G. Llenning – Russian Regiment S.V.C
Report Title: E.I. Kukuishko, applicant for enlistment in the Russian Regiment, S.V.C
Report date: June 19, 1940
Report number: 383
External archival references to this person: SH/62192

Evgeny Ivanovitch Kukuishko, Russian, was born on March 27, 1908 in Ekaterinoslav Province, Russia. In 1910 he proceeded to Harbin together with his family, where his father was employed with the Chinese Eastern Railway. In 1927 he graduated from the Harbin Commercial School and in 1930 proceeded to U.S.S.R. According to his own statement he escaped from the U.S.S.R. and returned to Harbin in 1933 and upon his return took out emigrants papers through the Bureau for the Affairs of Russian Emigrants in Manchoukou. The applicant's father who was a Soviet citizen left Harbin for the U.S.S.R. in 1935, after the sale of Chinese Eastern Railway to the Japanese.

The applicant arrived in Shanghai together with his mother on May 20, 19+40 and is not known locally.

Full Name in English:	Golbraih Vulf Haimovich
Full Name in Russian:	Гольбрайх Вулф Хаимович
Birth Year:	1914
Birth Place:	Manchouli, Manchuria.
Private Address:	Kungping Road, 35
Report Title:	V.H. Golbraih, applicant for enlistment in the Transport Coy, S.V.C
Report date:	June, 16, 1940
Report number:	384

External archival references to this person: SH/62192

Vulf Haimovich Golbraih, Soviet citizen of Jewish origin, was born on December 27, 1914 at Manchouli, Manchuria. According to his own statement, he left the U.S.S.R. for China in 1922 together with his parents and for the following 16 years resided in Tientsin where he attended the St. Louis College for five years. Leaving the College in 1928 he worked in a local garage as an apprentice for three years. Later he was employed as a chauffeur-mechanic in Mark Ferber's Hire Garage (1936) and with Mr. J.B. Affleck, British Consul-General at Tientsin, for about 7 months (1938). He holds a good testimonial from Mr. E.G. Jameson who succeeded Mr. Affleck on the post of Consul-General.

Applicant arrived in Shanghai from Tientsin sometime in September, 1938. Here he was employed as a chauffeur with various local firms including James Neil & Co, Steinberg's Transportation Service Co, Chevrolet Transport Co and Union Brewery Co. until September, 1939 when he secured his present position as a fitter in the China General Omnibus Co.

He resided at various addresses in the French Concession until April, 1940 when he moved to 35 Kungping Road together with his mother. According to him, his father, Haim Golbraih, a commission agent by occupation, is also in Shanghai, but on account of bad relations between them he even does not know his father's address. His former brother is employed with the Bakerite Bakery.

Applicant holds Soviet passport No. 76915 issued on 4-2-38 at the Soviet Consulate, Tientsin, Valid until 31-10-38. He is not registered at the local Soviet Consulate-General.

He holds a certificate dated 19-9-38 issued by Deputy Chief of Police, British Concession, Tientsin, to the effect that he resided in the British Concession for 14 years, during which period nothing had recorded against him by the British Municipal Police.

Full Name in English:	Bugaeff Viatcheslav Fedorovitch
Full Name in Russian:	Бугаев Вячеслав Федорович
Birth Year:	1905
Birth Place:	Harbin, Manchuria
Report Title:	V.P. Bugaeff, applicant for enrolment on the Transport Company, S.V.C
Report date:	June 22, 1940
Report number:	385
External archival references to this person:	SH/20927

Viatcheslav Fedorovitch Bugaeff, Russian, was born on September 12, 1905 in Harbin, Manchuria. In 1931 he graduated from the Harbin Institute of Oriental Science. In 1933 he proceeded to Dairen where he resided until April 1938 when he came to Shanghai. Here, he has been working as a private teacher, his pupils being mostly Chinese and Japanese.

The applicant was charged with Assault at the 2nd S.S.D. Court on November 23, 1939 and sentenced to a $120.00 fine. Apart from the above nothing is known against him

Full Name in English:	Rogoff Valentin Dmitrievitch
Full Name in Russian:	Рогов Валентин Дмитриевич
Birth Year:	1903
Birth Place:	Samara, Russia
Report Title:	V.D. Rogoff, applicant for enrolment in American Troop, S.V.C.
Report date:	July 3, 1940
Report number:	386
External archival references to this person:	SH/101189

Valentin Dmitrievitch Rogoff, Russian, was born on October 2, 1903 in Samara, Russia. In 1922, he arrived in Shanghai from Vladivostok. In Shanghai he was employed as a Riding Instructor in various Riding Schools until 1930, when he, together with another Russian, named Krikoriantz, established a Riding Academy of their own, under the name of Columbia Riding Academy. In 1937, he sold his share in this business and proceeded to Tsingtao, where, owing to his poor health, he resided until the end of 1939, after which he returned to Shanghai. Since his return he has been employed as manager of the Ascot Riding Academy, 200 Tunsin Road.

The applicant left Shanghai for Tsingtao on June 30, 1940 and is expected to come back in two months time.

Full Name in English:	Vedeniaeff Evgeny Alexandrovitch
Full Name in Russian:	Веденяев Евгений Александрович
Birth Year:	1917
Birth Place:	Moscow, Russia
Private Address:	Rue Massenet, 56
Known to:	Mr. P.T. Konovaloff, S/1 of S.M.P
Report Title:	E.A. Vedeniaeff and V.I. Petroff, applicants for enlistment in the Russian Regiment, S.V.C
Report date:	July 6, 1940
Report number:	387
External archival references to this person: SH/130931	

Evgeny Alexandrovitch Vedeniaeff, Russian, was born on November 12, 1917 in Moscow, Russia. He is reported to have left Russia together with his parents in 1919 and to have subsequently resided in Harbin. In August 1931 he arrived in Shanghai from Harbin and at the beginning of 1932 entered the Commercial School of the Russian Orthodox Confraternity, in which he studied up to 1936.

He failed to find any fixed employment and was supported by his sister, Baroness R.D. Auxion de Ruffe, 56 Rue Massenet.

Full Name in English:	Petroff Vassily Ignatievitch
Full Name in Russian:	Петров Василий Игнатьевич
Birth Year:	1922
Birth Place:	Harbin, Manchuria
Private Address:	Route Bourgeat, 682/5
Known to:	Mr. N.C. Borisoff, 149 Av.Haig
Report Title:	E.A. Vedeniaeff and V.I. Petroff, applicants for enlistment in the Russian Regiment, S.V.C

Report date: July 6, 1940
Report number: 387
External archival references to this person: SH/91291

Vassily Ignatievitch Petroff, Russian, was born on March 1, 1922 in Harbin, Manchuria. In 1928 he left Harbin for Tientsin together with his family and in 1931 arrived in Shanghai from the later city. Here for a period of one year, 1934-1935, he attended the First Russian High School. Later he worked for short periods as an apprentice and as a messenger at various shops in the Concession but mostly he remained unemployed.

His elder brother is at present serving with the Russian Auxiliary Detachment of the French police.

This applicant appeared in the First Shanghai Special District Court on April 19, 1938 on a charge of Larceny. He was found not guilty and released on the same day.

Full Name in English:	Hablieff Mihail Nikolaevitch
Full Name in Russian:	Хаблиев Михаил Николаевич
Birth Year:	1922
Birth Place:	Harbin, Manchuria
Private Address:	Route Lorton, 66/48 room 4,
Known to:	Mr. V. Kosterin 770-772 Rue Bourgeat.
Report Title:	M.N. Hablieff, applicant for enlistment in the Russian Regiment, S.V.C.
Report date:	July 19, 1940
Report number:	388

External archival references to this person: SH/41626

Mihail Nikolaevitch Hablieff, Russian, was born on April 23, 1922 in Harbin, Manchuria. In 1932 he arrived in Shanghai together with his parents. During 1933 and 1934 he studied in the Ecole Remi and between 1937 and 1939 in the Commercial School of the Russian Orthodox Confraternity.

From June 1935 to December 1939 he was an inmate of the St. Tichon's Orphanage. From December 1939 to April 1940 he resided at the Russian Orthodox Cathedral, Route Paul Henry, where he was employed as an assistant to Bishop John, the Head of the Russian Orthodox Mission in Shanghai.

Full Name in English:	Nikolaeff Vladimir Pavlovitch
Full Name in Russian:	Николаев Владимир Павлович
Birth Year:	1922
Birth Place:	Habarovsk, Maritime Province, Russia

Private Address:	Route Des Soeurs, 118 House 27.M.2
Known to:	Mr. N.N. Nikolaeff, 68 Route Paul Henry
Report Title:	V.P. Nikolaeff, applicant for enlistment in the Russian Regiment, S.V.C.
Report date:	August 12, 1940
Report number:	389

External archival references to this person: SH/81926

Vladimir Pavlovitch Nikolaeff, Russian, was born on July 28, 1922 in Habarovsk, Maritime Province, Russia. In the previous year his mother, Miss. V. Nikolaeff, became the common law wife of one P. Kgalevitch, but the applicant has always been known under his mother's maiden name. The applicant is reported to have left Russia, together with his mother his mother in 1923 and to have subsequently resided in Harbin. In 1930 he arrived in Shanghai from Harbin together with his mother and grand-father, Colonel N.N. Nikolaeff, Leader of the Russian Monarchist Legitimists in Shanghai.

During 1930 and 1931 the applicant attended the Commercial School of the Russian Orthodox Confraternity. In 1933 he proceeded to Tsingtao and resided there until 1937 during which period he studied in the Tsingtao American School. It is reported that during that time, his mother was either married to or cohabited with one Morton, American, Chief petty Officer of the U.S.S. Canopus, and that in Tsingtao the applicant was known under the name of Horton.

The applicant returned to Shanghai in 1937 and in December 1938 entered the St. Francis Xavier's College, where he studied until July 1939, since which date he has been without any fixed employment.

Full Name in English:	Grey Semen Leonidovitch
Full Name in Russian:	Грей Семен Леонидович
Birth Year:	1912
Birth Place:	Harbin, Manchuria
Private Address:	Av. Joffre, 544
Report Title:	S.L. Grey, applicant for enrolment in American Troop, S.V.C.
Report date:	August 10, 1940
Report number:	390

Semen Leonidovitch Grey, Russian, was born on July 22, 1912 in Harbin, Manchuria. He graduated from a Harbin high school in 1928 and subsequently proceeded to Shanghai, arriving in this port in August 1928. Here he resided unemployed, together with his mother until 1930 after which he took up work as a salesman with various local firms dealing in motor cars.

During the summers of 1934-35 and 36 he operated a shooting gallery in Chefoo and during the winters of the same years was employed as a physical instructor with the now defunct Knije's Physical Institute, corner of Seymour and Weihaiwei Roads.

From 1936 he has been a representative of the Gold and White Label, State Whisky and since December 1939 has a half share in the Dixie Bar, 544 Avenue Joffre, at which address he at present residence.

This applicant is not registered with the Russian Emigrants' Committee or any other Russian public organization.

Full Name in English:	Sadovschikoff Valentin Ivanovitch
Full Name in Russian:	Садовщиков Валентин Иванович
Birth Year:	1919
Birth Place:	Harbin, Manchuria
Private Address:	Rue Cardinal Mercieur, 326
Known to:	Mr. V.C. Egoroff, 246, Joffre Terrace
Report Title:	V.I. Sadovschikoff and P.P. Welts, application for enlistment in the Russian, S.V.C.
Report date:	August 26, 1940
Report number:	391

External archival references to this person: SH/101820

Valentin Ivanovitch Sadovschikoff, Russian, was born on March 22, 1919 in Harbin, Manchuria. He graduated from a Harbin high school in 1937 and subsequently continued his education in the North-Manchurian University until 1940.

On August 7, 1940, he arrived in Shanghai from Harbin and is not known locally.

Full Name in English:	Weltz Peter Petrovitch
Full Name in Russian:	Вельц Петр Петрович
Birth Year:	1919
Birth Place:	Verhneudensk, Transbaikal Province, Russia
Private Address:	Route Des Soeurs, 153.M.
Known to:	N.A. Booiloff, 1015, A.V. Joffre, Tel. 73404
Report Title:	V.I. Sadovschikoff and P.P. Welts, application for enlistment in the Russian, S.V.C.
Report date:	August 26, 1940
Report number:	391

External archival references to this person: SH/131033

Petr Petrovitch Weltz, Russian, was born March 10, 1919 in Verhneudensk, Transbaikal Province, Russia. He is reported to have left Russia together with his parents in 1922 and have subsequently resided in Harbin.

On July 29, 1940, he arrived in Shanghai from Harbin.

Being a new arrival here he is not known in the local Russian Community.

Full Name in English:	Singer Samuel Solomonovitch
Full Name in Russian:	Зингер Самуил Соломонович
Birth Year:	1911
Birth Place:	Harbin, Manchuria
Report Title:	S. Singer, applicant for enrolment in the American Company, S.V.C.
Report date:	August 26, 1940
Report number:	392

Samuel Solomonovitch Singer, Russian jew, was born on February 19, 1911 in Harbin, Manchuria. He arrived in Shanghai in November, 1926. In 1929 he obtained a position as a sales-man with the now defunct Far Eastern Drug Trading Company. He remained with that company until 1931 after which he worked in the same capacity with the Claude Neon Lights until February, 1932. He later worked as a sales-man with the following firms in Shanghai:-

1932-34 with the American Engineering Corporation

1934-36 with the Mustard and Company

1936-38 with the Union Brewery

In May, 1938 he obtained his present position with the Ewo Brewery.

Recovered files 394-421 (6 July 1940-May 1942)

Full Name in Russian: Иванов Василий Павлович
Report date: 28.3.1940
Report number: 370
External archival references to this person: SH/50452

Full Name in Russian: Браун Димитрий Георгиевич
Report date: 15.5.1940
Report number: 130
External archival references to this person: SH/20765
Notes: дата в карточке не соответствует времени.

Full Name in Russian: Петров Георгий Алексеевич
Report date: 6.7.1940
Report number: 394
External archival references to this person: SH/91293

Full Name in Russian: Готфрид Морис Аронович
Report date: 10.9.1940
Report number: 395
External archival references to this person: SH/41062

Full Name in Russian: Малахов Владимир Николаевич
Report date: 10.9.1940
Report number: 396
External archival references to this person: SH/70490

Full Name in Russian: Кирилюк Владимир Александрович
Report date: 14.9.1940
Report number: 397
External archival references to this person: SH/51883

Full Name in Russian: Петренко Василий Георгиевич
Report date: 5.10.1940
Report number: 400
External archival references to this person: SH/91253
Notes: 2 раза

Full Name in Russian: Шиверский Сергей Емельянович
Report date: 5.10.1940
Report number: 400
External archival references to this person: SH/111139

Full Name in Russian: Кучеров Александр Васильевич
Report date: 10.10.1940
Report number: 401
External archival references to this person: SH/60690

Full Name in Russian: Лаврушин Лев Николаевич
Report date: 15.10.1940
Report number: 403
External archival references to this person: SH/70455

Full Name in Russian: Протасов Александр Васильевич
Report date: 24.10.1940
Report number: 404
External archival references to this person: SH/100510
Notes: или 464?

Full Name in Russian: Сзегеди Евгений Петрович
Report date: 31.10.1940
Report number: 406
External archival references to this person: SH/121222
Notes: вероятно Сегеди

Full Name in Russian: Дмитриев Николай Иванович
Report date: 31.10.1940
Report number: 405
External archival references to this person: SH/30197

Full Name in Russian: Мирошниченко Федор Григорьевич
Report date: 1.11.1940
Report number: 408
External archival references to this person: SH/71835

Full Name in Russian: Штерензон Борис Соломонович
Report date: 6.11.1940
Report number: 411

External archival references to this person: SH/120795
Notes: опечатка - в индексе Штерезон

Full Name in Russian: Носовицкий Максим Бераевич
Report date: 6.11.1940
Report number: 411
External archival references to this person: SH/82073

Full Name in Russian: Тлатов Евгений Александрович
Report date: 11.11.1940
Report number: 412
External archival references to this person: SH/121786

Full Name in Russian: Хотнянский Евгений Георгиевич
Report date: 13.11.1940
Report number: 414
External archival references to this person: SH/42067
Notes: ошибка в индексе

Full Name in Russian: Голик Павел Назарович
Report date: 13.11.1940
Report number: 413
External archival references to this person: SH/40640

Full Name in Russian: Колесников Всеволод Николаевич
Report date: 19.11.1940
Report number: 414
External archival references to this person: SH/60384

Full Name in Russian: Морозов Олег Михайлович
Report date: 19.11.1940
Report number: 414
External archival references to this person: SH/72083

Full Name in Russian: Панов Михаил Васильевич
Report date: 19.11.1940
Report number: 414
External archival references to this person: SH/90702

Full Name in Russian: Репин Михаил Андреевич
Report date: 21.11.1940
Report number: 416
External archival references to this person: SH/100942

Full Name in Russian: Александров Борис Викторович
Report date: 28.11.1940
Report number: 417
External archival references to this person: SH/10304
Notes: 2 раза

Full Name in Russian: Самсонов Василий Федорович
Report date: 28.11.1940
Report number: 417
External archival references to this person: SH/101948

Full Name in Russian: Пекарский Павел Леонтьевич
Report date: 29.11.1940
Report number: 418
External archival references to this person: SH/91006

Full Name in Russian: Пермикин Валентин Константинович
Report date: 29.11.1940
Report number: 418
External archival references to this person: SH/91126

Full Name in Russian: Шадрин Александр Кузьмич
Report date: 29.11.1940
Report number: 418
External archival references to this person: SH/110509

Full Name in Russian: Шевцов Петр Петрович
Report date: 29.11.1940
Report number: 418
External archival references to this person: SH/110971

Full Name in Russian: Панайотаки Сергей Дмитриевич
Report date: 9.12.1940
Report number: 420
External archival references to this person: SH/90661

Full Name in Russian: Дубович Эльмень Виктор Иоганович
Report date: 12.12.1940
Report number: 421
External archival references to this person: SH/30480
Notes: 2 раза

Full Name in Russian: Николаев Георгий Георгиевич
Report date: 12.12.1940
Report number: 421
External archival references to this person: SH/81906

Full Name in Russian: Селезнев Борис Павлович
Report date: 19.12.1940
Report number: 422
External archival references to this person: SH/110223

Full Name in Russian: Шестаков Арсений Михайлович
Report date: 19.12.1940
Report number: 422
External archival references to this person: SH/110881

Full Name in Russian: Игошев Алексей Петрович
Report date: 27.12.1940
Report number: 423
External archival references to this person: SH/50132
Notes: 2 раза

Full Name in Russian: Стрелец Борис Петрович
Report date: 27.12.1940
Report number: 424
External archival references to this person: SH/120929

Full Name in Russian: Кибардин Юрий Михайлович
Report date: 8.1.1941
Report number: 425
External archival references to this person: SH/51776

Full Name in Russian: Лукин Николай Дмитриевич
Report date: 8.1.1941
Report number: 425

External archival references to this person: SH/80919

Full Name in Russian: Патент Иосиф Григорьевич
Report date: 12.2.1941
Report number: 428
External archival references to this person: SH/90778

Full Name in Russian: Четыркин Валентин Тихонович
Report date: 28.2.1941
Report number: 230
External archival references to this person: SH/21370
Notes: 2 раза

Full Name in Russian: Лепин Лавринович Сергей Леонидович
Report date: 28.2.1941
Report number: 430
External archival references to this person: SH/70431

Full Name in Russian: Танский Федор Яковлевич
Report date: 28.2.1941
Report number: 430
External archival references to this person: SH/121270

Full Name in Russian: Игошев Алексей Петрович
Report date: 3.4.1941
Report number: 432
External archival references to this person: SH/50132
Notes: 2 раза

Full Name in Russian: Тархов Борис Николаевич
Report date: 3.4.1941
Report number: 432
External archival references to this person: SH/121368
Notes: 2 раза

Full Name in Russian: Захаров Вадим Константинович
Report date: 3.4.41
Report number: 452
External archival references to this person: SH/140146
Notes: Записан в карточке отца. Опечатка в карточке.

Full Name in Russian: Мошкин Н. В.
Report date: 3.4.1941
Report number: 432
External archival references to this person: SH/72173
Notes: нет отдельной карточки

Full Name in Russian: Моравский Никита Валерианович
Report date: 3.4.1941
Report number: 432
External archival references to this person: SH/72043

Full Name in Russian: Четыркин Валентин Тихонович
Report date: 17.4.1941
Report number: 435
External archival references to this person: SH/21370
Notes: 2 раза

Full Name in Russian: Элтышев Павел Михайлович
Report date: 17.4.1941
Report number: 436
External archival references to this person: SH/30954

Full Name in Russian: Мошкин Александр Константинович
Report date: 13.5.1941
Report number: 432
External archival references to this person: SH/72177

Full Name in Russian: Мильштейн Рудольф Леонидович
Report date: 18.5.1941
Report number: 440
External archival references to this person: SH/71750

Full Name in Russian: Гроссе Лев Викторович
Report date: 24.6.1941
Report number: 443
External archival references to this person: SH/41436

Full Name in Russian: Рассушин Борис Владимирович
Report date: 4.7.1941
Report number: 445

External archival references to this person: SH/100756

Full Name in Russian: Швырянский Арнольд Михайлович
Report date: 20.7.1941
Report number: 446
External archival references to this person: SH/111496
Notes: Заявление подавал под фамилией Швир

Full Name in Russian: Воронов Николай Николаевич
Report date: 3.9.1941
Report number: 448
External archival references to this person: SH/131650

Full Name in Russian: Гальюнас Валентин Степанович
Report date: 15.10.1941
Report number: 450
External archival references to this person: SH/31982

Full Name in Russian: Пригоровский Вениамин Максимиллианович
Report date: 15.10.1941
Report number: 450
External archival references to this person: SH/100358

Full Name in Russian: Обелкин А. И.
Report date: 16.10.1941
Report number: 451
External archival references to this person: SH/90007
Notes: Нет карточки

Full Name in Russian: Волк-Левонович Сергей Николаевич
Report date: 21.10.1940
Report number: 453
External archival references to this person: SH/131472
Notes: Опечатка в дате. Должно быть 21.10.1941

Full Name in Russian: Попов Константин Евграфович
Report date: 21.10.1941
Report number: 453
External archival references to this person: SH/100023

Full Name in Russian: Никонов Валерий Иванович
Report date: 30.10.1941
Report number: 454
External archival references to this person: SH/81951

Full Name in Russian: Верник Антон Иванович
Report date: 4.11.1941
Report number: 455
External archival references to this person: SH/131107

Full Name in Russian: Швец Константин Дионисович
Report date: 1.12.1941
Report number: 456
External archival references to this person: SH/111481

Full Name in Russian: Матиньянц Константин Гайкович
Report date: 3.12.1941
Report number: 458
External archival references to this person: SH/70953

Full Name in Russian: Зайцев Петр Сергеевич
Report date: 3.12.1941
Report number: 458
External archival references to this person: SH/140224

Full Name in Russian: Байков Артемий Георгиевич
Report date: 3.12.1941
Report number: 459
External archival references to this person: SH/11108

Full Name in Russian: Рогожин Виталий Михайлович
Report date: 3.12.1941
Report number: 459
External archival references to this person: SH/101204

Full Name in Russian: Захаров Олег Сергеевич
Report date: 3.12.1941
Report number: 460
External archival references to this person: SH/140233

Full Name in Russian: Ханжин Михаил Владимирович
Report date: 9.12.1941
Report number: 461
External archival references to this person: SH/41709

Full Name in Russian: Пьянков М. Л.
Report date: 15.1.1941
Report number: 462
External archival references to this person: SH/91510
Notes: Нет отдельной карточки. Опечатка - должно быть 1942.

Full Name in Russian: Никонов Аркадий Валерьевич
Report date: 8.1.1942
Report number: 428
External archival references to this person: SH/81953
Notes: Опечатка в карточке. Вероятно февраль 1941.

Full Name in Russian: Минасенко Борис Степанович
Report date: 11.5.1942
Report number: 421
External archival references to this person: SH/71767
Notes: Опечатка в карточке. Дата и номер не совпадают.

Last Names Index

Белов Анатолий Емельянович 60
Белов Константин Миллианович 150
Беловчиков Павел Васильевич 67
Белоцерковец Николай Гермогенович 88
Бельдин Виталий Лаврентьевич 27
Беляков Юрий Александрович 57
Белятко Александр Антонович 60
Богословский Николай Владимирович 27
Богунский Святослав Николаевич 171
Болотненко Федор Еремеевич 116
Борисов Николай Константинович 183
Бородина Мария Николаевна 16
Бородин Виктор Сергеевич 50
Бородин Даниил Иванович 140
Брайнер Евгений ? 177
Браун Димитрий Георгиевич 188
Брейнер Евгений Иванович. *См* Брайнер Евгений Иванович
Бруздунов Владимир Федорович 150
Брызгин Олег Валентинович 86
Брянский Николай Николаевич 128
Бубелов Александр Максимович 115
Бугаев Вячеслав Федорович 182
Буйкис Юрий Михайлович 142
Бурков Сергей Александрович 76
Бусыгин Михаил Иосифович 179
Бутской Владимир Алексеевич 159
Буяновер Евгений Моисеевич 124
Важенин Николай Федорович 51
Вальтер Михаил Александрович 17
Васильев Вадим Петрович 32
Васильев Георгий Владимирович 118
Васильев Леонид Иосифович 170
Васильев Николай Николаевич 10
Вдовкин Петр Иванович 79
Веденяев Евгений Александрович 183
Веденяпин Петр Александрович 121
Велисов Виктор Васильевич 126
Вельгус Виктор Андреевич 119
Вельц Петр Петрович 186
Велюхов Илья Михайлович 24, 31
Вергасов Амрула 53
Веретенников Иннокентий Капикович 30
Верник Антон Иванович 196

Виллер Владимир Андреевич 154
Волк-Левонович Сергей Николаевич 195
Волков Владимир Иванович 61
Волков Михаил Яковлевич 74
Волошин Константин Васильевич 17
Волчков Георгий Васильевич 13
Вольский Владимир Александрович 31
Воронов Николай Николаевич 195
Воронцов Михаил Владимирович 10
Воропай Василий Васильевич 46
Габескирия Георгий Михайлович 32
Гаврилов Серафим Гаврилович 120
Гальюнас Валентин Степанович 195
Гарифулин Абдурахман 137
Гвоздев Борис Владимирович 45
Геккер Марк Григорьевич (Гиршевич) 121
Гелемиев Борис Тихонович 25
Гинтер Евгений Сергеевич 178
Гинх Глеб Николаевич 16
Гладченко Афанасий Анисимович 101
Глебов Вадим Иванович 15
Голдобин 43
Голик Константин Терентьевич 91
Голик Павел Назарович 190
Голован Евгений Михайлович 163
Головенко Иван Филипович 151
Головкин Постриг Юрий Константинович 104
Голос Виталий Е. 31
Голощапов Никита Иванович 171
Голубков Г. 20
Гольбрайх Вулф Хаимович 181
Гончаренко Иосиф Маркович 20
Горлинский Александр Викторович 18
Горовиц З. А. 59
Готфрид Морис Аронович 188
Грабовский Юрий Модестович 105
Грановский Павел Иннокентьевич 64
Грей Семен Леонидович 185
Грибов Евгений Иванович 113
Григорьев Леонид Васильевич 19
Григорьев Сергей Сергеевич 61, 157
Грикало Владимир Сергеевич. См Грякало Владимир Сергеевич
Гринберг Мейер 167

Грищев Михаил Степанович 25

Громов Федор Ермолаевич 108

Гроссе 10, 11

Гроссе Лев Викторович 194

Груздев О. И. 141

Грякало Владимир Сергеевич 83

Данилевский Константин Павлович. *См* Сычев-Данилевский Константин
    Павлович

Данилов П. Т. 31

Данько Сергей Ильич 62

Денисов Георгий Иннокентьевич 31

Денисов Федор Лукьянович 113

Деньгин Борис Павлович 130

Депрерадович Вера Михайловна 172

Депутатов К. 148

Диго Виктор Николаевич 13

Диканов Евгений Евгеньевич 20

Дмитриев Александр Александрович 86, 149

Дмитриев Борис Дмитриевич 157

Дмитриев Николай Иванович 189

Добровольский Александр Петрович 13

Долгов Иван Никитич 79

Доможиров Анатолий Григорьевич 83, 137

Донченко Сильвестр Николаевич. *См* Рудин-Донченко Сильвестр Николаевич

Дроздов Александр Петрович 68

Дронников Сергей Николаевич 16

Дубович Эльмень Виктор Иоганович 17, 192

Дунаев Владимир Николаевич 165

Дюдин Борис Алексеевич 14

Евстафиев Леонид Борисович 19

Егоров Виктор Константинович 186

Егоров Милий Николаевич 24

Еленский Евгений Спиридонович 61

Елисеев Михаил Николаевич 179

Еловитский Тадеуш Генрихович 62

Емельянов А. С. 11

Ефремов Илья Григорьевич 100

Жариков Николай Федорович 81

Жаров Леонид Георгиевич 20, 23

Жемчужин Борис Владимирович 29

Жилочкин Владимир Андреевич 149

Жуков Виктор Григорьевич 30

Жуков Михаил Васильевич 72

Кивикинг Павел Михайлович 167
Киреевский Дмитрий Дмитриевич 122
Кирилов Лев Сергеевич 173
Кирилюк Владимир Александрович 188
Кирьяков Константин Сергеевич 32
Кишкин Лев 173
Клачко М. 59
Коблей Иван Никитич 76
Ковыкин Виктор Дмитриевич 146
Козлов Онуфрий Андрианович 166
Козловский Владимир Иванович 11
Козулин Прокопий Иванович 109
Колесников Всеволод Николаевич 190
Колесников Георгий Николаевич 32
Колпачников Энвер Степанович 143
Колпинский Николай Николаевич 103
Комарницкий Владимир Федорович 26
Коновалов Павел Тимофеевич 183
Коновец Анатолий Анатольевич 125
Конышев Николай Григорьевич 180
Коптилин Александр Александрович 177
Копытов Владимир Федорович 109
Кореневский Вадим Федорович 138
Коркунов Илья Ильич 97
Коростелев Борис Алексеевич 58
Короткевич Лев Михайлович 18
Коротков Александр Степанович 27
Кортус Виктор Иванович. *См* Турлук-Кортус Виктор Иванович
Косовский Соломон Иосифович 169
Костерин Владимир Иванович 184
Костин Федор Семенович 9
Кочан Е. А. 151
Кочнев Георгий Дмитриевич 90
Кошман Юлиан Люцианович 73
Кравченко Ростислав Харлампиевич 58
Краковцев Владимир Михайлович 16
Красуля Виктор Павлович 85
Крейзельман Бина (Борис) Наумович 128
Криворучко Григорий Матвеевич 56
Круглик Игорь Иллиодорович 21
Крутиков Александр Петрович 141
Кублей Иван Никитич. *См* Коблей Иван Никитич
Кудрявцев Анатолий Никитич 65

Кудрявцев Георгий Никитич 141
Кузнецов Н. 148
Кукуишко Евгений Иванович 180
Кулинберг Алексей Сергеевич 42
Кулинберг Виктор Сергеевич 35
Кульчицкий К. И. 65
Кучеров Александр Васильевич 189
Лавринович Сергей Леонидович. *См* Лепин Лавринович Сергей Леонидович
Лаврушин Лев Николаевич 189
Ламбирис Иван Георгиевич 171
Ланге Александр Федорович 52
Ланге Федор Федорович 65
Лашкевич Георгий Алексеевич 21
Левонович Сергей Николаевич. *См* Волк-Левонович Сергей Николаевич
Левый Василий Дмитриевич 44
Леженин Петр Иванович 146
Леман Иван Федорович 154
Леонов Георгий Александрович 128
Лепин Лавринович Сергей Леонидович 193
Лимонников Борис Александрович 91
Лисуненко Георгий Петрович 31
Ломаев Семен Алексеевич 29
Лордкипанидзе А. А. 62
Лукин Георгий Димитриевич 29
Лукин Николай Дмитриевич 192
Луполов Иосиф Иосифович 33
Лушников Андрей Иванович 59
Лысик Александр Александрович 17
Лютов Георгий Игнатьевич 108
Ляпунов Евгений Михайлович. *См* Потемкин-Ляпунов Евгений Михайлович
Макаров Борис Николаевич 30
Макаров Е. К. 108
Македонский Василий Васильевич 88
Маклаевский Борис Степанович 96
Максимов Федорищев Виктор Петрович 24
Малахов Владимир Николаевич 188
Малаховский Михаил Федотович 151
Маликов Николай Емельянович 140
Малиновский Петр Иванович 117
Малых Константин Семенович 176
Мальцев Виталий Николаевич 151
Маркевич Георгий Александрович 56
Маркизов Анатолий Алексеевич 96

Марков Гавриил Иванович 28
Марков Георгий Алексеевич 15
Масол Александр Захарович 124
Матиньянц Константин Гайкович 196
Махов Сергей Гурьевич 28
Медвикус Анатолий Феофанович 103
Меди Николай Петрович 75
Мезавицев Виктор Михайлович 127, 128
Мезенцев Николай Иванович 17
Мелешко Александр Максимович 15, 25
Мельник Алексей Трофимович 179
Мельников Игорь Иродионович 17
Мельников Николай Петрович 52
Мельников Семен Иванович 35
Меннинг Георгий Генрихович 163
Меньков Владимир Михайлович 25, 28
Мерзляков Михаил Николаевич 60
Мешков Юрий Александрович 121
Мещеряков Игорь Александрович 56
Миллер Исаак Соломонович 74
Мильштейн Рудольф Леонидович 194
Минаев Валентин Дмитриевич 122
Минасенко Борис Степанович 197
Миронов Георгий Михайлович 21
Мирошниченко Михаил Васильевич 125
Мирошниченко Федор Григорьевич 189
Митчелл Аркадий Алексеевич. См Михайлов Митчелл Аркадий Алексеевич
Михайлов Митчелл Аркадий Алексеевич 79
Михалев Георгий Николаевич 111
Мишин Игорь Алексеевич 55
Моравский Никита Валерианович 194
Морозов Олег Михайлович 190
Мосичкин Николай Степанович 172
Мосол А. С. 84
Мочалов Борис Андреевич 72
Мошкин Александр Константинович 194
Мошкин Н. В. 194
Мраморнов Борис Алексеевич 43
Мрочковский Иван Константинович 153
Мусалевский Борис Михайлович 127
Мухаметзянов Г. 109
Муханов Александр Вивианович 22
Мюллер Лео Макарович 78

Мюллер Лео Оскарович. *См* Мюллер Лео Макарович
Найденьшев Евгений Петрович 23
Нарбут Владимир Дмитриевич 170
Нарышкин Юрий Сергеевич 30
Нежин Валентин Александрович 22
Нежин Георгий Александрович 35
Непомнящий Борис Павлович 11
Нестеров Владимир 12
Нестеров Владимир Дмитриевич 162
Никитин Андрей Петрович 13
Николаев Владимир Павлович 184
Николаев Георгий Георгиевич 192
Николаев Михаил Витальевич 92
Николаев Николай Николаевич 127, 185
Николаев Семен Николаевич 37
Никонов Аркадий Валерьевич 197
Никонов Валерий Иванович 196
Нилус Александр Евгеньевич 12
Новгородов Евгений Максимович 129
Новиков Юрий Кузьмич 77
Новицкий Олег Вениаминович 34
Новожилов Василий Сергеевич 28
Носков Борис Артемьевич 18
Носков Семен Васильевич 24
Носовицкий Максим Бераевич 190
Обелкин А. И. 195
Огнев Иосиф Алексеевич. *См* Запольский (Огнев) Иосиф Алексеевич
Окружнов Павел Михайлович 111
Оксаковский Анатолий Леонтьевич 82
Онищук Виктор Кузьмич 48
Орлов Виктор Васильевич 165
Осадчий Александр Иосифович 132
Осипов Михаил Артемьевич 149
Павлов Василий Иосифович 81
Павлов Леонид Витальевич 30
Павлов Мартиан Петрович 33
Павловский Георгий Николаевич 123
Панайотаки Сергей Дмитриевич 191
Панов Михаил Васильевич 190
Парицкий Серафим Петрович 160
Патент Иосиф Григорьевич 193
Пахомов Борис Константинович 94
Пекарский Павел Леонтьевич 191

Приходько Виталий Степанович 19
Просвирнин Игорь Иванович 107
Протасов Александр Васильевич 189
Прудников Георгий Иванович 105
Пьянков М. Л. 197
Пятаков Петр Михайлович 32
Рабинович Эдуард Иосифович. *См* Робин (Рабинович) Эдуард Иосифович
Радецкий-Микулич Георгий Васильевич 104, 125, 171
Райко Николай Константинович 162
Рассушин Борис Владимирович 194
Редров Георгий Геннадьевич 16
Репин Михаил Андреевич 191
Робин (Рабинович) Эдуард Иосифович 174
Робустов Вадим Александрович 99
Робустов Викентий Александрович 16
Рогов Валентин Дмитриевич 182
Рогожин Виталий Михайлович 196
Розенберг Александр Альфредович 59
Романов Александр Федорович 170
Романов Леонид Тимофеевич 18
Романов Тимофей Фирсович 81
Рубин Михаил Лазаревич 63
Руденко Василий Васильевич 116
Рудин-Донченко Сильвестр Николаевич. *См* Рудин Сильвестр Николаевич
Рудин Сильвестр Николаевич 14
Руднянский Александр Михайлович 77
Руссет Константин Константинович 143
Руссиян Владислав Викторович. *См* Русский Владислав Викторович
Русский Владислав Викторович 38
Рухлядев Владимир Викторович 21
Ручьев Иван Павлович 83
Рымович Владислав Владиславович 10
Ряшинцев Евгений Иванович 164
Ряшницев Евгений Иванович. *См* Ряшинцев Евгений Иванович
Садовщиков Валентин Иванович 186
Салищев Петр Петрович 16, 91
Самсонов Василий Федорович 191
Санотский Леонид Антонович 142
Сахно Иван Иванович 37
Сдобников Юрий Андреевич 175
Сегеди Евгений Петрович. *См* Сзегеди Евгений Петрович
Селезнев Борис Павлович 192
Семенин Николай Михайлович 66

Семибратов Яков Семенович 9
Сергиевский Лев Николаевич 9
Сердюк Анатолий Николаевич 34
Сережников Георгий Николаевич 56
Сесько Борис Георгиевич 141
Сзегеди Евгений Петрович 189
Сидамонидзе Константин Юрьевич 69
Симинютин Георгий Иванович 110
Сицинский Франц Николаевич 45
Скалин Николай Иванович 23
Скаредов Олег Николаевич 14
Скарятин Георгий Александрович 27
Скобяев Павел Флегонтович 14
Сколин Николай Иванович. *См* Скалин Николай Иванович
Скопин Федор Ильич 156
Скрейтул Альфред 143
Скуев Викторин Валерьевич 26
Слоссман Б. А. 103
Согрин Николай Михайлович 40
Соколов Борис Владимирович 139
Соколов Владимир Михайлович 149
Соколов Георгий Алексеевич 152
Соколов Игорь Иванович 95
Соколов Михаил Афиногенович 129
Сомнительнов Геннадий Иванович 26
Сорокин Александр Сергеевич 164
Сорочинский Сергей Арсентьевич 41
Сосновский Валентин Михайлович 26
Сосновский Константин Михайлович 86
Сосновский Леонид Михайлович 27
Спирин Павел Григорьевич 29
Стариков Василий Ефимович 176
Стариков Иван Гаврилович 87
Стеер Всеволод Николаевич 155
Стеклов Константин Алексеевич 77
Степанищев Николай Михайлович 87
Степанов Борис Иванович 27
Степанов Георгий Александрович 142
Степанов Игорь Алексеевич 89
Стогней Николай Константинович 19
Столица Юрий Сергеевич 142
Стоцкий Владимир Владимирович 20
Страут Павел Карлович 84

Чиркович Вячеслав Петрович 80
Чувствин Михаил Николаевич 87
Чудинов Иван Сергеевич 9
Чудовский Дмитрий Николаевич 82
Чуйков Михаил Алексеевич 112
Шавикин Александр Павлович 70
Шаврин Николай Всеволодович 34
Шадрин Александр Кузьмич 191
Шайдитский Владимир Иоаннович 58
Шастин Николай Меркурьевич 12
Швец Константин Дионисович 196
Швир Арнольд Михаилович. *См* Швырянский Арнольд Михаилович
Швырянский Арнольд Михаилович 195
Шевелев Олег Владимирович 22
Шевелев Ростислав Борисович 18
Шевцов Петр Петрович 191
Шестаков Арсений Михайлович 192
Шестаков Георгий Васильевич 93
Шестаков Михаил Иванович 34
Шестаков Феодор Алексеевич 22
Шиверский Сергей Емельянович 189
Шикалов Виктор Иванович 124
Шик Виктор Владимирович. *См* Щекин Виктор Владимирович
Шимановский Александр Евгеньевич 104
Шимохин Александр Петрович 30
Широков Владимир Викторович 111
Шмулевский Леонид Израелевич 27
Штерензон Борис Соломонович 189
Шулигин Леонид Максимилианович 153
Шульгин Константин Иванович 105
Шульгин Николай Павлович 126
Щекин Алексей Алексеевич 11
Щекин Андрей Алексеевич 11
Щекин Виктор Владимирович 98
Щирский-Чернский Иван Яковлевич 9
Элтышев Павел Михайлович 194
Эльмень Виктор Иоганович. *См* Дубович Эльмень Виктор Иоганович
Эпов Владимир Алексеевич 19
Юмшанов Владимир Иванович 63
Юмшанов Георгий Иванович 63
Юшков Афанасий Гаврилович 9
Языков Иннокентий Афанасьевич 28
Яковкин Михаил Гаврилович 66, 100, 145